Attacks on the Press

Attacks on the Press

2013 EDITION

Journalism on the World's Front Lines

Committee to Protect Journalists

WILEY | Bloomberg PRESS

Cover image: French photographer Rémi Ochlik covers a demonstration in Cairo. Ochlik was killed on assignment in Syria in February 2012. (AP/Julien de Rosa)
Cover design: John Emerson

Editorial Director: Bill Sweeney
Senior Editor: Elana Beiser
Deputy Editors: Kamal Singh Masuta, Shazdeh Omari
Edition Editor: Lew Serviss

Published by John Wiley & Sons, Inc., Hoboken, New Jersey.
Published simultaneously in Canada.

For general information on our other products and services or for technical support, please contact our Customer Care Department within the United States at (800) 762-2974, outside the United States at (317) 572-3993 or fax (317) 572-4002.

Wiley publishes in a variety of print and electronic formats and by print-on-demand. Some material included with standard print versions of this book may not be included in e-books or in print-on-demand. If this book refers to media such as a CD or DVD that is not included in the version you purchased, you may download this material at http://booksupport.wiley.com. For more information about Wiley products, visit www.wiley.com.

Library of Congress Cataloging-in-Publication Data:

ISBN 978-1-118-55055-7 (Paperback)
ISBN 978-1-118-61137-1 (ePDF)
ISBN 978-1-118-61137-1 (Mobi)
ISBN 978-1-118-61129-6 (ePub)

Printed in the United States of America
10 9 8 7 6 5 4 3 2 1

MIX
Paper from
responsible sources
FSC® C005928
www.fsc.org

Contents

From the Editors

A fledgling Committee to Protect Journalists first published *Attacks on the Press* in 1986. It was, literally, a list of attacks against journalists, produced simply on typed pages that were held together with staples. The organization quickly expanded its efforts, publishing bound editions of the annual survey, each year adding substance and context to the reporting. *Attacks on the Press* soon became a leading resource on international press freedom, all the while evolving to put greater emphasis on analysis and include ever-more ambitious digital companions. With the publication of this new edition, CPJ takes another important step in the evolution of *Attacks on the Press*. We're proud to announce a new partnership with Bloomberg, which is underwriting the publication of *Attacks on the Press*, and Wiley, our new publisher. With their expertise, the new edition of *Attacks on the Press* leverages CPJ research to look ahead at the emerging issues confronting journalists across the world. In this new anthology of essays, you'll read the stories of international journalists writing about matters of life and death in the field, the views of the pre-eminent journalists who serve on CPJ's Board of Directors, and the analysis of CPJ staff working to protect the press in every corner of the world. We continue to publish our detailed, country-by-country research reports on cpj.org. With this volume, we begin dating the editions in the year in which they are published to reflect the currency of CPJ's research. We've also changed the subtitle to *Journalism on the World's Front Lines* to highlight the extraordinary challenges facing journalists working in dangerous and repressive places worldwide. Their stories illustrate the importance of a free press to every citizen of the world.

1

THE FRONT LINES

In Syria, Facing Danger From All Sides

By Paul Wood

A dozen smugglers were squatting next to their mules. We should have left hours earlier. The four of us in the BBC team worried that if we didn't go soon it would be dawn before we reached Lebanon. A Syrian patrol might spot us on the bare hillside. We were on the edge of the mountains that run along Syria's border with Lebanon, falling away into the Bekaa Valley, and not all that far from the official border crossing on the Damascus-Beirut highway. There had been a gunfight in the next village, they told us, a battle for control of the smuggling routes (and for the big profits from selling weapons to the rebels). Three men had been killed. The mules' owner was on the winning side. But he'd be late.

When he did arrive, we set off up a steep hill, the rocky ground luminous white under the full moon. Some of the mules were loaded with rocket-propelled grenades and a heavy machine gun for a village on the way. The others, we rode. The smugglers were "the scum of the earth," said one of those in our group. It was Ramadan, but they weren't fasting. They swore. When we parted ways 12 hours later, one got very aggressive as we checked the mules' panniers for anything left behind. "Back off or I shoot," he snarled from atop a black horse. "F--- you and f--- your sister." He had stolen a flak jacket, we discovered later.

We were using this criminal gang because rebel fighters were unable to take us back the way we had come, through the town of Zabadani. There was too much shelling. We could hear it in the distance as the sun came up, volleys of far-off thunder from the tanks and artillery pieces we had seen ringing the town two weeks earlier. That crossing, into Syria, hadn't been easy, either. It was too steep for mules so we walked for three nights, legs aching, lungs burning, stopping to rest before we edged round Syrian army posts as quietly as we could in the dark.

■ ■ ■

That journey was in August 2012, one of a half dozen covert trips across the border that we made for the BBC over the past year. The crew consisted of a cameraman, Fred Scott; a medic, Kevin Sweeney; our translator, Ghassan (who was not using his real name); and me. We did this to be able to cover the insurgency from the inside. But, mostly, we had to sneak in because the regime was not granting visas. Despite the government's promise to the United Nations that foreign reporters would be given access, visas were often impossible to obtain. A hard slog with low-life smugglers was a small price for avoiding the Syrian security forces. "Seven years for crossing the border illegally. Another 10 for having a sat phone," an activist warned when we were setting up our first trip, in November 2011. "Do you really want to do this?"

The regime's grip was still strong everywhere on those first covert trips in 2011. We'd spend days or even weeks hiding out in safe houses. Activists and Free Syrian Army fighters risked their lives to look after us. Getting caught was a real risk. There was always a government checkpoint nearby. Informers, we were warned, were everywhere. An activist told me that a Lebanese reporter for an international news agency had been arrested and tortured for a month with electric shocks. A Western journalist was detained and badly beaten, her captors urinating on her as she lay on the cell floor, he said. As anyone reporting from Syria will tell you, the activists sometimes exaggerate, but such stories seemed alarmingly plausible. They were in line with what we'd heard about others who had run into trouble in Syria. The uprising was still quite new and it seemed the authorities were trying to scoop up activists' networks by arresting journalists. The reporters who were detained for meeting with opponents of the regime were in the country legally. At the very least, we thought, we would be jailed as spies if caught. Our interpreter expected he would be killed.

The official media blamed Syria's troubles on "foreign infiltrators" and "agents of Israel." In Homs last February, my host came in to say he had seen me on Dounia, a private channel known for putting out pro-regime propaganda even more virulent than that of state television. He told me that Dounia showed one of my pieces on camera while the anchor accused me of using certain words and gestures to send coded messages to the Israeli intelligence agency Mossad. I found this too ridiculous to believe, even for Dounia. Why wouldn't I just phone Mossad? But other Syrians told me later that they had seen the broadcast, too.

Later, as Syria became more a civil war and less an uprising, there was an identifiable front line and rebel-held territory. Still, we got the same warning from activists as at the beginning: It's more dangerous to go out with a camera, they said, than with a Kalashnikov. Mika Yamamoto, an experienced Japanese correspondent, was shot dead in Aleppo in August. The commander of the Free Syrian Army unit with which Yamamoto was traveling told me he had no doubt she was killed deliberately. The FSA said a captured government sniper admitted carrying out orders to target foreign reporters. It is hard to know if that is true, but Syria's citizen-journalists believe the regime is out to get them—and foreign journalists, too.

The highest-profile media casualty was Marie Colvin, one of the best and bravest correspondents of her generation. An American working for the U.K.'s *Sunday Times*, she went to the Baba Amr district in Homs when it came under bombardment in February. She died, along with the French photographer Rémi Ochlik, as shells or rockets hit a makeshift media center in Baba Amr. We had stayed there only the week before. It was really just an activist's apartment with a generator, hot water, and Internet. Between the members of the BBC team, we had been to two dozen wars, but the shelling there was the worst we had ever seen. Government tanks were already at the edges of Baba Amr. After only four days, we decided to leave.

Marie came to see me before she went in. She thought the regime might do anything to prevent stories and pictures from getting out that could make foreign intervention more likely. Although citizen-journalists sent out shaky pictures of the shelling day after day, the presence of international correspondents did focus attention on Baba Amr. Marie was all over the BBC, CNN, and Sky with a gut-wrenching account of a baby that had been hit by shrapnel dying in an ill-equipped field clinic. "The doctor said 'I can't do anything,'" she told the BBC. "His little tummy just kept heaving until he died." She was killed less than 24 hours later. If the regime was trying to suppress coverage of Baba Amr before its ground offensive, it failed. An editor in London stated a fact when he said of Marie's death: "This has put rocket boosters under the story."

■ ■ ■

Did the regime deliberately attack the media center? After Baba Amr's fall, I visited Marie's photographer, Paul Conroy, who was recovering in a London hospital with a fist-sized hole in his thigh. He had been a soldier in the British Royal Artillery before he became a journalist and thought that Katyusha rockets were carefully aimed at them. "There were two [impacts] happening and they appeared to be bracketed in on our location," he said. "They got a fix and then four [more] hit. As an artilleryman, I think that was a good day's work for a well-trained team. Nothing smacked of randomness." He told me how, using an Ethernet cable as a makeshift tourniquet for his leg, he stumbled out through thick black smoke and tripped over a body half buried in the rubble. It was Marie.

There were five days of agonizing uncertainty over whether he would be able to leave, along with other foreign journalists caught in the attack. One of the leaders of the Farouq Brigade, the main FSA group in Homs, was accused of keeping the journalists there so the world would not ignore Baba Amr's fate. The commander, Abu Jasim, denied it when I met him later, saying his men had died trying to get the journalists out of Homs. Still, such was the mistrust and recrimination amid Baba Amr's fall that another group of FSA fighters we were staying with nearby insisted on escorting us in case we were kidnapped by the Farouq Brigade.

Paul Conroy did not believe the regime's promises of safe passage and so, despite his grave wounds, he chose to leave using the tunnel that was Baba Amr's only tenuous link to the outside world. He was being taken through by an FSA fighter when they found a man carrying a 10-year-old boy whose legs had been stripped of their flesh by an explosion. A shell had collapsed the tunnel at one point. There was just a small crawl space at the top of a pile of rubble. Paul helped the boy pull himself through the hole, bare bone scraping across jagged concrete. Paul got out, but those following had to turn back when the tunnel was attacked. They included the Spanish correspondent Javier Espinosa, the French photographer William Daniels, and the French writer Edith Bouvier, who, with a shattered femur, was taped to a stretcher. All of the foreign journalists did eventually escape Baba Amr. Remaining behind were the local reporters who had been there throughout 25 days of shelling.

Among them was "Jeddi" ("grandfather" in Arabic, though he was only 34). Jeddi had been a vegetable seller before taking up a camera in the revolution. Often brave to the point of recklessness, he stayed as the FSA pulled out—to spare Baba Amr further bombardment, the rebels said. Most of the activist-reporters in Baba Amr I spoke to thought the fighters had made a mistake. One told me by phone: "The FSA are sitting in Qusayr, drinking tea and chit-chatting while Baba Amr is destroyed. They are cowards." Jeddi told me he had dug a hole in the garden behind his house. He would hide in it when the army arrived.

We heard nothing more of Jeddi, whose real name was Ali Othman, until a few weeks later when he was arrested in Aleppo. Other activists said he was tortured, giving up dozens of names. The following month, he appeared in a bizarre and disturbing special program on Dounia, giving a two-hour interview, or "confession" as the show's anchor described it. In the lurid title sequence, the camera moves down a darkened corridor as dramatic music blares out. A cell door swings open to reveal Jeddi sitting in the corner, head bowed, in a pool of blue light.

"Were gunmen among the demonstrators?" asked the interviewer.
"I didn't see any, only the security forces," Jeddi replied. "We heard
shots and ran. A guy next to me got a bullet in the back of the
head."
"Who do you think shot him?"
"The bullet was from behind. That's where the security were."
"Does that necessarily mean, in your opinion, that the security
targeted him?"
"Maybe. Maybe not."
"So, nothing proving that?"
"No, no."
"Would the security shoot this guy when they want the citizens'
welfare?"
"Of course not."

The pendulum swung back and forth. Jeddi did not denounce the
revolution. Nor did he throw the questions back in the interviewer's
face. It was a skilled performance and courageous, given the enormous pressure to say what was expected of him. The FSA was still furi-
ous. One commander called him a traitor. The reaction was unfair but
explained by the fact that the FSA would previously have seen Jeddi as
"their" journalist and the Baba Amr media center's function to put out
propaganda for the armed uprising.

■ ■ ■

Some citizen-journalists saw themselves this way, too. Most had taken
to reporting to help the revolution. Some were, literally, spokespeople
for the FSA, and a few were armed themselves. People, including those
in the FSA ranks, expected their media to be on their side. Many, probably most, of the Arabic TV stations or newspapers seen by the average
Syrian were highly partisan. People reacted to them as such.
    One afternoon in November 2011 in Baba Amr, we heard shout-
ing outside in the street. A small crowd surrounded a car. A reporter
and cameraman had just driven in. They were recognized as being
from Lebanese Al-Manar TV. Al-Manar is a Shia channel affiliated with
Hezbollah, and therefore the Syrian regime; Baba Amr, stronghold of

the uprising, was mostly Sunni, like the revolution itself. The reporter had been given the blessing of a Sunni religious sheik to come into Baba Amr. He had miscalculated.

The reporter—a Lebanese Shia, we learned later—took off at a sprint and reached the government checkpoint a couple of hundred yards away. His cameraman, a Syrian Sunni, was grabbed and hustled away. There was a debate over what to do with him. Our host, Abu Sufian, a leading figure in Baba Amr, had lost three members of his family in the uprising and was enraged. "I lost my brother. My brother. They killed my brother," he screamed.

Another man tried to calm him. "We can't harm him," he said. "That is not our religion."

The cameraman was taken to see the body of a 6-year-old boy shot dead as he played on his doorstep. Male relatives, tears running down their faces, were standing silently over the boy, laid out in the nearby mosque. Our hosts informed us that the cameraman was shocked and said he'd been wrong to support the regime. They asked if we would film his statement to show he hadn't been harmed. We refused. They tried to use the cameraman in a prisoner swap. That failed, but he was released that night in exchange for the return of two bodies, we were told. The next day we laughed as state television announced that two kidnapped journalists from Al-Manar had been freed in a "special forces raid" on Baba Amr.

I wondered if he would have been killed if we hadn't been there. The unspoken attitude of the fighters toward reporters was: You're either with us or against us. FSA officers would nod and agree when we told them we were not there to put out propaganda. But there was little real understanding of objective journalism. At the beginning, the rebels thought foreign reporters would bring Western planes to bomb the regime, as in Libya. By late 2012, they told us there's no point in helping journalists—they know they are on their own. But, though they are bitter about the outside world's failure to help, fighters and activists have continued to welcome us to their homes, feeding us, moving us around the checkpoints.

Syrian state TV accused the rebels of killing Gilles Jacquier, the first Western correspondent to die in Syria's civil war. He was hit by a mortar shell or rocket-propelled grenade in January 2012 while on

a government-sponsored trip to Homs. He was in a neighborhood of
Alawites and affluent Sunnis loyal to the regime. But two Swiss journalists with him thought it was a setup, a government attack made to
look like the work of rebels. Jacquier's wife, Caroline Poiron, was also
there, on assignment for *Paris Match*. "Everything was orchestrated—it
was like theater," she told me. "Gilles and the 12 other journalists were
targeted by the regime to show the world that there are terrorists in
Syria." A French judge is now investigating.

■ ■ ■

Alex Thompson of Britain's Channel 4 made another accusation against
the rebels. He believes that FSA fighters pointed his crew down a road
where they knew the regime's forces would fire on any approaching
vehicle. "The rebels deliberately set us up to be shot by the Syrian
Army," he wrote on his blog. "Dead journos are bad for Damascus."
Thompson said that the rebels he met didn't trust anyone coming from
Damascus on an official visa. We traveled with activists or fighters
from start to finish. But I never felt, as he did, that the rebels might get
you killed just so they could blame it on the government. We still had
problems: hostile questions about stories that, it turned out, the rebels
had not actually seen, or about the actions of "BBC journalists" when
we knew there had been no one from the BBC present.

An FSA spokesman in northern Lebanon, for example, began telling armed groups inside Syria that I was a spy. How did he know?
A source inside the regime, he said. Had he spoken to this informer?
No, others had. What had been said exactly? He wasn't sure. This might
have been a lie by the regime to discredit us, we said. Had he thought
of that? We began to suspect that this was fallout from emails written
by Nir Rosen, the controversial American journalist and commenta-
tor. Among the thousands of emails uncovered when activists hacked
into President Bashar al-Assad's private account in February 2012 were
forwarded messages from Rosen. He had written to officials to inform
them that reporters were sneaking into Homs. He did this to help his
own visa application. He named me. This was not helpful. We assumed
the regime knew we had been in Homs—we had broadcast from

there—but Assad was apparently not aware himself. We worried that if he were to take a personal interest, the security services would really start looking for us.

Rosen mounted a vigorous defense, writing articles and enlisting activists to deny that he was a regime stooge or a spy. I suspected that on seeing my name and the word "spy" in the same article, the FSA spokesman and others had simply gotten things backward. Other journalists faced similar, flimsy accusations, often just the result of muddle on the part of the FSA. "What made you think he was a spy?" one reporter asked when a colleague came under suspicion. "He asked what weapons we were using," a fighter replied. A French reporter found herself the subject of a tense discussion in Homs. "They thought you were a spy and were debating whether to execute you," an activist told her when she got back to Lebanon.

All of this might be the product of 40 years of state-sponsored paranoia about outsiders, especially Westerners, and the fact that the Free Syrian Army is not one organization but a brand name for hundreds of local militias. The chaos has also allowed jihadist groups to join the fight, a dangerous development for Western journalists in Syria. The British photographer John Cantlie and a Dutch colleague, Jeroen Oerlemans, stumbled into a foreign jihadists' camp in the north in July. There were 40 fighters, from Bangladesh, Pakistan, Chechnya, and Turkey and 10 to 15 speaking with southern English accents. The journalists were blindfolded, handcuffed, kicked around, and put in stress positions. Some of the worst treatment was from the Britons, Cantlie said. They were young, on their first jihad and "very excited" to have Western hostages. They were calling us "Christian filth," and saying "die, kafir" (infidel), he recalls. A knife was sharpened, to behead them, they were told. They ran for their lives across the plain leading away from the camp. The jihadists sprayed automatic fire in their direction. Both were wounded and dragged back.

They were patched up and prepared for transfer to a "more serious" Al-Qaeda-affiliated group. Cantlie said they would have been killed if the FSA had not arrived to rescue them. "The implications are that the longer this goes on, the more complicated it will become," he said. "And the longer this goes on, the nastier it will get, for all of us."

They were both lucky not to join the list of those who have died covering Syria's civil war, some foreign correspondents, many more local reporters. Whether it is the presence of jihadist groups or the regime's use of aerial bombing, new risks are being added to those that journalists faced at the beginning. As Syria endures its second winter of war, the dangers for journalists are multiplying.

Paul Wood is a BBC Middle East correspondent covering Syria. He has reported on more than a dozen conflicts, including in Afghanistan, Iraq, Libya, Darfur, the Balkans, and Chechnya.

Africa's Media-Savvy Insurgents Pose New Threat

By Mohamed Keita

It was midmorning on April 26, 2012, and Grace Chimezie, an intern in the newsroom of the Nigerian daily *ThisDay* in the capital, Abuja, was checking email and reviewing newspapers for the next editorial meeting when an explosion ripped through the office complex. "I found myself on the floor, groaning in pain," Chimezie recalled in a story in her paper. In a split-second move that probably saved her life, Chimezie evaded a chunk of debris that came crashing down on her laptop. The explosion killed five people; Chimezie was among at least eight injured.

The blast was one of two simultaneous bombings that targeted the offices of three newspapers, in Abuja and the northern city of Kaduna. The militant Islamist sect Jama'atu Ahlis Sunna Lidda'awati Wal-Jihad, popularly known as Boko Haram, claimed responsibility for both. "We have just started this new campaign against the media and we will not stop here—we will hit the media hard," warned Abul Qaqa, a spokes-man for the group.

Journalists have long been caught in the crossfire, literally and fig-uratively, between opposing sides in armed conflict and where nonstate actors such as insurgents or criminal groups operate: Afghanistan, Somalia, the Democratic Republic of Congo, and Mexico are powerful examples of the past decade. But with the rise of mobile Internet technology and social media, both insurgent groups and the governments they are fight-ing have become more cognizant, and apparently more sensitive, to how they are portrayed. The result is increased danger for journalists, who are squeezed between threat of violent attack from one side and pressure of censorship or prosecution from the other. At the same time, nonstate actors are trying to leverage social media for themselves, bypassing tradi-tional journalists to disseminate their messages directly.

"One of the most potent modern threats to emerge against jour-nalists is the rise of extremist groups who deliberately target journal-ists," Peter Bouckaert, emergencies director of Human Rights Watch, told CPJ by email. "The changes in technology and accessibility of media over the Internet also mean that human rights abusers are much more aware of what is being written about them, and that can result in more direct and immediate threats against the journalists who are writing critically about these individuals or groups."

The problem has gained attention at the highest international lev-els. In September 2012, the United Nations Human Rights Council expressed "concern that there is a growing threat to the safety of jour-nalists posed by nonstate actors, including terrorist groups and criminal organizations."

The menace of terrorist groups grew exponentially for the press in Mali and Nigeria in 2012, as these two nations battled violent Islamists in their respective northern regions. Brutal actions by the militants forced some journalists into hiding and induced others to self-censor—a cycle of intimidation already familiar to reporters covering some of Africa's longest-running conflicts, such as in eastern Democratic Republic of Congo and Somalia. "West Africa is confronted with a new wave of challenges to governance, peace consolidation, and conflict pre-vention," Said Djinnit, the U.N. special representative in the region, said in July.

■ ■ ■

Journalists in Mali—a model of stability and democracy for more than two decades—were subject to a record number of attacks by insurgents and government security forces as the country slipped into instability. After the military ousted the elected government, having criticized its handling of a separatist Tuareg rebellion in the vast Saharan north, the rebels allied with radical jihadi militants and seized northern town after town. Separatists, particularly jihadi militants, accounted for the over-whelming majority of attacks on journalists, according to CPJ research, as they imposed draconian censorship measures and brutal intimidation tactics. Speaking of the insurgent groups, Yéhiha Tandina, a journalist based in the fabled northeast town Timbuktu, said, "They don't like to see photos of child soldiers among them or anything portraying their fighters in a bad light."

In the northeastern town of Ansongo, militants from the Salafist group Ansar Dine took over Radio Soni in April and forced the station to replace its female editor, Fatoumata Abdou, with a man and limit its programming to Quranic recitations. In the town of Gao, on at least two occasions, fighters from the Movement for Oneness and Jihad in West Africa dragged the Radio Adar Khoïma host Malick Aliou Maïga away from live programming at gunpoint and assaulted him for report-ing on public discontent with the brutal rule of the Islamists. Across northern Mali, radio stations were forced to drop any musical content, including jingles, local journalists told CPJ. "When you want to cover an event, you must present a letter [to the militant groups] with your questions in advance," Tandina said.

At least two journalists fled northern Mali in 2012 because of direct intimidation, and many others have left because they were unable to carry on their professional duties, according to CPJ research. Towns of the sparsely populated region have limited electricity and mobile network coverage; radio is the most widely available medium. As a result of the censorship and intimidation, residents have been stripped of discussion platforms and forced to rely on international radio broadcasts for independent information.

"The human rights situation in West African countries affected by political instability and insecurity, such as Mali . . . and in those affected by the growing threat of terrorism, such as Nigeria, remains a source of concern," U.N. Secretary-General Ban Ki-moon noted in a report to the Security Council in June 2012.

In Nigeria, Boko Haram has been waging war on the federal government since 2009 in an effort to impose Shariah law in the country's northern, predominantly Muslim states. In the conflict, "the mass media have been very crucial to publicizing the violent activities of nonstate armed and terrorist groups in Nigeria and state security measures to contain them," Olusola Isola and Michael Akintayo wrote in the October 2012 edition of *International Journal of Social Science Tomorrow*. In October 2011, Boko Haram claimed responsibility for the murder of Zakariya Isa, accusing the state media cameraman of spying. In May, Boko Haram followed the twin bombings in April 2012 with a chilling video released on YouTube that singled out three international news outlets and 11 Nigerian papers for attacks. In the same video, which registered more than 86,000 views, the Boko Haram spokesman Qaqa accused *ThisDay* of inaccurately attributing to Boko Haram attacks it did not carry out. News outlets "should understand that for us there is no difference between those fighting with arms and with the pen," Qaqa said in August, accusing the media of taking sides.

Boko Haram accounted for only one-fifth of attacks against the press in Nigeria in 2012—most were committed by government forces and officials, according to CPJ research—but the group's brutal tactics caused much greater fear. "To say there are increased security risks facing journalists this year compared to previous years is an understatement of the fact," said Aishatu Sule, deputy president of the Nigerian Guild of Editors.

Boko Haram did not immediately follow through on the threats in its May video, but the open-ended warning prompted many news outlets to pull their correspondents out of the group's strongholds in northern Nigeria. Some reporters have gone underground or suspended work altogether, while others have simply adapted their reporting to the group's demands, local journalists told CPJ.

"Generally, there is a shift on the part of the media from blaming all attacks and killings on the group unless it claims responsibility. So, you now find the media using 'gunmen' and 'attackers' to describe suspects of attacks that are without clear signatures of the insurgents," *Daily Trust* investigative editor Nuruddeen Abdallah told CPJ in an email. "We are now being more careful with all the information," he said, and that includes "the usual security agencies' spins on their 'successes' in tackling the militant group."

■ ■ ■

Government responses to coverage of the insurgents put further pressure on journalists. In a September 2012 keynote address at the All Nigerian Editors Conference, Presidential National Security Adviser M. S. Dasuki urged media to play down reporting of Boko Haram attacks and refrain from embarrassing the government. "This is particularly important in the advent of social media and the Internet when all your newspapers are being read around the world, almost as instantly as you finish your columns," he said. "Bad press about Nigeria affects the ability of our nation's level of entrepreneurship and job creation."

In Mali, the government resorted to blocking websites and phone numbers belonging to the Islamists. According to Diakaridia Dembélé, a freelance reporter based in the capital, Bamako, a call to spokesmen for the militants on one of the country's largest mobile networks yielded this voice recording: "You are not authorized to call this number because it belongs to persons with bad intentions."

Though insurgent groups are a relatively new menace for the press in West Africa, they have long established a trail of censorship and journalists' blood in Somalia, Africa's deadliest nation for the press. At least 20 journalists have been murdered in Somalia since Al-Shabaab militants emerged in the country in 2007, according to CPJ research—more than the number killed in the prior 14 years of civil war. Al-Shabaab, which is affiliated with Al-Qaeda, has claimed responsibility for only five of the murders, and while it is possible that other criminal or political groups could be behind some of the deaths, the hard-line jihadi group represents the most fearsome threat. Somali authorities have never brought to trial any suspect in the murder of a journalist, affording killers total impunity.

Governments in Nigeria and Mali have not done much better. In the twin bombings in April, the Nigerian police arrested one of the bombers, but have not brought anyone to trial, according to local journalists. Frank Mba, Nigeria's federal police spokesman, referred questions about the government's efforts to ensure the safety of journalists to the press itself. "If you speak to the Nigerian media, they'll tell you the steps we are taking," he said. "We don't go about telling the whole world what we are doing." He added that police don't treat the press differently than any other sector of society. In response, Sule of the Nigerian Guild of Editors noted that the press constitutes a particularly vulnerable group, which should merit commensurate police attention. She also said authorities generally refuse to make exceptions for journalists and media workers during curfews related to terror attacks, making it difficult for them to work.

In Mali, where the insurgency and the coup have divided the country in two, with both halves in chaos, journalists have little more to rely on than their wits. Veteran reporter Moussa Kaka, who has been reporting on Islamist militants in Mali, said he relies on his extensive experience as a reporter to keep himself safe and circumvent limitations. Ultimately, however, "you must establish total trust" with your subjects, he said.

Governments, however, can be quick to arrest journalists like Kaka who secure interviews with insurgents. Kaka was once imprisoned in his native Niger for more than a year on anti-state charges, based on recordings of his phone conversations with Tuareg rebels. In June 2012, a court in Burundi sentenced radio reporter Hassan Ruvakuki to life in prison on terrorism charges based on his embedded reporting with a new rebel movement.

Though the Nigerian government hasn't arrested journalists for reporting on Boko Haram, reporters told CPJ they believe their actions are being closely watched by the authorities. "Most of us know that our phone lines are bugged by the security agencies. We are operating between the devil and the deep blue sea," said *Daily Trust*'s Abdallah. Freelance journalist Ahmad Salkida, who has extensively covered Boko Haram, reported in March 2012 that he had been put under surveillance and had received threatening phone calls from suspected state security agents. He went into hiding.

■ ■ ■

To some extent, journalists can take advantage of technology to reduce the hazards of reporting on armed groups. "The electronic nature of social media and mobility of modern telephones makes it relatively easy to communicate from a safe and remote distance," said Judith Matloff, a veteran international correspondent and journalist security consultant. One Nigerian journalist, who did not want to be named for fear of reprisal from Boko Haram, said, "It is very common to see a journalist writing about Maiduguri," a northeastern city badly afflicted by the conflict, "from Abuja, Kaduna, Lagos, or even Port Harcourt because it is suicidal to stay in one place."

Yet, even as insurgent groups like Boko Haram intimidate journalists in a bid to influence coverage, they also bypass the mainstream media by disseminating their own messages via Facebook, Twitter, YouTube, and other social media. In Somalia, for example, Al-Shabaab militants release statements via a Twitter account with more than 16,000 followers. In their research paper, Isola and Akintayo wrote that insurgent groups "deliberately use the new media to intensify the fear they create among the public and to reach the elite and younger elements of the population who may not be too exposed to the traditional media."

This dual strategy to control information is a striking contrast to the insurgencies of previous decades, when the press served as a conduit at times in delivering the messages of militant groups.

"It's funny to think back to the 1980s, before we had readily available cellphones or social media," Matloff said. "Fax was the main form of communication, and it was rare to find a Mozambican or Angolan rebel who could quickly send a message from the jungle." Digital connectivity means insurgents can "be their own media," said David J. Betz, an expert on counterinsurgency and information and professor of War Studies at King's College London. Betz told CPJ by email, "News editors who once played a very important role as gatekeepers are not nearly so powerful as they were."

To the insurgent and criminal groups operating today, the press is instead a rival in disseminating information—and events in Nigeria, Mali, and Somalia make plain that journalists are vulnerable as a result.

Mohamed Keita is advocacy coordinator for CPJ's Africa Program. He regularly gives interviews in French and English to international news media on press freedom issues in Africa and has participated in several international panels.

In Taliban's Media Evolution, Press Became An Enemy

By *Ahmed Rashid*

W hen I first met the Taliban in 1993 in Kandahar they had no concept of journalism. Their leaders had told them to avoid all foreigners, even non-Taliban Pashtuns who come from the same ethnic group. The Taliban suspected all foreigners and journalists to be spies. Many came from the backward and conservative rural areas of southern Afghanistan that had hardly been touched by the Soviet occupation, making them extremely secretive about their political structures and intentions.

After conquering Kabul in 1996, their leaders went on a blitz, banning all news media except the Taliban-run Radio Afghanistan and hanging television sets from lampposts to make their point. Television, newspapers, magazines, photography were all forbidden. So for years before the September 11 attacks, Afghanistan was without any kind of domestic media.

The Taliban made it extremely difficult for a foreign journalist to carry out normal reporting because they offered no news, facts, or opinions. They failed to understand that ignoring the media only fueled the negative images the world and Afghans had of them. Yet they were never hostile, threatening, or corrupt toward journalists. I was denied a visa by the Taliban in 2000, but the Taliban and I knew the denial had been ordered by Pakistan's Inter-Services Intelligence Directorate, or ISI, which supported the Taliban and was critical of my reporting. When I accidentally met Mullah Wakil Ahmad Muttawakil, the Taliban foreign minister, on a flight to Central Asia, he apologized to me and with a wink and nod said that the ban was not his fault. The ISI still tries to be the gatekeeper for anybody trying to contact the Taliban.

By 2000, some Taliban commanders developed a much more hostile attitude toward the media, largely because of the presence of Arab militants and the influence of a very paranoid Al-Qaeda. First welcomed as a guest, Al-Qaeda began to dictate social mores in the major Afghan cities. It encouraged the Taliban to carry out ethnic cleansing against the Shia Hazaras and other minorities like the Hindus and Sikhs in Kabul. Al-Qaeda threatened all foreigners in Kabul, including United Nations and Red Cross officials. The few foreign journalists who did travel to Kabul knew they had to avoid any accidental meeting with the Arabs of Al-Qaeda.

■ ■ ■

Surprisingly, it was Al-Qaeda and Pakistani extremists who taught the Taliban how to use the media more effectively in the post-9/11 era. After their defeat in Afghanistan in 2001, both the Taliban and Al-Qaeda leadership came to live in exile in Pakistan's northwestern border provinces. Although the Taliban remained extremely secretive about their new political and military structures and their relationships with Al-Qaeda and the ISI, by 2004 they were actively promoting jihad against U.S. occupation forces and what they termed the puppet regime of President Hamid Karzai.

The Taliban thus had a public political stance to win sympathizers. On the defensive, fighting a guerrilla war, they also had to create their own publicity if they wanted to show their military successes.

Al-Qaeda militants, who by then had set up video film studios in northwest Pakistan churning out gory scenes of suicide bombings and military attacks inside Afghanistan, helped the Taliban do the same.

The Taliban provided video clips of their battles to journalists, sold propaganda DVDs in the markets in Peshawar, and offered instant comment via mobile phone from official spokesmen who were usually based in Pakistan but pretended to be in Afghanistan. They created blogs and websites and eventually Twitter and Facebook accounts. Trained camera operators accompanied particularly audacious attacks against U.S. forces.

The Afghan Taliban's new relationship with Al-Qaeda had enormous moral impact on many Taliban commanders, who became excessively brutal in the belief that they were justly forcing Afghans to embrace their interpretation of Shariah law. One of those commanders, Mullah Dadullah, a close friend of Osama bin Laden, killed a Red Cross engineer in 2003 and had no compunctions about killing journalists. Some of the worst atrocities took place in Helmand Province, Dadullah's area of command. After Dadullah was killed, his brother continued in the same way. In March 2007, the Taliban seized an Italian journalist and his Afghan interpreter. The Italian, Daniele Mastrogiacomo, was freed in exchange for five Taliban prisoners; the interpreter, Ajmal Naqshbandi, was executed.

Several journalists were to die in suicide bombings, including Abdul Qodus, a cameraman for Aryana TV, who was killed in Kandahar in July 2006, and Carsten Thomassen of Norway, who died in the bombing of the Serena Hotel in Kabul in January 2008 carried out by the network of Jalaluddin Haqqani. At the same time, journalists were being picked up for ransom or in bids to get the Americans to release Taliban prisoners. Such tactics became a new form of fundraising and political messaging, all encouraged by the Taliban high command and Al-Qaeda.

The attraction of kidnapping was enhanced by the safe havens afforded by Pakistan's Federal Administered Tribal Areas, or FATA, where hostages could be held indefinitely. Much of this region was controlled by the Haqqani network, which emerged as the leader and adjudicator for both the Afghan and Pakistani Taliban. Thus, in 2008, David Rohde of *The New York Times* and Afghan colleague Tahir Ludin were abducted outside Kabul, taken to FATA and kept there while negotiations went on. Rohde and Ludin escaped on foot after seven months of captivity. A year later, Stephen Farrell of the *Times* and Afghan journalist Sultan Mohammed Munadi, were kidnapped. Farrell escaped in a British-led rescue attempt, but Munadi was killed.

Finally, journalists suffered as casualties of war: blown up by land mines, caught in Taliban ambushes, or victimized by suicide bombers. By 2007 it had become extremely dangerous if not impossible for Kabul-based media to trust the Taliban for a face-to-face conversation or to go with them on forays into the countryside. Journalists were forced to become Kabul-bound or to leave town only with adequate security.

■ ■ ■

In Pakistan there was an even more complicated war taking place between the army and the Pakistani Taliban. The Pakistani Taliban were made up of many different factions, the most extreme having been influenced about media and foreigners by Al-Qaeda. Later, extremist groups from Punjab and other parts of Pakistan were to set up bases in FATA, and they were even more hostile to journalists.

The ISI itself played a dubious role. It sided with some Taliban groups, especially those who fought the Americans in Afghanistan, while going after those Taliban who attacked the Pakistan army. Local Pashtun journalists often were caught in the crossfire or found themselves punished either by the Taliban or the ISI because they could not keep up with the constantly changing connections between various Taliban groups and the intelligence service.

War took a toll among local Pakistani Pashtun stringers, who became inadvertent targets of Pakistani airstrikes, Taliban suicide bombings, U.S. drone missile strikes, and other instruments of death. Many Pashtun journalists in FATA, increasingly targeted by all sides, left the region and moved to Peshawar. Many were not regularly paid by the local media and depended on stringing for Western media networks, which invariably asked them to take greater risks. War deaths included Abdul Shaheen, a reporter killed in a Pakistani airstrike while being held prisoner by the Taliban in 2008; Mohammed Sarwar, a driver killed in a suicide bombing in Quetta in 2010; and Abdul Wahab and Pervez Khan, reporters killed in a double suicide bombing that claimed 50 lives in FATA in 2010.

The Taliban publicly gunned down journalists they considered to be traitors or spies—or to have simply covered them insufficiently. The victims included Afghan journalist Janullah Hashimzada, shot by the Pakistani Taliban while riding a public minibus in FATA in 2009. Journalists may well have reported what the Taliban wanted them to report, but there was no guarantee that news desks would use the material, thus creating enormous risks for the stringers.

It soon became apparent that the lower echelons of the ISI who were based in FATA adopted the same attitudes as the Taliban. They expected local Pakistani journalists to be loyal to them, not divulge their secret deals with the multiple Taliban factions, not say who was on their payrolls, and, above all, to maintain the myths that drone attacks were carried out by the Americans without ISI intelligence support and that the military was wholeheartedly fighting an all-out war with the Pakistani Taliban. Journalists were arrested or disappeared for months. Some did not return home. In all, 38 journalists were killed in Pakistan in direct relation to their work between January 2005 and October 2012, placing it among the deadliest countries in the world for the press.

Hayatullah Khan, who disclosed that the United States was firing drone missiles into FATA while the military was trying to hide the practice, disappeared in December 2005 and was found dead in June 2006. His body was emaciated, and he had been tortured and shot several times. Doctors said one hand had been manacled in handcuffs typically used by the ISI. After enormous media and international pressure, a judicial investigation into his death took place, but the results were never made public. In November 2007, his wife was murdered in a bomb attack outside her home, leaving behind five orphaned children.

FATA and the Afghan border region have been off-limits to journalists for several years. There is no independent information from the tribal agencies as political activists, NGO workers, and tens of thousands of people opposed to the Taliban have left FATA and become refugees. The military keeps a tight lid on what is reported from FATA, even if the reports emanate from Peshawar. The Taliban react immediately if anyone tries to report the true facts from anywhere in the northwest.

The lack of information has created a vacuum in which it becomes impossible even for experts to assess the impact of the drone attacks, gauge whether the army or the Taliban control particular regions, measure the strength and ideological basis of the various Taliban factions, and determine the condition of Taliban kidnap victims, both Pakistani and foreign. The Pakistani media, by and large, have gone along with such restrictions so as not to anger either the army or the Taliban. It is one more instance in which the loss of sovereignty over a large area by the Pakistan state and the subsequent widespread suffering of the people is going unreported.

Ahmed Rashid, a CPJ board member, has covered Afghanistan since 1979 for numerous publications and has written five books on the wars in Afghanistan and the politics of Pakistan and Central Asia. His latest book is "Pakistan on the Brink." CPJ's Sumit Galhotra contributed research for this essay.

2

CENSORED

The Zacatecas Rules: Cartel's Reign Cannot Be Covered

By Mike O'Connor

An anonymous phone call tipped police to the body dumped in a field near the hamlet of El Bordo in central Zacatecas state. Police would say only that the victim was a peasant farmer in his 40s who had been beaten and shot, and that his body had been there for a few days. But the reporter knew the pattern: A poor person in a rural community had not paid extortion money to the ruling cartel, or had somehow crossed the gang. Much more information was waiting in the hamlet, from family members and neighbors. But the reporter wasn't going, though it was only an hour or so from the state capital where he worked. He could never write such a story. In fact, just learning what really happened would put his life in danger.

"They'll kill you, and I have children. So, I guess even if you don't think about it every time you write a story, you never forget about it, either," the reporter said. "It must be there all the time, somewhere, always. Because you automatically know the things you can write about and the things you can't say."

These are the rules for reporters in the state of Zacatecas, Mexico.

What reporters can't tell the public is that organized crime has taken over Zacatecas, from the deserts to the mountain ranges. Journalists told CPJ that gangs control each of the 58 counties either completely or almost so. In most of the state, they said, control is in the hands of the Zetas, the most vicious and feared cartel in Mexico. The municipal and state police, reporters said, are terrified or have been bought off. Some police stations are abandoned and others have officers who seldom leave the building. Beginning about a year ago, army, navy, and federal police patrols have made the main highways somewhat safer, along with a very few rural areas, but the state does not belong to its citizens, journalists said.

In other states the press has been forced into silence after the murders of journalists—sometimes, a stream of murders. But in Zacatecas, the cartels haven't had to kill a single journalist to silence every journalist. According to CPJ research, this is the pattern now in many Mexican states: Cartels gain control, the press is intimidated, and the public is uninformed. And since there are no deaths among local journalists, there is no attention drawn to the pervasive problem of self-censorship.

"We know what organized crime does to reporters who don't follow orders in other states. They kill them," a journalist known for his bravery said on the patio of a bar near the state capitol. Speaking of a reporter murdered in January 2010 in the neighboring state of Coahuila, he added: "We knew Valentín Valdéz—he came here once. He sat at this table. Here, this very table. They killed him."

There are two false but broadly held beliefs among the political and social elite in Mexico City. The first is that every reporter in the states is corrupt. The second is that murdered reporters were singled out because they worked for a cartel and had either angered their gang bosses or crossed a rival group. There is some truth in this broad caricature. CPJ research has found that corruption has tainted the press corps at times. That may happen because journalists want the extra money. But when a cartel of killers takes over your town and tells you to follow orders if you want to keep your family alive, well, corruption is not exactly the right description.

Still, this stereotype of the corrupt journalist has had the effect of absolving national leaders of their obligation to address the murderous attack on free expression across the country. Why protect the corrupt? Why investigate a journalist's murder if everyone knows the victim was working for a cartel? So even as Mexico has taken important steps like the adoption of a constitutional amendment that federalizes anti-press crimes, it's not going to make any real progress until its leaders understand that their cynical views are wrong.

They can go to Zacatecas to learn this.

There, journalists express a profound responsibility for their work and an anguish that it can no longer be done properly. Their torment comes spilling out in interviews across the state. In the city of Fresnillo, when CPJ met with a group of reporters, a veteran journalist was on the edge of tears. She stood, head down, chin nearly to her chest. Then she pulled her head up to speak to 12 other reporters, her suffering spread across her face. At first, she said it was the personal frustration of knowing the reality and not being able to report it. Then, a deeper truth came out. "We have failed the people here who counted on us to tell them what was happening all around us. We had the responsibility to tell them, but we could not. So we failed them." Some agreed with her. Others said that telling the truth was suicidal and that self-censorship was the only way to survive.

A lone reporter, too afraid to speak in public, came instead to a CPJ representative's hotel room, where he collapsed in uncontrollable weeping, a trembling human ball in a corner chair. "These things chase me in my sleep," he said. "Sometimes it feels physical because they pull you in two directions. You have to report what is happening. You must. But you can't."

CPJ spoke with 32 reporters, photographers, and editors in Zacatecas. Some of the editors hold senior positions for statewide papers; some of the reporters work for small-town broadcast stations or weeklies. All were told their identities would be kept confidential. All agreed that organized crime operates at will in every corner of the state, and that journalists saw the wave rolling across Zacatecas and were afraid to report it.

■ ■ ■

It's strange the things journalists can no longer report. Not only things like threats and payments to police and public officials—those wouldn't

be visible. But in the city of Fresnillo, the state's largest, journalists said
they all knew that one of Mexico's top Zeta leaders often lived at 301
Huicot Avenue. Of course, they said, if journalists were on to it, then
the city police knew, and so did the army and the navy, which are
in the state supposedly doing what the police won't do. The avenue
is perhaps the city's most high-end street, four lanes and pruned pine
trees down the divider. The Zeta leader's house was one of the newest.

Not a word of any of that was reported, journalists in Fresnillo said.
Then, a murderous dispute exploded between the gang leader, known
as Zeta 50, and a rival called Zeta 40. In the first week of September
2012, according to neighbors and reporters, construction machinery showed up at the home and partially demolished it—a humiliating public assault by Zeta 40 on Zeta 50. Afterward, debris from the
Huicot Avenue home ran across the yard, onto the sidewalk, and into
the street. But nothing about the event was reported. Even talking
about it, reporters whispered. And, those who work for statewide news
organizations said they didn't tell their editors in the city of Zacatecas,
the capital, because they assumed their phones were tapped by
either the Zetas or the authorities. In any event, even a story as obvious as this was much too dangerous to publish. (U.S.-trained Mexican
marines arrested Zeta 50, identified as Ivan Velázquez Caballero, on
murder charges in late September, Mexican officials said. Although half
the city of Fresnillo knew where Zeta 50 was living, the tip that led to
his arrest had come from Washington, according to a U.S. law enforcement official.)

The Zeta cartel began slithering into the state virtually unnoticed
because there were few gunshots. About five years ago, a small force
of midlevel cartel leaders arrived with magnificent SUVs, assault rifles,
and thick rolls of pesos wrapped in rubber bands, according to reporters. The weapons and money were distributed to the young sons of
impoverished bean and chili farmers; the payoffs made them important people in their isolated, scrub desert and mountain communities.
These young men knew the canyons and the country trails far better
than the soldiers and federal police sent from the outside to control
them. Though they now exploit their own, they are also the sons of
Zacatecas. As that was happening, there was a coup against the police
in nearly every county. "It was very smart," a reporter told CPJ. "They

went to the local police chiefs and the local small-time criminal gangs and said, 'We're here and we're in charge.' Some of the police were killed, just to make a climate of terror. It was for an example. Then the rest went over to the cartel."

Zacatecas has only about 1.5 million residents. But it's just about in the middle of the country, so major highways—the drug routes to the North—run through it. Since it is mostly empty, it is also a very good place to train, hide, and then dispatch cartel soldiers in any direction they're needed. And 1.5 million people with little police protection still represent a good opportunity for drug sales, robbery, extortion, and kidnapping.

Mexicans hardly ever see a thing about this state in their press, except its gorgeous colonial buildings and museums. Mexico is a country of 112 million, making Zacatecas barely worth counting amid the crime and death occurring nationally. And with more than 50 journalists and media workers killed or disappeared nationwide since 2007, Zacatecas would not seem to register as a press freedom concern. But that would miss two important facts. There isn't as much bloodshed in Zacatecas precisely because the Zetas have so much control. Despite a split in the cartel and firefights with other gangs nibbling at the edges of the state, the Zetas' lock is strong.

The other factor is this: Although there are correspondents from national news organizations based in Zacatecas, they can't report the truth, either. They are no safer than the local press, and they work under local rules. Even if correspondents were foolhardy enough to file stories that gave a true picture of what happened at the beginning of the Zetas' takeover and what is happening today, editors in Mexico City tell CPJ they won't publish stories that will put their correspondents' lives in danger. So the Mexican public as a whole has been kept in the dark about Zacatecas. The state has been taken over by homicidal gangsters, and people who rely on the Mexican national press still don't know.

"We had to decide to take a step back from giving a full view of the national picture," said Mireya Cuéllar, national editor of the newspaper La Jornada. "I would definitely call it a step back. That's a very clear decision because no story is worth the life of one of our correspondents. Our people who cover the states live there and their families are there. They are very vulnerable." The larger issue, then, isn't just about one small state but rather how many other, seemingly quiet states are really just like Zacatecas?

Because the journalists of Zacatecas were not able to tell the public about the cartel takeover, they were not able to expose the state government's failures either. "The fact is that the criminals got in and the state government should have been watching," state legislator Saúl Monreal said. "Why it wasn't watching is what we all want to know. Because now these guys are everywhere and no one knows how to handle them. The state government is completely overwhelmed." Running his hand above his head, as if to show the government drowning, he added: "Now, were the state officials only inept? That's very inept. Were they threatened also? Did some get payoffs? We don't know."

Journalists said they can't get to the bottom of what went wrong originally for the same reason they can't find out if state officials are involved with the problem today: The cartels are too dangerous to even ask about. There is some limited coverage of the gunfights between cartels, and those between government forces and cartels. That's spot news, stories about an event, not stories that give readers a panoramic view of what is going on. But almost always, reporters said, it's either too dangerous to get close to the fighting or, more likely, government forces seal off the area.

The result is that most news stories have to be written from what the state or federal government claims happened. And that's where reporters learn not to ask questions. A reporter explained: "If I call a police official and push for too much information about a shootout, then he begins to give me subtle threats, like 'Why are you so curious?' In Zacatecas that's a threat." Another reporter said, "Maybe I could go to the county records department to research how much a legislator's suspicious new house cost. But a clerk will report me, I'll have to leave my name, somehow it will get out. Why don't I just shoot myself instead? That will be quicker."

It is not just the cartels that keep the news from the public, according to reporters and top editors. Their own news organizations are afraid to lose vital advertising contracts from the state, and the official state policy has been that there was no problem with the cartels. Zacatecas' economy is fairly simple. It has mines and farms, some tourism, and money sent back by relatives working in the United States. It is hard for any news organization to find substantial advertisers. "Most of us survive only because of what the state pays for ads," said the publisher of a major newspaper. An editor said: "There is no doubt that makes the owner listen to what the state says. If the governor calls the owner and says such and such is the truth, well, you better take that into account." Two governors ago, when reporters said the Zetas were beginning to arrive, the governor's position was that there was no problem. The current governor says there's a problem but it's being handled.

■ ■ ■

Jerez is a little town founded in the 1500s. Its sidewalks are framed by high stone arches, and its plazas are surrounded by wrought ironwork and green ivy. Not only does nearly everyone know each other, nearly everyone's great-great-grandmother knew everyone else's. Its small stores were left open when shopkeepers went to lunch, and bicycles were left leaning unlocked against lampposts. That was until three years ago, people said, when the spread of the Zeta cartel reached the rural settlements around Jerez and then the town itself. Now, Jerez is noteworthy for its terror. There were no news stories about it, journalists here said.

A woman in her 50s said she had moved away for university and a career, and came back for her hometown's quiet ways and to care for her elderly parents. "Just don't put down my name," she said, taking a careful look around. "The nights used to be nearly as lively as the days because we lived in the plazas and walked from one friend's home over to a cousin's or things like that. There were musicians who came on a route they had from other towns." Not now. Those nights are gone. The streets are quiet before dark. Friends don't get into details with one another, people said. Everyone feels the terror alone, or maybe they share it with their closest family members. "I heard that they were extorting the taxis on the main plaza and my cousin has a taxi there," a man said. "My cousin wouldn't say yes and he wouldn't say no. That means yes. They steal our money first, then they steal the life we had together." Until recently a family in Jerez would be proud to say they had relatives in the United States who were doing well. Now, no one wants it to get out that their relatives in the north may be better off than broke because that could mean a nasty visit from a group of Zetas demanding a monthly payment.

In their new isolation from the friends and families they have known for generations, the people of Jerez are also isolated from the truth about the rest of the state. In their own small town they learn only guarded rumors of what might be happening. They cannot see how their lives sync up with other lives in other towns and in the vast, wild stretches in between.

The highway from Jerez to the state capital is four lanes and is sometimes patrolled by the army. It takes about an hour for the run. People on both ends said that in early 2012 the Zetas routinely set up roadblocks and stole cars or robbed people in buses. It was the Old West of the U.S. come south. Journalists said it was like that all around the state, although the military has more or less retaken the major highways. The trouble is that the state is all open space with just slivers of pavement. Even if the federal government did have control of the highways, it wouldn't have control of Zacatecas.

On the way back from Jerez to the capital, along the right side of the highway, close, maybe 250 feet away on a hard dirt road, there were two SUVs with civilians carrying assault rifles. They were on patrol, covering their zone.

Mike O'Connor is CPJ's Mexico representative. He is the co-author of CPJ's 2010 report, "Silence or Death in Mexico's Press."

Extremists Are Censoring The Story of Religion

By Jean-Paul Marthoz

T wenty years ago, on May 22, 1993, Algerian journalist Tahar Djaout, the founder of the independent weekly *Ruptures*, left his home, walked to his car, and sat at the wheel. A few seconds later he was hit by two bullets shot through the window. A gifted and rebellious writer, Djaout had forcefully denounced the Islamist groups fighting the Algerian military regime. His murder inaugurated a killing spree, mostly attributed to armed Islamic groups, which eventually cost the lives of 60 Algerian journalists.

In the following two decades, hundreds of local and international reporters have been targeted by violence in the name of religious faith. The attacks have had a chilling effect on the coverage of religion and the many issues and conflicts that surround it. Many editors think twice before sending reporters to regions where religious extremists could abduct or kill them. In countries riven by religious sectarianism, some journalists do not dig too deeply. Even in more peaceful countries, the mainstream media are wary of the potential for violence, offense, or the trespassing of blasphemy laws. Columnists choose their words carefully or avoid inflammatory topics. Cartoonists blunt their pencils.

"You risk your life on the front lines or you are taken out of the story because of the red lines—the fear of inflaming a minority or of creating a backlash for you and your media," John Owen, former CBC chief news editor and professor of international journalism at London City University, told CPJ.

The religion story, however, has to be told because religion pervades local and international news. Its coverage determines the capacity of societies to address freely and thoroughly issues that are central to the rooting of democracy and the respect of human rights. And it is all the more crucial because religion has become a global issue. Globalization, if it is to be a new intersection of freedom, requires a journalism that is uninhibited and robust.

"Journalists should be free to cover religion without intimidation," Aidan White, director of the Ethical Journalism Network at the Global Editors Network, told CPJ. "Their decisions should not be determined by their fear of violence or prosecution but by their professional and ethical judgment."

"Every major religious tradition has served as a resource for violent actors," Mark Juergensmeyer wrote in his seminal book "Terror in the Mind of God." In the 1980s, the Ulster conflict pitted Catholics against Protestants, and in the 1990s, the Balkan wars raged among Catholic Croats, Orthodox Serbs, and Muslim Bosnians. Although other faiths are involved in violence against journalists, the focus of recent international news is mostly Islamic extremism—a political current that targets non-Muslim journalists as well as Muslim moderates, modernizers, and reformers.

■ ■ ■

In 1966 when *Time* magazine published a cover story headlined "Is God Dead?" many pundits predicted an inexorable trend toward increased secularization in the wake of modernization and globalization. The reverse has been true. "We now live in a world where religion is a robust global force. It is increasingly vibrant, assertive, and politicized the world over," wrote Timothy Samuel Shah and Monica Duffy

Toft in "Blind Spot: When Journalists Don't Get Religion." According to the 2012 Pew Research Center's Global Index of Religiosity and Atheism, 59 percent of the world population calls itself religious. Although Western Europe is generally an exception and atheism is slightly on the rise in the United States, other regions with booming demographics have experienced a sustained religious surge, especially through the rise of Islam, Pentecostalism, and Evangelical Protestantism.

This trend is reinforced by globalization, which gives greater influence to religious diasporas, according to Scott Thomas, an expert at the U.K.'s University of Bath. The rise of global media and the emergence of transnational social media add a particular volatile mix to religious controversies. As illustrated by the row over Danish cartoons that caricatured the Prophet Muhammad in 2005–06 and the film "The Innocence of Muslims" in 2012, which provoked angry protests in Egypt and other Muslim countries, a local religious story can nearly instantly become viral and global.

Religious extremism does not usually stand out as such in press freedom groups' statistics; it is blurred with other causes of violence (politics, corruption, terrorism) or other categories of perpetrators (nonstate actors, political groups). In fact, in many conflicts it is often difficult to disentangle religious extremism from causes such as nationalism, ethnicity, or politics.

But religious extremism appears to be in a class by itself as a source of violence. And as with all types of attacks on the press, a majority are committed against local, not international, journalists.

Among the attacks in 2012 was a killing in March in Somalia's semi-autonomous region of Puntland, where Al-Shabaab insurgents claimed responsibility for shooting to death Ali Ahmed Abdi, a journalist with Radio Galkayo. In April, a Frankfurt-based Salafist group released a video directly naming and threatening German journalists who had criticized its campaign to hand out free copies of the Quran to every household in Germany. In May, Canadian journalist and Muslim reformist Irshad Manji suffered minor injuries when a mob attacked her at a book launch in Yogyakarta, Indonesia.

Similarly, Bosnian journalist Stefica Galic was beaten by a group of men and women in July, two days after the screening of her documentary film "Nedjo of Ljubuski," dedicated to her late husband, Nedjeljko

Nedjo Galic, a Croat who had helped Muslim citizens avoid ethnic cleansing. In August, gunmen from the Movement for Oneness and Jihad in West Africa, a Salafist militant group affiliated with Al-Qaeda, stormed the studios of Radio Adar Khoïma in the northeast town of Gao in Mali and attacked Malick Aliou Maïga, a local stringer for Voice of America, beating him unconscious. In Tunis in September, local and foreign reporters were attacked by Salafists while they were covering protests against "The Innocence of Muslims" near the U.S. Embassy.

Pressure on journalists comes not just from religious actors but also from state authorities who conflate the coverage of radical groups with complicity with religious extremism. For example, in June 2011, Urinboy Usmonov, a reporter for the BBC World's Uzbek service, was arrested in Tajikistan and convicted of "extremism" after meeting with members of the banned Islamist group Hizb-ut-Tahrir. Although he was released on bail in July and later granted amnesty, his conviction sent a chilling message to reporters covering sensitive religious stories.

In March 2012, Ahmad Salkida, an independent Nigerian journalist who had been reporting for years on the activities of the Islamist sect Boko Haram, received death threats that he suspected came from government security agents accusing him of being a member of the extremist group. And in Ethiopia, the authorities arrested Yusuf Getachew, editor of the *Ye Muslimoch Guday* (Muslim Affairs), and suspended three Muslim news outlets in August after they covered protests opposing policies that Muslims said were interfering with their religious institutions.

■ ■ ■

In some countries the resurgence of religious extremism has coincided with a countercurrent: the rise of a new generation of independent journalists, bloggers, and social media activists. Often hailed as heroes of international press freedom, they work according to values and standards that by definition question dogma, break taboos, and investigate all social actors, including religious groups.

"In Northern Africa, many of these journalists tend to be more secular, more liberal, and Westernized, especially in the Francophone media," independent Moroccan journalist Ali Lmrabet told CPJ. They are also often denounced as traitors, agents of the West, or apostates by extremists, and even by old-style journalists.

In countries with strong religious identities, many in the media have traditionally conformed to the prevalent religious norms or aligned themselves with a particular religious group. "In an average Indonesian newsroom, most media workers identify closely with an Islamic and nationalist identity," says Human Rights Watch consultant Andreas Harsono. In Nigeria, "many of what we have as national newspapers—both private and state-owned—are in fact religious," writes Leo Igwe, research fellow at the University of Bayreuth in Germany. "They are extensions of their churches and mosques."

Sometimes the most radical journalists even call openly for violence against those they see as infidels or apostates. "In Pakistan there are big sectarian divisions in the media," said White of the Ethical Journalism Network. "When Punjab Gov. Salman Taseer, a vocal opponent of blasphemy laws, was murdered by his bodyguard in January 2011, there was support on TV for his killing."

In this environment, the supposed religious affiliation of journalists affects their ability to report safely. From northern Mali to Afghanistan, large swaths of land are considered off-limits; editors are concerned not only by the obvious physical risk involved in being on the ground, but they also fear publishing stories or opinions that might antagonize radical religious groups and expose their reporters in the field to reprisal.

Western journalists, even if they insist they are neutral, are particularly at risk. "In areas afflicted by religious conflicts, the alleged faith of the reporters matters," said Morocco's Lmrabet. "Contrary to his/her Western colleagues, a Moroccan journalist will not have any problem covering Hamas in Gaza. Al-Jazeera reporters, who are often seen as close to the Muslim Brotherhood, are allowed in by Islamic armed groups who deeply mistrust the Western media."

Some reporters are even targeted in retaliation for their government's policies. In 2004, Iraqi Islamic militants forced their French hostages, Christian Chesnot of Radio France Internationale and Georges Malbrunot of *Le Figaro*, to call on the French government to repeal a law banning the Muslim headscarf in public schools.

■ ■ ■

Threats and physical violence are not the only form of attack; the gavel of the magistrates can be very effective in muzzling the media. In many autocracies, from Saudi Arabia to Pakistan, blasphemy laws sternly restrict freedom of expression. "Blasphemy laws provide a context in which governments can prevent the peaceful expression of political or religious news, including those on the role of religion in law, society, and the state," Human Rights First wrote in a March 2012 survey. "By restricting these essential freedoms in the name of protecting religion from defamation, governments are able to stifle the healthy debate and discussion of ideas and essentially determine which ideas are acceptable and which are not."

Blasphemy laws can be harsh. In early 2012 a Saudi journalist, Hamza Kashgari, who had posted Twitter messages that were judged blasphemous, was detained in Malaysia while trying to flee to New Zealand and handed back to Saudi Arabia, where he may face the death penalty. Accusations of religious defamation often provide a ready-made justification for mob violence. On Facebook, thousands of people called for Kashgari's execution.

In Europe, where there is no constitutional freedom-of-speech tradition, blasphemy laws are still on the books in many countries, and even if they are dormant they offer a legal opportunity for those who seek to curb what they consider offensive speech. Increasingly, however, laws against hate speech or racism are used as instruments in the fight against alleged defamation of religion. "These laws in some countries go beyond protection from effective harm and prohibit any statements which are perceived as offensive," White said.

At the United Nations, the 57-member Organization of the Islamic Conference, together with some authoritarian countries, has been trying for years to impose a global ban on the "defamation of religion," prescribing penalties for those who criticize, insult, or ridicule religion, particularly Islam. In September 2012, in the wake of the rage triggered by "The Innocence of Muslims," the OIC vigorously relaunched its campaign against what it called "the deliberate and systematic abuses of freedom of expression."

Fear of the law, however, is not the only factor. Many mainstream journalists are wary of being accused of inciting hatred, breaching ethics, or insulting religious feelings, especially in the context of a resurgence of far-right movements, which abusively present themselves as the heroes of free speech. "Some politicians, particularly on the left, are quick to accuse us of inciting hatred when we cover stories deemed to paint Islam or an ethnic minority in an unfavorable light," Béatrice Delvaux, chief editorialist of the liberal Brussels daily *Le Soir*, told CPJ. "Some journalists are reluctant to proactively cover issues like the rise of fundamentalism, crime, or women's sexual harassment in migrant neighborhoods, out of fear of playing into the hands of the far right."

In March 2012, Paul Berman referred in *The New Republic* to "a vogue all over the world for an entirely voluntary self-censorship— a custom of downplaying certain topics that are deemed sensitive, or declining even to utter certain controversial words."

Some extremists take punishment for perceived blasphemy into their own hands. Kurt Westergaard, the Danish cartoonist who created the image of the Prophet Muhammad wearing a bomb in his turban, was the target of several murder attempts. In November 2011, *Charlie Hebdo*'s offices were firebombed after the French satirical weekly published a "Sharia Hebdo" issue with a cover adorned with a cartoon depiction of the Prophet Muhammad threatening "100 lashes if you don't die laughing."

■ ■ ■

The delicate equation between a commitment to practice responsible journalism and the fear of conceding too much space to religious groups divides the journalistic community. Already dramatized in the controversy over Salman Rushdie's book *The Satanic Verses* in the late 1980s, this tension was exacerbated by the fury over the 2005–06 Danish cartoons. The publication of caricatures of the Prophet Muhammad by the newspaper *Jyllands-Posten* not only raised a global storm, but also sharply split the press. Some media stood squarely behind the Danish paper in the name of freedom of expression, even republishing some of the cartoons as a sign of solidarity. Most media, however, decided against running the cartoons. "That seems a reasonable choice for news organizations that usually refrain from gratuitous assaults on religious symbols, especially since the cartoons are so easy to describe in words,"

The New York Times wrote in an editorial on February 7, 2006. In a *Washington Post* op-ed, William Bennett and Alan Dershowitz strongly disagreed. "To put it simply," they wrote, "radical Islamists have won a war of intimidation."

When in September 2012, in the middle of the uproar over "The Innocence of Muslims" the French satirical weekly *Charlie Hebdo* published cartoons, some of them obscene, of the Prophet Muhammad, the issue again deeply fractured the profession. The Catholic daily *La Croix* lambasted the weekly's "antireligious obsession" and its "provocation," while the left-leaning *Libération* defended editorial freedom and underlined that the "road between self-censorship and capitulation is extraordinarily short and without return."

Amid these concerns and controversies, a number of journalists associations, media companies, and foundations have set up projects to address the coverage of religion. In 2012, for instance, the U.S.-based International Center for Journalists established an award for religion reporting in honor of Christiane Amanpour, the longtime international correspondent and a CPJ board member. The center also helped create an International Association of Religion Journalists. The London-based Media Diversity Institute, together with the European Federation of Journalists and the U.K.-based press freedom group Article 19, published a detailed handbook on the reporting of ethnicity and religion.

These initiatives support cross-cultural understanding, promote conflict-sensitive reporting, and offer guidelines on diversity reporting. "That is an important part of being a journalist, to be able to use your skills to tell the people that religion should be used as a harmonizing factor rather than a dividing factor," said Tanzanian journalist Erick Kabandera.

But some journalists stress that disengaging from the story out of fear to offend or to be hurt is not an option. "We are acutely aware of the particular sensitivity of the religion issue," *Le Soir*'s Delvaux said, "and we take particular care to consult widely when we anticipate controversies, but these stories should be told."

The press is called on to assert its autonomy and freedom in order to perform its most crucial role. "You cannot let Salafists or others set your own news agenda and you cannot outsource these kinds of stories" to freelancers, said Owen, the former CBC chief news editor. "The press has to take its responsibilities. It must adopt the measures that will allow it to cover these issues and controversies fairly and seriously, by painstakingly assessing the risks and preparing reporters for the front lines and the red lines."

CPJ Senior Adviser Jean-Paul Marthoz is a Belgian journalist and writer. He is a foreign affairs columnist for Le Soir *and journalism professor at the Université Catholique de Louvain.*

In Asia, Three Nations Clip Once-Budding Online Freedom

By Shawn W. Crispin

W hen a Bangkok court ruled that website editor Chiranuch Premchaiporn was criminally liable for an anti-royal comment posted by an anonymous visitor to one of her news site's Web boards, the landmark verdict effectively shifted the onus of Internet censorship in Thailand from government authorities to Internet intermediaries. Judges ruled that by failing to remove the comment quickly enough—it remained on Chiranuch's *Prachatai* website for more than 20 days—she had "mutually consented" to the critical posting. Chiranuch, who was acquitted on nine other, similar counts, was sentenced to an eight-month suspended prison term under the 2007 Computer Crime Act, legislation passed in the aftermath of a military coup that, among other restrictions, applies the country's strict *lèse majesté* law to online content.

The May 2012 ruling represented the first time the Computer Crime Act was used by the state to criminally convict a Thai journalist for a freedom of expression–related offense. The authorities had already applied the law's vague and arbitrary national security-related provisions to censor tens of thousands of anonymously posted Web pages, mostly for material deemed offensive to the monarchy. While the ruling sent a stark warning to all online journalists in Thailand, it also implied that Web managers of user-generated platforms like political chat rooms, social media applications, and e-commerce hubs could also be held accountable for content posted to their sites deemed as offensive to the royal family, a criminal offense punishable by 15 years in prison under Thai law.

"The verdict confirmed that the [Computer Crime Act] could be implemented to restrict Internet freedom by requiring intermediaries to police Internet content," said Chiranuch, who appealed the decision and had another *lèse majesté*–related case pending against her in late 2012. "It has had direct effects on freedom of expression and free flow of information because Internet intermediaries now must practice self-censorship."

■ ■ ■

Across Southeast Asia, governments have curtailed Internet freedoms through increasingly restrictive practices, including prohibitive laws, heightened surveillance and censorship, and threats of imprisonment on various national security-related offenses. But Thailand, Malaysia, and Vietnam—countries that once had some of the region's most promising online openings and vibrant blogospheres—stand out as the most egregious backsliders due to official crackdowns.

Through critical postings and commentaries, online journalists in the three countries had challenged officialdom's traditional control over the mainstream media. Their independent reporting opened once untouchable institutions and largely unaccountable politicians to more public scrutiny and criticism. It wasn't until the latter part of the previous decade that officials came to view Internet-delivered news as a threat to their authority.

But now governments in Malaysia, Thailand, and Vietnam are fighting back with a vengeance, employing increasingly harsh tactics including the imposition of intermediary liability and local data hosting requirements, and the use of underlying anti-state and national security laws to crack down on Internet freedoms. Other countries in the region, including Cambodia, the Philippines, and Singapore, are moving more tentatively, mostly through legal measures governing the Internet, in the same restrictive direction.

They have only partially succeeded. Despite the threats, tech-savvy reporters have made effective use of proxy servers and other technological roundabouts to circumvent state-administered blocks and maintain their online anonymity and security. In Vietnam, for example, pseudonymous bloggers have gravitated from domestic to foreign-hosted platforms to conceal their identities.

Though the three countries' Internet controls are not as invasive or sophisticated as those in China, journalists believe their respective governments have taken certain cues from Beijing's repressive model. For instance, governments have recently deployed Internet agents, known respectively in Malaysia, Thailand, and Vietnam as "cybertroopers," "cyberscouts," and "red guards," to flood online political forums with pro-government propaganda or undermine critical bloggers through *ad hominem* attacks—tactics that journalists believe have been imported from China.

Earlier hopes that more Internet-enabled journalism would usher in a new era of regional press freedom have been diminished by the mounting crackdowns. But the repression has come at a high reputational and economic cost to governments: Civil society groups, business associations, and international technology companies have all sounded alarms about growing online restrictions, pressuring governments to strike a more progressive balance between online freedoms and controls. In Thailand, for instance, Chiranuch's case served as a rallying point against a wider government crackdown on Internet freedoms. Though Chiranuch was convicted on only one of 10 counts, "convicting her for something she never wrote sends a clear message to the entrepreneurs and business leaders who run Internet platforms in Thailand that they can and will be penalized for the independent actions of users," Ross LaJeunesse, Google's Asia-Pacific public policy head, wrote on the company's blog.

■ ■ ■

Vietnam's Internet crackdown has targeted individual bloggers: Thirteen of the 14 journalists imprisoned in Vietnam in late 2012 were jailed primarily for their online writings. In September, three prominent bloggers—Nguyen Van Hai, Ta Phong Tan, and Phan Thanh Hai—were sentenced respectively to 12, 10, and four years in prison for online postings that a judge ruled had "abused the popularity of the Internet" and "destroyed people's trust in the state." In August, bloggers Dinh Dang Dinh and Le Thanh Tung were sentenced to six and five years on criminal charges of conducting propaganda against the state for their online writings.

In recent years, Vietnam has enacted a series of progressively restrictive decrees and directives that have given authorities the legal powers to censor online content and prosecute bloggers. A 2008 decree made it illegal for users to access government-banned websites, including Vietnamese-language sites that promote multiparty democracy or habitually criticize the ruling Communist Party and its policies. Later that year, the Ministry of Information and Culture issued a directive that required blogs to refrain from political reporting and to remove on demand any postings the authorities deemed as sensitive, including reprinted international news articles. In 2011, an executive decree brought bloggers under the same national security–related restrictions, including vague and arbitrary anti-state legislation, traditionally used by state authorities to censor and control the mainstream media.

A draft decree pending in late 2012 would require international technology companies to establish data centers and representative offices in Vietnam, a provision that online journalists fear would compromise the security of their IP addresses. Company representatives complained it could force them to uphold the decree's many freedom-curbing measures. The decree would also make it illegal for bloggers to maintain anonymous or pseudonymous online identities. The draft decree poses "a significant threat to free expression and privacy, obliging Internet companies and other providers of information to Internet users in Vietnam to cooperate with the government in enforcing over-broad provisions that are inconsistent with international human rights standards," said David Sullivan, policy and communications director of the Global Network Initiative, a coalition of technology companies, academics, investors, and human rights defenders. "Internet companies have helped to enable the free flow of information in Vietnam, where other forms of media remain tightly controlled, but that could change as a result of the decree by raising the risks of remaining in the Vietnamese market for rights-respecting companies."

Vietnamese authorities maintain extensive filtering of online content. The OpenNet Initiative, a global academic project that monitors Internet surveillance and censorship, found in technical testing results conducted in 2012 that the blocked content was generally specific to Vietnam, and included websites associated with imprisoned bloggers, the U.S. government-funded Radio Free Asia, and the exile-run political party Viet Tan, which has campaigned on press freedom-related issues. Still, certain Vietnamese bloggers are skeptical of the government's online tracking capabilities. "In Vietnam we live in a jungle of rules and laws," said a Hanoi-based mainstream journalist who moonlights as a blogger under a pseudonym. "Where there is a firewall, there is a way to break it. And technically many [of the regulations] are not enforceable." She notes, for example, that the authorities were unable to stifle independent blogs that reported in 2010 on a fireworks accident that killed as many as 40 people during a government-sponsored, millennial celebration of the founding of the national capital, Hanoi. State-censored mainstream media, she says, were forced to report that only four people had died in the accident, the severity of which was played down. "In many cases now, bloggers are leading [mainstream] journalists," she said.

■ ■ ■

In Malaysia, where the government tries to maintain the illusion of an uncensored Internet, curbs against online freedom have been less overt but similarly disruptive for journalists. In 1996, in an effort to lure foreign investment to the Multimedia Super Corridor, a state-led information technology development project, then-Prime Minister Mahathir Mohamad and other senior officials vowed not to censor the Internet. The no-censorship promise was also included in the corridor's 10-point "bill of guarantees" and the 1998 Communication and Multimedia Act. Although it's not clear that Malaysia directly filters online content, the authorities have openly harassed and pressured critical bloggers and probing news sites. Despite the Internet freedoms guaranteed under the Communication and Multimedia Act, bloggers have been detained and charged under provisions of the Official Secrets Act, the Sedition Act, and the Security Offenses Act for postings on such sensitive topics as race, religion, and official corruption. The vague national security-related laws have recently been extended to stifle online criticism of Malaysia's royal sultans.

In July 2012, police briefly detained blogger Syed Abdullah Syed Hussein al-Attas under the Official Secrets Act over a series of investigative articles he posted about the sultan of the state of Johor. In 2010, Khairul Nizam Abd Ghani, who blogs under the name Aduka Taruna, was detained under the Sedition Act for postings considered insulting to Johor state's royal family. He was acquitted in June 2012 after state prosecutors failed to present evidence to justify the charges. *Malaysiakini*, the country's leading online news portal, has been persistently singled out for harassment, both from official and anonymous sources. Days before a pivotal state election in 2011, *Malaysiakini* and two other news websites were hit by debilitating denial of service attacks of unknown origin that forced them to publish through alternative domain names and platforms. *Malaysiakini* has been hit by unexplained cyberattacks at least 35 times since the site was founded in 1999, according to CPJ research.

In other instances, censorship pressure has been more overt. In 2009, the state-run Malaysian Communications and Multimedia Commission ordered *Malaysiakini* to take down two videos, one of which included footage of Malay Muslim demonstrators parading a severed cow's head in protest against plans to relocate a Hindu temple to their neighborhood. Editors stood by the clips' news value and refused to comply with the order. By late 2012, the popular news site faced possible punitive legal action from the attorney general's office.

A new law threatened to further erode Internet freedoms. In April 2012, parliament passed an amendment to the 1950 Evidence Act that made intermediaries liable for any seditious postings made by anonymous visitors to their online platforms or over their Wi-Fi networks. The amendment threatened to "open the door to selective, politically motivated prosecutions," the U.S. government-funded Freedom House said in a September report on global Internet conditions. "The amendment has sent a chill down the spine of Internet users," said Anil Netto, a prominent Malaysian political blogger. "It makes me more careful about moderating comments that are posted on my blog . . . just to be on the safe side against seditious or potentially libelous remarks."

For bloggers like Raja Petra Kamarudin, founder of the collective *Malaysia Today* blog, rising restrictions on online freedoms are symptomatic of a wider censorship problem. "Discussing whether the monarchy should be abolished in favor of a republic, whether Islam should be removed as the religion of the federation in tune with the ideals of a secular state, whether meritocracy should prevail rather than special rights for ethnic Malays—all are taboo subjects," said Kamarudin, who was detained for several months on pending sedition charges for his online journalism in 2008. "Hence why even bother to discuss Internet freedom?"

■ ■ ■

Thailand's crackdown has been driven by political polarization caused by the 2006 military coup that ousted the elected prime minister, Thaksin Shinawatra, and by anxieties over the approaching royal succession from 85-year-old King Bhumibol Adulyadej to his son, Crown Prince Vajiralongkorn. While in power, both pro- and anti-Thaksin sides have touted their pro-royal credentials by aggressively censoring commentaries posted anonymously online that criticize the monarchy.

Because different ministries and agencies maintain independent censorship powers, the precise extent of the crackdown is unclear. C. J. Hinke, founder of Freedom Against Censorship Thailand, an Internet freedom monitoring organization based in Bangkok, said that by mid-September 2012 the authorities had blocked more than 950,000 URLs, an estimate that included banned pornographic, gambling, and pharmaceutical websites but with approximately half of the total dealing with politics or the monarchy. "A lot of the censorship is tied to the personal issues of [political] leaders," said Hinke, whose own site is blocked by the Ministry of Information and Communications Technology, or MICT. "They're killing the Internet for their own self-interests." Hinke says that while local Internet service providers are quick to block content on government orders, there is no precedent for the authorities' unblocking a site after it has been targeted for censorship.

In 2009, in the name of shielding the monarchy from criticism, the previous Abhisit Vejjajiva–led government began a controversial Internet monitoring scheme that trained civilian volunteers, including university students, to serve as "cyberscouts" assigned to comb the Internet for anti-royal material. The number of *lèse majesté* complaints filed under Abhisit's tenure nearly tripled year on year from 2009 to 2010, rising from 164 to 478 cases, according to Thai court records.

Prime Minister Yingluck Shinawatra expanded the government's Internet surveillance capabilities in 2011 through a US$13 million investment in an undisclosed "interception" system, according to local news reports. That same month, her cabinet approved a directive that allowed the national police Department of Special Investigations to collect evidence, including through the intercept of Internet-based communications, without a court order in Computer Crime Act-related investigations. Yingluck also established a 22-member committee dedicated specifically to suppressing *lèse majesté* content online. By mid-2012, MICT authorities claimed to have blocked 90,000 Facebook pages because of anti-monarchy content. That censorship followed on a late 2011 warning by MICT Minister Anudith Nakornthap that Internet users could be charged under the Computer Crime Act for "liking" online comments critical of the royal family.

"If you want to criticize the prime minister or other ministers, there's seldom a crackdown on political opinion, whether in newspapers or online," said Sinfah Tunsarawuth, a Bangkok-based independent media lawyer who monitors Internet freedom cases. Although he maintained that since the 1960s Thailand has allowed greater freedom of expression than most of its Southeast Asian neighbors, he added, "but *lèse majesté* offenses have always been different."

Faced with these rising threats and restrictions, journalists and civil society groups have fought back in their respective countries in different ways. In Thailand, activist groups have campaigned against the Computer Crime Act's many draconian provisions, prompting a government-appointed review through the Human Rights Commission of the law's use in *lèse majesté* cases. In Vietnam, where public protests and rights-related advocacy campaigns are strictly prohibited, bloggers recently produced and distributed the underground book, *F Generation*, which chronicles the history of Vietnam's blogging movement and provides tips on how to access and use Facebook as a secure platform.

And in Malaysia, news organizations, bloggers, academics, and nongovernmental organizations voluntarily took down their websites in August 2012 in a symbolic "Blackout Day" to protest the government's Internet freedom-eroding amendment to the 1950 Evidence Act. "Malaysians cherish the freedom they have on the Internet," said Masjaliza Hamzah, executive officer of the Centre for Independent Journalism, a Kuala Lumpur-based press freedom advocacy group that spearheaded the blackout. "If push comes to shove, they will fight back and resist the control the authorities want to impose on them."

CPJ Senior Southeast Asia Representative Shawn W. Crispin is based in Bangkok, where he is a reporter and editor for Asia Times Online. *He is the author of the 2012 CPJ report, "As Vietnam's Economy Opens, Press Freedom Shrinks."*

3

HEROES IN THE CROWD

Harnessing Power In the Stories of Ordinary People

By Kristin Jones

On March 9, 2008, Dechen Pemba, a British-born teacher living in Beijing, boarded an overnight train for Xian, a city about 560 miles to the southwest. She was met there by Dhondup Wangchen, who had traveled from his home in Amdo, a region of the Tibetan plateau that takes up most of China's Qinghai Province. The two were strangers to each other, linked only by heritage and a loose global network of activists and exiles who hope, in various ways, for a freer Tibet.

Spring starts early in Xian, and the day was bright. When they spoke about the purpose of their meeting, they talked quietly in the Lhasa dialect of Tibetan in the open air and away from passers-by, or in the apartment of a trusted friend of Wangchen. They were being followed, maybe. It was hard to know. When Pemba left that evening, she was carrying a bundle of tapes, the final installment of Wangchen's project for the previous year, with the intention of smuggling it out of the country.

Five months later, the Summer Olympics began. On the same day, Wangchen's 24-minute documentary, "Leaving Fear Behind," made its premiere. "I am not an educated man," he tells the camera. "I have never been to school. However, I would like to say a few things."

What followed was a series of clandestine conversations made public. Wangchen asked ordinary Tibetans to talk about the Olympic Games, and about China. A monk on an empty road says the Games should stand for freedom and peace, and "as a Tibetan, I have neither freedom nor peace." A creased old man in a light-starved room says he doesn't know what to make of the Games. "I feel very uncertain, as though I'm wandering in the dark and don't know where it's safe to step," he said. "I don't trust the Chinese at all. Not one bit."

■ ■ ■

Who is allowed to talk, what are they allowed to say, and to whom? In November 2012, CPJ awarded its International Press Freedom Award to four journalists from around the world—Dhondup Wangchen, Mae Azango, Azimjon Askarov, and Mauri König. All four came up against these questions and found their own ways to answer. The stories they ultimately told are the stories of ordinary people—not politicians, not wealthy power brokers, not criminal masterminds. They didn't rely on databases of stockpiled information. Their sources were people who had something to say about their own lives, and wanted to be heard.

There is power in ordinary voices. That much is clear from the threats and attacks that followed the telling. Part of it—both the power of their work and the reason for the attacks—had to do with the secrets revealed. Mae Azango, one of only a few women working as journalists in Liberia, reported on a brutal initiation rite known to many but kept deliberately hidden. Azimjon Askarov recorded what went on in southern Kyrgyzstan's detention centers, where people accused of crimes are held without trial. Brazilian reporter Mauri König traveled along the country's invisible borderlands, where drugs, weapons, and humans are bought and sold and used. Dhondup Wangchen told a story—in contradiction to the one told in the opening ceremony of Beijing's Games—of an empire's faltering power to impose happiness through prosperity.

The four journalists were also attacked for who they are. An African woman criticizing her own society. An Uzbek in Kyrgyzstan at a time of ethnic violence. A Brazilian journalist on the wrong side of a border.

Wangchen knew the risks he was taking. Before he even started on his documentary, he sent his wife and children to the Tibetan exile city of Dharamsala, India. Just after he finished filming in March, protests began in Tibet, as the slow simmer of anger against Chinese rule erupted into a boil. All Tibetans came under suspicion.

Police knocked on the door of Dechen Pemba's apartment in Beijing in July 2008 and escorted her to the airport. The last few months had been frightening ones; she had been stopped and questioned, her apartment searched. At least, she thought, she had the protection of a British passport; being deported wasn't the worst thing that could happen. "I was more worried for my Tibetan friends," she said. For them, "terrible things could happen and nobody would even know."

By that time, Wangchen had already disappeared into China's prison system.

■ ■ ■

During the Liberian civil war, Mae Azango spent four years living as a refugee in the Ivory Coast. Some days she went without eating. Walking down the street wasn't safe. "Someone will come up and slap you," she said. "They will say, 'This road is not for you.'"

She could have learned almost any lesson from that. The things she learned were empathy for the most vulnerable people, and respect for her own fight. "When I came back home, I lived a poor life," Azango said. "I know what it feels like. That's why I have so much passion in reporting on ordinary people."

Azango has written about sexual violence, poverty, police brutality; she writes about things she wants to change. It was natural that she would write about female genital cutting. Girls who go through the initiation rite, common in the Sande society in Liberia, are told never to speak about it. Government officials, who sometimes owe their power to the tribal elders who protect the practice, are hesitant to condemn it. The local media won't touch it.

"Nobody talks about it," said Azango. "Everybody knows."

But Azango asked questions, and people began talking. One woman recalled the day, 34 years earlier, when it happened to her: Five women held her down and another cut out her clitoris. "It can hurt much more than delivery pain when they be cutting your clitorises with a knife because they cannot numb the place but only put leaves to cover the sore," the woman told her, in a story that appeared in March 2012 in *FrontPage Africa*, the newspaper in Monrovia for which Azango works.

The outrage followed swiftly after publication—not against the practice, but against Azango. She was threatened with violence. People turned up at her office looking for her, and Azango was forced into hiding. It wasn't that anyone denied the truth of what Azango was reporting. Nobody called her a liar. What they called her was a traitor.

"They say I'm Liberian. I'm African. I should protect our culture. They say I take our culture and serve it up to the white people," said Azango. "You will see me to be a hero in the Western world. In my home, I'm a violator."

When *FrontPage Africa* reports on corruption, or even child prostitution, other media tend to pile on with related stories of their own, says Rodney Sieh, the newspaper's editor and publisher. But not in this case. Sieh got a call from an editor at another publication. "He told me that we shouldn't allow white people to come into our country and tell us how to conduct our culture." Both Azango and Sieh rejected that argument. After all, Azango says, she published the story for a reason: She wanted the practice of female genital cutting to end.

"That is why I use my pen. I believe my pen has the power to make the government shift," said Azango. If she had been a white woman reporting on it, Azango says, she would have simply been ignored. There would have been no threats. But there would have been no national conversation, either. As it was, the government—called out on the complicity of its silence—spoke out against the practice. Tribal leaders agreed to suspend female genital cutting for four years.

Without enforcement, it's a long way from the ending Azango wants. But the journalist, who has since emerged from hiding, isn't done yet. "Push until something happens," she said, explaining the term behind an acronym. "That's my motto. PUSH!"

■ ■ ■

In April 2010, protests in northern Kyrgyzstan led to the ouster of President Kurmanbek Bakiyev and the installment of an interim president, Roza Otunbayeva. The new government proved unable to exert full control, however, leaving space for old tensions to rise to the surface. In southern Kyrgyzstan, a pro-Bakiyev faction worked to consolidate power and came into conflict with an Uzbek minority, prevalent in the region and seen as politically ascendant.

In June, riots erupted in southern Kyrgyzstan, lasting less than a week but taking a brutal toll. By the end, according to Human Rights Watch, 400 people were dead, thousands had been forced from their homes, and Uzbek neighborhoods were in ruins. Most of those killed were Uzbek. Most of those arrested in the aftermath were also Uzbek. One of them was Azimjon Askarov. The unrest and the confusion—and Askarov's ethnicity—had given his enemies a perfect opportunity to silence him.

Askarov made a living as a painter, depicting pastoral scenes of life in the southern Kyrgyz town of Bazar-Korgon, as well as a series of self-portraits. His face, with its craggy cheeks and bushy eyebrows, was a landscape all its own. In 1998, Askarov learned from a brochure about a new human rights organization and made his way to the nearby city of Jalalabad to volunteer, says Valentina Gritsenko, who had founded the group.

"He was an artist," said Gritsenko, "really open and sensitive to people's problems. He could see what was happening around him and wanted to do something." The painter threw himself into this new project, which consisted of interviewing people who were detained without trial, recording instances of torture, and monitoring treatment of minorities, who experienced frequent, often subtle discrimination. He once succeeded in freeing someone accused of murder by producing the alleged victim, alive; the prosecutor was dismissed. He wrote about a woman who was raped repeatedly during her seven-month pretrial detention; she was freed.

Askarov went on to form a separate local rights group, called Vozdukh, meaning Air. His work was published in its weekly bulletins, and on regional news websites. He upended the careers of police officers and prosecutors. Most of the police in his area were Kyrgyz; many—but not all—of the people whose cases he advocated were Uzbek.

Askarov took photos and video, too, in June 2010 as violence ravaged his town. He visited hospitals, and provided journalists with details about the movement of weapons, as well as police abuses, including two shootings, he told CPJ. On June 15, he was arrested and beaten "like a soccer ball." He was charged and convicted of complicity in the murder of a Kyrgyz police officer killed during the violence, inciting ethnic hatred, and other crimes. His case was riddled with inconsistencies and heavily reliant on the testimony of police officers who knew the victim and had reasons to resent Askarov.

The painter, human rights defender, and journalist was sentenced to life in prison. Masha Lisitsyna, a lawyer with the Open Society Justice Initiative, is working on a complaint to the U.N. Human Rights Committee calling for Askarov's release. She visited him in prison, where he is kept in a cold and damp basement cell. Askarov recalled to her the words spoken by a police officer in the first days of his detention: *Because of the article criticizing us, we will get even with you. We will make you die slowly. Now we have the opportunity and time to punish you.*

In the wake of the violence of June 2010, CPJ has documented the near disappearance of Uzbek-language media in southern Kyrgyzstan. Osh TV and Mezon TV, two independent TV stations with Uzbek owners, were both heavily vandalized and ordered to close, accused of inciting violence. Osh TV resumed operations, but transferred to ethnic Kyrgyz ownership; Mezon TV never did.

Now there are fewer ways to talk, and less to hear.

■ ■ ■

The border regions of large countries can often be nearly invisible to those in the urban centers. Think of the scrublands and desert of southern Texas or Arizona, where thousands of immigrants each year hope to remain unseen as they travel north. Borderlands—neither here nor there—can also be perfect places to hide crimes.

Mauri König has spent his career illuminating the borders that Brazil shares with its neighbors. In a series of investigations in 2004 and 2005, he was able to map out the routes of child sex trafficking along the borders with Paraguay, Uruguay, Argentina, and Bolivia. In another investigation, he showed how Brazilian police had linked with criminal groups in Paraguay to form a car-theft ring.

In 2000, his work took him to San Alberto, Paraguay, 50 miles from the border of Brazil, where he was investigating the mysterious deaths of teenagers at the hands of the Paraguayan army. Pulled over at an apparent police roadblock, König was dragged from his car and beaten and kicked by three men. One of his attackers wrapped a chain around his neck and tightened it to the point of suffocation. "You will never come back to Paraguay again," they told him. His camera was destroyed and its film, showing children inside the Paraguayan army headquarters, was unspooled. "Down with the Brazilian press" was scrawled on the hood of his car.

König's attackers were counting on the protection of the border, even as they were profiting from its porousness. He was on their turf, after all; they thought they could evict him. They weren't figuring in the ability of news to cross borders, too, to forge a larger global community out of a fragmented and divided population.

The assault on König had the opposite effect from the one intended. It became international news, drawing attention to the story that König was telling: Paraguay's army had been recruiting under-age soldiers. He continued with his reporting and told a complete story, publishing the names of 109 children and teenagers from Brazil, Argentina, and Paraguay—the youngest 12 and the oldest 18—who had died under questionable circumstances while in military service.

The story had real impact. International and domestic pressure on Paraguay led to changes in the army's behavior. The unexplained deaths stopped, and the national legislature made military service voluntary rather than required. König says the main motivation for his work is to provoke anger, so that his journalism can be a tool for transforming realities and people, for stemming injustice.

"My primary intention is to give visibility to excluded people and their problems, which are in fact the problems of all humanity, only on a smaller scale," said König. "I write hoping to plant a seed of indignation in each reader, so that each one, within possibility, does something to improve the situation."

■ ■ ■

The slim documentary that Dhondup Wangchen made about Tibet in 2007 and 2008 was extraordinary, says Robert J. Barnett, who directs the modern Tibetan studies program at Columbia University. Other documentaries have been complaints about suffering and victimhood in Tibet, appealing for sympathy and for condemnation of the aggressor, says Barnett. Or they've been fragments collected by Westerners, in the model of the intrepid outsider braving the dangerous.

Wangchen's film, instead, poses a question: Do the Chinese state and media represent us?

"It treats Tibetans as intelligent agents in contract with the [Chinese Communist] Party, and invites them to discuss what they think of the contract, and whether it's kept its promises," said Barnett. "It's quite a different way of thinking that we don't see, and it's typical of internal discussions."

The film was made as the Chinese government was cracking down on expression and religion in the eastern Tibetan region where Wangchen lived, which had previously enjoyed more leeway than central Tibet. The end of Wangchen's filming coincided with the start of protests that swept across Tibet. The answer he found in his documentary—that no, the Chinese state does not represent Tibetans—was the same conclusion that thousands of others were reaching at the same time.

It is hard to know exactly what happened to Wangchen. He has been unable to contact his family; fragments of information have come from Jigme Gyatso, a monk who assisted in making the documentary and has been in and out of jail over the past several years. Wangchen's family knows that he was sentenced to six years in prison on subversion charges, and that his appeal was denied. His wife, Lhamo Tso, says he has contracted hepatitis B in prison.

Wangchen's crime was articulating for a global audience what he and others—ordinary people—were thinking. His crime was being one among many.

Tso, an unassuming bread maker and mother of four, now takes his message around the world. "My main concern is for the release of my husband Dhondup," said Tso. "But I also talk on behalf of all the prisoners in Tibet, and people who are suffering like me. I talk on behalf of the Tibetan people."

Kristin Jones is a reporter living in New York. In 2011, she was part of a team that won a Robert F. Kennedy Journalism Award for "Seeking Justice for Campus Rapes," a collaboration between NPR and the Center for Public Integrity. Jones was CPJ's senior Asia research associate until 2007.

Running Toward Danger, Syria's Citizens Become Journalists

By Oliver Holmes

'**I**s he shooting at us?" I asked. The flaring red tracer bullets fired from a Syrian Army attack helicopter hit just in front of my feet, spitting up the dust of Aleppo's streets. Sheltering behind an old car engine—the nearest thing I could find—I should have been able to answer the question for myself.

I had covered Syria's uprising since it began, for the most part from outside the country, given the government restrictions on media access and the dangers on the ground. I had reported on the targeted killings of Syrian and foreign journalists. In Aleppo, I had seen the body of a boy lying in a street—he had been shot in the head by a government sniper as he walked home from market. I had spoken to Syrian journalists who had been beaten nearly to death by President Bashar al-Assad's security forces.

Yes, he was shooting at us.

Inspired by the Arab Spring's dramatic sweep across the Middle East, Syrians took to the streets in March 2011 to protest four decades of oppressive rule by the Assad family. In the months that followed, peaceful demonstrators were shot dead or simply went missing, taken by Assad's ubiquitous secret police. The defection of soldiers who refused to kill their own gave an armed wing to the uprising, backed further by farmers with hunting rifles. In response, the government used artillery and airstrikes to hit rebel groups positioned in civilian areas, like the deprived Aleppo suburb where I was attacked. A full-scale civil war was raging countrywide.

In Aleppo and Damascus, I reported from both sides of Syria's conflict—in rebel-held territory where the risks were almost prohibitive, and in the government-run capital where restrictions made it impossible to get a rounded picture of the crisis. Journalists were not seen merely as observers in Syria. Assad's media machine painted the uprising as a foreign conspiracy fought by terrorists, and declared that anyone critical of the regime was a terrorist and deserved death. Before entering Syria, journalists are advised to rip off the "PRESS" decal from their protective vests. The designation confers no safety.

■ ■ ■

I visited Aleppo, a sprawling metropolis of 2.5 million people, in August 2012, when roughly half the city was in rebel hands. The night before I ventured in, a Japanese video-journalist, Mika Yamamoto, had been shot dead at close range by government militia when she turned the wrong corner. Her husband, who worked as her cameraman, said the assailants had recognized her as a journalist before firing.

CPJ research now ranks Syria as the most dangerous place in the world for journalists. At least 28 journalists were killed covering the conflict from January through December 2012. And it is not just government forces behind the killings; rebel forces have been blamed for an increasing number of attacks against journalists seen as pro-government.

I was staying in a rebel-held town an hour's drive north of the city with a photographer who had a hunger for front-line images and a burly British security adviser who was worryingly conspicuous in his

Oakley sunglasses. Entering Aleppo, we found a city being demolished from the top down. The multistory buildings provided some protection on the streets from incoming artillery fire, but floor by floor the buildings were being wiped out by shelling.

Despite its status as a war zone, Aleppo was still full of civilians. "We might be able to leave Aleppo, but what then? We have no money," said a tobacconist who lived only a few hundred meters from where rebels and soldiers were fighting. I saw mothers, dressed in the conservative black veil, walking along streets with a line of young children behind them as black smoke rose and tank shells boomed in the distance. After months of battle, they appeared numb to the brutality of war.

During the Libyan conflict a year before, NATO forces had taken down Muammar Qaddafi's air power, and journalists were able to advance to the battleground and then retreat to a safer distance. But in this war that Assad is waging against his own citizens, fighter jets and helicopters batter residential districts of towns and cities. Residents in Aleppo told of government spies who were giving away rebel positions and informing on foreign press in the city. Nowhere was safe.

Syria has a long history of repression. A year after President Assad took over from his father in 2000 he legalized private media, which had been banned since 1963. Yet the move was seen as largely superficial, with the state controlling media through intimidation and censorship, or through ownership by proxy. The Syrian journalists I know who were trained before the uprising were taught to write and broadcast propaganda for government media, not to criticize or expose.

But our guide in Aleppo was one of the many Syrians who, in the absence of a free press, had decided to become a citizen journalist and document the atrocities. A young man who was finishing a bachelor's degree in international law when the uprising began, Abu Zaid started filming protests in the wider Aleppo Province when the government was still in control.

"The regime prevented foreign journalists from coming in, and I needed to show the world that police were shooting dead peaceful protestors," he told me one morning as we made our daily drive past farms along the flat roads that lead to Aleppo. After a year and a half of fighting, the rebels had pushed government forces out of Abu Zaid's hometown. He had become a combat journalist during that time, spending his days filming the conflict in Aleppo. As we spoke, I noticed that he kept a pistol tucked in the back of his jeans.

"Why do you carry that?" I asked. "Just in case," he said, offering me the gun for my time in Aleppo.

"If I hold a gun, then I can be considered a military target and not a journalist," I said, with a tad too much self-righteousness. He burst out laughing: "You're a target anyway." Abu Zaid had been wounded three times before we met. A few weeks after I left, I heard a bullet had sliced through both his legs. Yet Abu Zaid laughed off his close calls with death. His life, like that of many Syrians, had been devastated by the war that had engulfed his country.

Before advancing to the front line, rebels would frequently tell me, they prayed to God asking for the gift of death. Once we were there, with bodies in the streets, tank shells hitting buildings and the whiz of bullets cutting the air, I would berate myself for advancing with people who appeared to want to die. One afternoon, I spoke to a rebel fighter about my body armor. "Is it bulletproof?" he asked, dressed in camouflage and wearing an ammunition belt. "Let's see if it is," he said, pointing his rifle at my chest. I stood there in shock as his men laughed. A mortar landed across the street, and I felt shrapnel ping near my face. They barely flinched.

I didn't want to die. I wanted my friend Abu Zaid to show an appreciation for his safety, too. Yet without his blasé attitude, how could he return to work in that city every day?

■ ■ ■

After I left, I called a friend, a Syrian journalist from Damascus. "Aleppo is really bad," I said, sitting exhausted in my hotel room in Turkey. "Is that what it is like all over Syria now?" My friend, who like many Syrians does not want her identity known, goes by the name Leila. She had just returned to Damascus from her native Deir al-Zor, an eastern desert city close to the border with Iraq. "My city is being destroyed, too," she told me.

I had met her a year earlier, just as people were starting to protest across the country, first in rural areas and then in major towns and cities. Nobody could believe it was happening. Many states in the Middle

East had vast security agencies, but Assad and his father before him had perfected the art of silencing dissent through fear.

Just out of university, Leila was smart and confident. She had started working for a pro-government news website but slowly became disillusioned and was quietly told to leave. We were introduced by mutual friends, and I asked her to work for me as a fixer. She helped me find doctors who had treated torture victims and protesters who had been shot. Leila used her network of friends around the country to get an idea of what was happening outside the capital.

When we met, she asked me to teach her how journalists worked abroad. She knew she had a talent for gathering information and said she wanted to help her country. But her friends were worried that she was being too vocal. She had been posting photographs on her Facebook wall of the men, women, and children who had been shot while protesting. And I worried about our professional relationship; she risked interrogation and jail for working with a foreign journalist.

With more than 20 intelligence agencies, Syria has had thousands of informants and secret police on the streets. Conspicuous in their leather jackets and beige trousers, standing idly on street corners, the security agents' lack of discretion was intentional. Their presence was intended to incite fear among civilians, keenly aware that they were under constant surveillance.

I had entered Syria on a student visa that time, intent on pursuing a number of freelance assignments. The authorities had restricted foreign journalists, either by refusing entry or granting short trips under tight government supervision. Those who were found reporting illegally were arrested, sometimes beaten. Wary of the secret police, Leila and I would meet sources in rooms with the windows closed. Open reporting was impossible, and phones were tapped. I conducted nightly phone interviews with international radio and television broadcasters over Skype, using encryption software to try to conceal my identity.

"We now go live to Faris Amato, who cannot give his real name for security reasons," the anchors would say before I talked about the situation in the capital. I'd selected the pseudonym to protect both myself, and the people I'd spoken to. I'd heard stories of Syrians being seized by the police after journalists were too open about speaking with them. I didn't want that on my conscience. I wish the viewers could have seen me. I imagine they thought I was the typical foreign correspondent, standing in a dusty street with a notepad. The reality was far from that. For each interview, I would hide with my laptop under a thick bed blanket and lie there only in boxers, sweating copiously in the summer heat. The crowded Old City of Damascus offered ramshackle accommodations, and I worried that my neighbors would overhear conversations through the thin walls.

Leila is still working in Damascus. Like many journalists in government-held areas, she has to work in secret and cover her tracks. In contact with a handful of news organizations outside the country, Leila gives first-hand accounts of both government and rebel abuses, much needed as foreign journalists are few on the ground. The uprising and civil war, in a country filled with paranoia and fear, has turned Leila, as it did Abu Zaid, into a reporter. Learning the craft as they go, constantly working in peril, Leila and Abu Zaid and many others like them are getting the story out to the world.

Oliver Holmes is a correspondent for Reuters based in Lebanon. He previously worked as a freelancer for Time *and* The Wall Street Journal. *He has worked across the Middle East including Syria, Yemen, and Libya.*

4

MURDERED
AND MISSING

Disappearances Unexplained Amid Hints Of Cover-Ups

By María Salazar-Ferro

I n the early hours of January 25, 2010, Sandhya Eknelygoda walked to the police station nearest her home on the outskirts of Colombo, Sri Lanka. She had been up all night, frantically looking for her husband. Over the past five months, Prageeth Eknelygoda, a political cartoonist and columnist, had been kidnapped, followed, and threatened. Fearful, the couple had agreed that Prageeth would frequently check in with Sandhya, but he had failed to do so the night before. At the station, the police were dismissive. Eknelygoda was first told that she was at the wrong jurisdiction. Officers then said she was lying, insinuating that her husband was hiding at home. They said staged disappearances were common among those seeking easy fame. Finally, in the evening, a reluctant officer took down her complaint.

Prageeth Eknelygoda has not been heard from since. He is among 35 journalists around the world who have vanished over the past two decades, according to CPJ research. Twenty-nine were local journalists.

Most covered conflict, crime, or corruption. Their families struggle to get by financially and psychologically. Their colleagues, fearing a similar fate, censor their own reporting. Without a body or a clear-cut crime, the cases dwell in legal limbo. In at least three cases—including Eknelygoda's—the sensitive nature of the journalists' work and the stubborn lack of investigative progress suggest cover-ups by the authorities, who may be linked to the disappearances.

More than half of the disappeared have gone missing in Mexico, Russia, Iraq, and Sri Lanka—countries with high rates of impunity in media murders, according to CPJ's Impunity Index. Mexico, one of the most dangerous countries for the press, accounts for 11 cases over the past 10 years—all but one under the tenure of President Felipe Calderón Hinojosa. Among the disappeared is María Esther Aguilar Casimbe, a veteran police reporter for the regional dailies *El Diario de Zamora* and *Cambio de Michoacán*, who vanished in 2009 near her home in Zamora, a small town in the central state of Michoacán.

Around 11 a.m. on November 11, 2009, Aguilar Casimbe left her house to cover a routine evacuation exercise at a nearby child-care center. She had only her cellphone and a notepad in hand, her sister Carmén told CPJ. Aguilar Casimbe never returned home to take her two young daughters to school. In prior weeks, she had reported on police brutality and a local official accused of corruption.

At least 15 of the journalists who have disappeared worldwide covered crime and official corruption. They include the Franco-Canadian investigative freelancer Guy-André Kieffer, who disappeared from a supermarket parking lot in Abidjan, Ivory Coast's economic capital, on the evening of April 16, 2004. A commodities expert who specialized in cocoa and coffee, Kieffer had linked the Ivorian cocoa trade to arms deals in recent articles. Although threats, assaults, and harassment of the news media are common in the Ivory Coast, Kieffer long believed that his standing as a foreign journalist would protect him. Only in the days immediately before he went missing did Kieffer admit to a colleague that he was scared, his wife, Osange Silou-Kieffer, told CPJ.

■ ■ ■

Prageeth Eknelygoda also believed his life was at risk. Days before he disappeared, the journalist told his wife about a hit list on which his name supposedly appeared. It was the pinnacle of an escalating pattern of intimidation, Sandhya Eknelygoda said. In August 2009, the cartoonist had been picked up near his home by unidentified individuals in a white van and held for nearly a day, tied up and blindfolded. After his release, Eknelygoda noticed a vehicle without plates frequently parked outside his home, and heard clicking noises on his phone that made him think it was tapped. He also received menacing calls from individuals who said they would break his arms and legs if he did not stop writing, Eknelygoda's wife told CPJ.

But the threats were never investigated, according to Sandhya Eknelygoda. Even his 2009 abduction remained unsolved. In fact, attacks on the media have largely gone unpunished during Mahinda Rajapaksa's time in power. During his eight years as prime minister and now as president, nine journalists have been killed and not a single perpetrator has been brought to justice. CPJ research shows that all those killed had reported on politically sensitive issues and were critical of the government. At the time of his disappearance—two days before the 2010 presidential election—Eknelygoda's work for the website *Lanka eNews* was focused on alleged corruption among members of the Rajapaksa family, Sandhya Eknelygoda told CPJ.

Kieffer's reports apparently also hit a nerve with the Ivorian presidential family. In the months after his disappearance, local and French authorities opened independent investigations that pointed to Michel Legré, a local businessman with whom Kieffer was last seen and who was related by marriage to the first lady at the time, Simone Gbagbo. Legré was arrested in June 2004 and charged in the Ivory Coast with Kieffer's kidnapping and murder, although no body has been found. In October 2005, Legré, who had accused several officials in the Laurent Gbagbo administration of complicity in the Kieffer affair, was released for lack of evidence. None of those mentioned were ever arrested.

Since, the investigation has had more false starts. In January 2006, French authorities arrested former Ivorian army officer Jean-Tony Oulaï in Paris under suspicion that he headed the commando unit that had abducted Kieffer. Oulaï denied any involvement and was released a month later. Other tips and rumors have followed, including one that led investigators to a body buried in the western region of Issia in January 2012, reviving media attention to the case. But within days, DNA tests determined that the remains were not Kieffer's, and the investigation returned to Square 1. Judge Patrick Ramaël, who leads the French investigation, did not respond to a CPJ email seeking comment.

The inquiry into Aguilar Casimbe's whereabouts has stalled in part due to a lack of witnesses. Some have not come forward out of fear, the journalist's sister speculates. Others, she said, have died since the investigation began. But the process has also been convoluted. Zamora authorities did not begin to look for the journalist on the day she vanished, asking her family to wait in case Aguilar Casimbe returned. Once an inquiry was opened, it was moved every few weeks to different jurisdictions within the state, with little result. In 2010, the special prosecutor for crimes against the press in Mexico City opened a parallel federal investigation focusing on Aguilar Casimbe's work. But to date, there have been no answers. The lead investigator on Aguilar Casimbe's case at the special prosecutor's office declined to comment, citing official protocol.

In Colombo, frustrated with the lack of progress, Sandhya Eknelygoda has driven an unyielding campaign to find answers. Days after filing her initial complaint, she filed a second with the Human Rights Commission of Sri Lanka, where officials did little more than take her statement. Eknelygoda told CPJ that she wrote to the Commission several times subsequently, but was told in mid-2011 to stop contacting its members. She has also reached out to key figures in the Rajapaksa government. "I have written to the president and first lady, to the attorney general and other cabinet ministers, and to members of parliament appealing for help," Eknelygoda said. "There has been no answer."

In February 2010, she filed a writ of *habeas corpus* before a Colombo court of appeals, asking for information on her husband's whereabouts or for his remains. Since then, periodic hearings have taken place, but police officers and government officials called to testify about the investigation have not volunteered anything substantive. The lack of government commitment has been obvious from the beginning, said Ruki Fernando, a local human rights activist and Eknelygoda family friend who has attended the hearings. "It's all technicalities, bureaucracy, and that's holding them back," he told CPJ. "If the government is not responsible, then authorities should be eager to find out who is behind it and prove that it's not them." Even if Sri Lankan authorities were not behind the disappearance, their lack of action makes them complicit, Fernando said. CPJ sought comment from the Sri Lankan permanent mission to the United Nations in New York, where an official directed inquiries to the embassy in Washington. An embassy official declined to comment.

Abroad, Eknelygoda has made appeals to the U.N. Human Rights Council and to Secretary-General Ban Ki-moon. She has traveled to the United States and Europe to speak about the case. At home, she has assumed the role of spokeswoman on the issue of disappearances, organizing vigils and religious services, and has become an advocate for freedom of expression. "There is rarely a protest where Sandhya is not present," her friend Fernando told CPJ. Eknelygoda's quest to find her husband has redefined her as public figure—a role that Fernando says seems to engulf her personal life.

■ ■ ■

Family members of missing journalists are typically more invested in police investigations and other proceedings than those of journalists who have been killed, CPJ found. "More than anything, they want to know what has happened to their loved one," said Laurence de Barros-Duchêne, mental health coordinator for the International Committee of the Red Cross, in a 2010 interview about the families of missing people. "It becomes an obsession and a source of constant anguish." According to the family members who spoke to CPJ, however, their pursuit is not for justice, or even details of the alleged crime. The information they seek is simpler: They want to know whether their loved one is alive or dead.

Without remains, said Silou-Kieffer, mourning is impossible, and moving on absurd. "When I'm being practical, I think that he is dead, that he died the night that he went missing," Silou-Kieffer said of her husband. "But until I have a body, I will never admit that he is dead because the truth is that if he is alive somewhere, and hears me saying he is dead, that is when he will truly die."

Perseverance in their quest for answers can isolate immediate family members from their communities, friends, and even extended family networks. In Silou-Kieffer's case, she said, rifts have occurred when friends ask her to admit that her husband is dead. "They say everybody knows that he was murdered, but I don't know that. I tell them I have no proof," she said. Eknelygoda said some friends have also stopped associating with her and her children. She told CPJ she believes that some have distanced themselves out of fear, and others because they work for the government and don't like what she is doing.

Uncertainty permeates the lives of families of the missing. For Silou-Kieffer, after seven years, her husband's disappearance still casts doubt even on who she is. "How do I describe myself when filling out a routine form? Am I married, single, or a widow?" she asked.

But the psychological impact is perhaps most severe on children. Carmén Aguilar Casimbe said her two nieces, Frida Sofía, 11, and Fátima del Carmén, 10, "live in permanent uncertainty." "They say very little, but when they see their mother's photo or something that reminds them of her, they cry and shut down." Both girls have needed psychological counseling, as have Eknelygoda's adolescent sons, Sathyajith, 18, and Harith, 15.

Then there are serious financial concerns. In most cases, families have lost their main source of income, requiring significant adjustments to ensure survival. In some, dedication to the case supersedes basic needs. Eknelygoda, for instance, quit her job as an insurance broker after her husband vanished so she could work full time writing letters, making phone calls, and attending events. She and her boys live off the sale of a book of Prageeth Eknelygoda's cartoons and writings, supplemented by small donations from family, friends, and organizations like CPJ.

Support from other journalists and human rights groups, abroad and in-country, has been crucial to these families. "There is great comfort in solidarity," said Eknelygoda. Sri Lankan journalists continue to be harassed, she said, especially her husband's *Lanka eNews* colleagues, whose offices were set on fire, forcing the outlet to close and at least one journalist to flee the country. Nonetheless, local journalists have worked relentlessly to keep Eknelygoda's cause alive.

Likewise, journalists who worked with Kieffer have banded together to demand answers. In the months after his disappearance, a group led by Kieffer's colleague Aline Richard formed the Truth for

Guy-André Kieffer Association, which has closely monitored the case and organizes annual events on the anniversary of his disappearance. "We exist because if there is no pressure on authorities, there is no case," Richard told CPJ. Ivorian journalists have also supported the case and kept it in the public eye, sending a message to local authorities that they will not stop being vigilant, Silou-Kieffer told CPJ. "Colleagues should never stop seeking answers; they should never give up when one of their own is missing," said Silou-Kieffer, herself a journalist.

In Mexico, however, the response has been the reverse. Local journalists have generally stayed away from investigating or even publicizing Aguilar Casimbe's case for fear of reprisal, according to one Michoacán-based journalist who asked not to be identified. "A case like that has a deep effect on colleagues working in the area. It spreads fear," the journalist said. "It affects all journalists because we do not want the same thing to happen to us." He told CPJ that most local news outlets steer clear of the Michoacán crime beat that Aguilar Casimbe covered, publishing only official statements. "We have to self-censor because it is the only way to protect ourselves," he said.

Fernando also believes that the disappearance of Prageeth Eknelygoda was intended to do more than silence a single journalist; it was a message to all Sri Lankan journalists. "When something like this happens," Fernando said, "journalists are always thinking about when their turn will come, and what they should and should not be printing." But Sandhya Eknelygoda says self-censorship is not the answer. "Why should I have stopped [my husband] from working?" she asked. "He was not doing anything criminal. He was not doing anything wrong."

María Salazar-Ferro is CPJ's Impunity Campaign and Journalist Assistance program coordinator. A native of Bogotá, she has represented CPJ on missions to Mexico and the Philippines, among other nations.

Bloggers Targeted as Murders Spike in Brazil

By John Otis

On April 23, 2012, Décio Sá, the most influential journalist and blogger in the northern Brazilian state of Maranhão, was shot three times in the head by a gunman who fled on a motorcycle. Sá was killed two months after the murder of Mario Randolfo Marques Lopes, a combative blogger who ran a local news website in Barra do Piraí, a town about 90 miles northwest of Rio de Janeiro.

The deaths of Sá and Randolfo, the first Brazilian news bloggers to be killed for their reporting, are part of a wider increase in journalist murders in the country since 2011. Randolfo's case is also emblematic of a common plight for provincial journalists in Brazil: Without ties to major urban media outlets, these journalists lack visibility and the support of colleagues on a national level. Such a low profile can mean that the authorities feel little pressure to solve attacks on the provincial press. Unsolved attacks on journalists, in turn, can dissuade provincial reporters from investigating crime and corruption in their regions.

"When you have any kind of violence against journalists, this threatens other reporters who might want to do the same kind of work," said Marcelo Moreira, editor-in-chief of TV Globo in Rio de Janeiro and president of the Brazilian Association for Investigative Journalism, or ABRAJI. "This is especially true in Brazil where the number of attacks is increasing. That's why we are so worried."

Journalists and law enforcement officials told CPJ during visits in September 2012 to São Luis, Barra do Piraí, and Rio de Janeiro that Sá and Randolfo were likely targeted for their aggressive reporting on local political corruption and organized crime—stories that were largely ignored by the country's major media based in Rio de Janeiro and São Paulo.

Radio journalists have often been gunned down in outlying areas of Brazil for their aggressive, often politically slanted reporting. But news bloggers, seen as more independent than radio reporters, have grown influential in many of the country's second-tier cities and towns. Thus, bloggers have become the newest targets of those who want to muzzle the Brazilian media. "Traditionally, the largest number of journalist deaths in the interior was among radio journalists," Jose Reinaldo Marques, an investigator for the Brazilian Press Association, an industry group based in Rio de Janeiro told CPJ. "But that was until the bloggers came along."

There are no official figures on the number of reported news blogs in Brazil. A 2011 survey by the Brazilian government's Internet Facilitation Committee (Comitê Gestor da Internet no Brasil) found that 16 percent of online users in urban areas and 11 percent in rural areas had created blogs. The data revealed nothing about the nature of the writings, but it's clear that serious blogs and Internet news sites focusing on current events are popping up across the country. For example, in the northern city of São Luis, the capital of Maranhão state where Sá was killed, about 20 widely read blogs cover news and politics, according to Marco Aurélio D'Eça, a blogger who was one of Sá's closest friends.

D'Eça told CPJ that blogs and Internet news sites have shoved aside radio as the most important media in many provincial capitals and towns. These regions often lack aggressive hometown newspapers or TV stations, and they are largely overlooked by Brazil's major media.

Radio stations once filled some of the gaps, but many are owned by politicians, and their reporters often produce accounts that favor their bosses, he said. Although some bloggers are also aligned with and paid by politicians, D'Eça said, he and many other independent bloggers "have more freedom to investigate" issues like drug smuggling, human trafficking, and environmental crimes.

In addition, radio news is generally aimed at a less educated audience and airs for just a few minutes before disappearing. By contrast, D'Eça said, local news stories and commentary published online can have more impact because these posts are usually aimed at a more literate audience of politicians, business leaders, and opinion makers. In addition, blog posts are available on the Internet for months and can be reposted and emailed to reach a broader audience. As a result, corruption, political scandals, and gossip in rural Pernambuco, Mato Grosso, Bahía, and other states—stories that in the past would have remained local—can now be read by Internet users across the nation and reproduced by the mainstream media.

■ ■ ■

Sá, 42, was a veteran political reporter at the region's largest newspaper, *O Estado do Maranhão*, which is owned by the Sarney family, a political dynasty headed by former President José Sarney, whose daughter, Roseana Sarney, is the state governor. The newspaper generally shies away from investigations or critical reporting about the Sarneys, said Saulo McClean, a police reporter for *O Estado do Maranhão*. McClean writes stories based on police reports, but he said his editors rarely push him to dig deeper.

Sá, however, made a name for himself outside the newspaper by starting in 2006 the independent *Blog do Décio*, which aggressively covered the intersection between politics and organized crime. "Décio had to follow the editorial line in his work at the newspaper but not on his blog," McClean said. "His blog was more informal. It included gossip and rumors, but he always went after the big fish." It quickly became one of the most widely read blogs in the state. Sá's sources were so good that sometimes he went too far and compromised police investigations, Maranhão Police Chief Aluísio Mendes said. "He was very aggressive," Mendes told CPJ. "Everybody read his blog."

The postings that might have led to Sá's killing concerned the March murder of a local businessman. Mendes said that Sá got ahead of the police investigation by linking the case to a network of Maranhão loan sharks who often doled out huge sums to political candidates in return for government contracts once their clients were elected. The murdered businessman, Fábio Brasil, had apparently failed to pay back his debt, Mendes said. Although Sá did not name names, several comments published beneath his original blog post alleged that the murder had been ordered by Gláucio Alencar and his father, José de Alencar Miranda Carvalho—the reputed leaders of the loan shark ring.

Because the ring leaders had corrupt police officers and politicians on their payroll, Mendes said, they were more concerned about what Sá might reveal on his blog than about the official police investigation. As a result, they hired the same gunman who had killed Brasil to murder Sá, Mendes said. Sá was shot dead while sitting in a bar in São Luis. He is survived by his wife, who was pregnant at the time of his death, and an 8-year-old daughter.

Mendes told CPJ that solving the crime was a huge priority. Not only did the reporter work for the Sarney family, which demanded results, but Sá was the best-known journalist in Maranhão. "There was a sense that if they could kill Décio, they could kill anyone," Mendes said. A man was quickly arrested, confessed to being the gunman, and claimed the crime had been ordered by the Alencar family, according to Mendes. Gláucio Alencar, his father, and seven other suspects— including a police captain alleged to have provided the pistol used to kill Sá—were arrested, Mendes said. Alencar and the other suspects have denied the charges and, along with the alleged gunman, were awaiting trial in late 2012.

■ ■ ■

The Sá killing attracted widespread attention in the Brazilian press and was considered solved within 50 days. By contrast, the murder of Randolfo remains under investigation and has barely registered, according to Moreira, the ABRAJI president. Unlike Sá, Randolfo did not work for a major newspaper and had no heavyweight political connections. He was also based in a much smaller city, Vassouras, in southern Rio de Janeiro state, where he was founder, editor-in-chief, and the main blogger for the news website *Vassouras na Net*.

Like many independent Internet journalists, Randolfo supported himself by selling ads on his site to local businesses, according to Wilians Renato Dos Santos, a crime reporter for RBP Radio in the city of Barra do Piraí where Randolfo was killed. In his blog posts, Randolfo frequently accused local officials of corruption and had reported on an alleged network of hit men run by a former Vassouras police chief. "He challenged everybody," Dos Santos said. "He denounced crimes. He put a lot of people into difficult situations, and they wanted to make him shut up."

He described Randolfo as an honest, ethical reporter. J.C. Moreira, a friend of Randolfo and president of the local journalists union, said the blogger often proclaimed: "No one can buy me." But Barra do Piraí Police Chief José Mário Salomao de Omena told CPJ that Randolfo also published rumors and delved into the personal lives of officials, even reporting on their extramarital affairs. "He was like an unarmed sniper. He had no limits," said Omena, who was not a subject of Randolfo's investigations. "In a small town, that kind of reporting can be devastating. Wouldn't you want to kill someone if he said your mother was a whore and your father was unfaithful?"

In July 2011, an unidentified gunman entered the *Vassouras na Net* newsroom and shot Randolfo in the head, which left him in a coma for three days with a bullet lodged behind his right ear. He survived and later claimed on his website that he had been targeted in retaliation for his reporting on irregularities in the investigation of a local murder. No one was charged or arrested in that attack. For his safety, Randolfo moved in January from Vassouras to Barra do Piraí, a town of 88,000. But the two towns are just 15 miles (25 kilometers) apart, and Randolfo did not stop reporting for his website. "After the attack, I told him to be careful and to forget about doing journalism," his friend, Moreira, told CPJ. Because Barra do Piraí is so close to Vassouras, Moreira said, "I thought he was crazy to move here."

Randolfo was killed on February 9, 2012, along with his companion, Maria Aparecida Guimarães. Omena said their bodies were found by the side of a highway on the outskirts of Barra do Piraí. Both had been abducted from Randolfo's home the night before and shot to death early that morning.

Omena said the vast majority of homicide cases in Barra do Piraí are solved, but he acknowledged a lack of progress in the Randolfo case. Shortly after Randolfo's death, he told reporters that the journalist had "created such a large volume of enemies that it is difficult to know where to start" the investigation. In responding to written questions from CPJ, Ramon Leite Carvalho, the public prosecutor in charge of the Randolfo case, refused to discuss details, citing the continuing investigation.

In the wake of the Sá and Randolfo killings, President Dilma Rousseff's government has tried to play down the notion that Brazil is turning into a red zone for journalists, according to Moreira, the ABRAJI president. He pointed out that the 2014 World Cup will be played in 12 cities across Brazil and that amid the increased international scrutiny, the government is trying to push the idea that the nation is peaceful and reporter-friendly. But at least seven Brazilian journalists were killed in direct relation to their work between January 2011 and November 2012, making the nation one of the world's deadliest for the press. And the government has at times appeared insensitive to the problem. In April 2012, the Brazilian delegation opposed a UNESCO-led plan to combat impunity in journalist killings worldwide. After Brazil's position drew heavy criticism from ABRAJI and others, U.N. Ambassador Maria Luiza Ribeiro Viotti said in June that the country would support the plan as it moved forward at the United Nations.

■ ■ ■

Sá and Randolfo took a delight in tweaking the powerful, yet neither took any special measures to protect themselves, according to friends and colleagues. Fellow bloggers have reacted in different ways to their deaths. Gildean Farias, the Web editor for *O Imparcial*, São Luis' oldest daily newspaper, said Sá's murder persuaded him to steer clear of politics in the blog he writes for the paper. D'Eça, by contrast, has been using his blog to continue with Sá's investigation of Maranhão loan sharks.

Reporter friends of Sá have kept his blog alive. But in rural Rio de Janeiro state, Randolfo's Internet site has been taken down and his death has meant one less watchdog in a part of the country with few journalists to begin with. There's been almost no follow-up in the Brazilian media about his case. And according to Moreira of ABRAJI, that means far less pressure on local authorities to find the killers.

Moreira said reporters based in Rio de Janeiro and São Paulo often view provincial journalists as biased, corrupt, and in bed with local politicians. Thus, he said, the major media pay less attention when these reporters and bloggers come under attack. Randolfo's murder did not make TV Globo's main newscast in Rio de Janeiro even though the blogger was gunned down in a nearby town. "If they are not writing for the big media, they are seen as nothing," Moreira told CPJ. "Yet these bloggers had the courage to write about the bad things that were happening in their communities."

John Otis, Andes correspondent for CPJ's Americas program, also works as a correspondent for Time *magazine and the* Global Post. *He wrote the 2010 book "Law of the Jungle," about U.S. military contractors kidnapped by Colombian rebels. He is based in Bogotá.*

Seeking Justice in Russia, A Mother Turns To Europe

By Elisabeth Witchel

When Rimma Maksimova last spoke with her son, investigative journalist Maksim Maksimov, in a phone call on June 26, 2004, they talked about the comings and goings of family life: his approaching birthday, her plans to visit him the next month in St. Petersburg. Mother and son swapped calls in the next couple of days but missed each other. She rang him up one last time on July 3, leaving a message that wished him a happy 41st birthday.

By that time, Maksim Maksimov was gone. His mother would spend her trip to St. Petersburg, and the next eight years, trying to find out what had happened to Maksimov, who was last seen on June 29, 2004, in downtown St. Petersburg. He was never found.

Today, Maksimova is 73 and battling bone marrow cancer. She is also waging war on Russia's political and judicial machinery. Having sought justice, without success, from police, prosecutors, and the president's office, Maksimova turned to the European Court of Human Rights (ECHR) in Strasbourg, France, where she filed a case in 2011 claiming that Russian authorities failed to uphold her son's rights to life, liberty, and freedom of expression. "Over the years, I have been through all the circles of hell imaginable—pain, helplessness, terrible suffering," Maksimova said in written testimony submitted to the court. "The pain of my situation was exacerbated from the very beginning by the attitude of the investigative authorities."

The case has implications not only for Maksimov's family but for journalists throughout Europe and Central Asia. If admitted, the case would be among the first heard in Strasbourg on a journalism-related killing in Russia. More significantly, Maksimova's representatives will also argue that her son's murder is part of a pattern of impunity in attacks on the press in that country.

"Because of the evidence that this was a systemic problem— because the number and nature of attacks on journalists is and has been for a number of years hugely concerning, hugely worrying, and it has not been dealt with—bringing proceedings in the Strasbourg court is one way of raising that problem and trying to tackle it," said Philip Leach, lawyer and project director of the London-based European Human Rights Advocacy Centre (EHRAC), which is representing Maksimova and which specializes in taking cases to Strasbourg.

Maksim Maksimov started working as a journalist in 1986 with a youth newspaper called *Smena* (Change). He then spent several years working for AZHUR, an investigative news agency, where he developed a reputation for reporting on corruption in law enforcement and the contract-style murders of local politicians. In July 2003, he went freelance, writing a regular column for *Gorod* newspaper. Around the time of his disappearance, colleagues say, Maksimov was investigating corruption in the 6th section of the operational detective bureau of the Ministry of Internal Affairs.

After their last phone conversation, Rimma Maksimova, who lives in Potsdam, Germany, traveled to Moscow in early July 2004 and on to St. Petersburg, her concern growing over lack of contact with her son. On July 9, she and two of Maksimov's colleagues went to the police station, where her statement was taken. Over the next two weeks, Maksimova hounded the police and an investigator from the Central

District Prosecutor's Office, waiting hours in his office to find out what steps were being taken.

She got little information. Often it was suggested that Maksimov was simply away with a woman or had been sighted. When she asked the Central District investigator if the people who had last seen her son had been interviewed, she was told no—one of many leads the police appear not to have followed.

Maksimova went back to Germany in late July but returned to St. Petersburg near the end of the year at the distressing news that the public prosecutor's office had suspended work on the case. In April 2005, the suspension was revoked on grounds that the investigation was incomplete. This decision cited unexplored lines of inquiry, including an analysis of fingerprints found in Maksimov's car in late July 2004; interviews with Maksimov's colleagues; and a study of his computer. There was no explanation of why those steps had not been taken.

■ ■ ■

In 2009, CPJ conducted an investigation into the flawed official inquiry into Maksimov's disappearance, the results of which were published as part of a wider report on unsolved journalist killings in Russia, "Anatomy of Injustice." At the time, Sergei Baluyev, *Gorod*'s chief editor, told CPJ that Maksimov's property, car, and savings had been found intact within a few weeks of his disappearance—but investigators conducted only a cursory review of the reporter's notes and his conversations with colleagues.

What evidence eventually emerged came mainly from Maksimov's colleagues at AZHUR. Yevgeny Vyshenkov, AZHUR's deputy director, told CPJ that he and his staff interviewed two people who said they were involved in Maksimov's disappearance. One person said he had been hired to lure the journalist to a local sauna under the guise of a business meeting, and that two Interior Ministry officers and two others were waiting there. After being ordered to leave the room, the person told Vyshenkov, he heard the men assault Maksimov.

Vyshenkov said he had also met with one of the assailants, an ex-convict, who told him that the men had strangled Maksimov, put his body in the trunk of a car, and driven in two vehicles to woods outside

St. Petersburg. There, the two officers drove off on their own with the body and returned a half-hour later, Vyshenkov said he was told.

AZHUR presented its findings to the regional prosecutor's office. Vyshenkov said he had persuaded the front person and the assailant to tell prosecutors their story. Nikolai Sirotinin, the Maksimov family lawyer and a former government investigator, said that AZHUR's information was credible enough to warrant official investigation, but the prosecutor's office did not appear interested in following up. Sirotinin told CPJ that investigators would not clarify what leads they checked.

A.V. Zaitsev, a senior official with the regional investigative committee, told CPJ in a written statement in 2009 that his staff had indeed checked whether Interior Ministry officers were involved in the crime. He did not elaborate on what investigators had done or found. The two officers implicated in AZHUR's account were at one point charged with forgery, false statement, and abuse of office in an unrelated case (they were later acquitted) but have never been charged in the Maksimov case.

The Dzerzhinsky District Court in St. Petersburg declared Maksimov dead on November 30, 2006, at the behest of the family, which was seeking emotional closure as well as greater legal rights and more official attention to the case. A concerted search for Maksimov's body was finally undertaken in spring 2007, also at the insistence of his family. Sirotinin said he traveled to Moscow to persuade former colleagues in the Prosecutor General's Office to send a forensics team to assist. The search came up empty.

In total the investigation was suspended and restarted three times between 2004 and 2011, with no substantial information provided to Maksimova on what steps were taken and why. Her phone calls were largely ignored, and from 2005 to 2009, Maksimova traveled from Potsdam to St. Petersburg more than a dozen times at her own expense. "The little I did find out was because I kept asking questions," Maksimova said in her testimony.

During this time, Maksimova wrote letters to officials at all levels of Russia's criminal system, including the minister for internal affairs and the Public Chamber, a governmental oversight body, requesting a thorough investigation, new personnel to oversee the case, or resumption of proceedings following a suspension. She made two appeals to

President Vladimir Putin, one a 2006 open letter published in *Moscow Pravda* titled "Will the President hear a mother's voice?" To all of these she has testified that she received cursory replies or nothing at all.

The toll on her physical and mental health was immense. She recently described to CPJ her last visit to St. Petersburg and a meeting she had in December 2011 with the general prosecutor for the Northwestern Federal District. "He turned our conversation upside down, as if I am demanding to prosecute an innocent person and they're guarding law and order," she said. "Following that meeting I had a nervous breakdown and contracted pneumonia, so they sent me to the airport in a wheelchair." In her last telephone exchange with the investigator, in August 2012, Maksimova told CPJ, "He openly told me that they did not restart the case, that all the investigative measures were fulfilled, and that there's nothing left to be done."

Sirotinin, the family lawyer, said his own requests to review the official case file were turned down. Russian procedural code gives investigators discretion to disclose details of an active inquiry to a victim's family and legal representatives; a family is entitled to access only when the investigation is formally finished. Although Maksimov's case is suspended, it has not been officially closed, which would allow the family and its lawyer to review the file.

■ ■ ■

Such languishing investigations into attacks against journalists are endemic in Russia. There have been no successful prosecutions in more than 90 percent of cases of journalists murdered or violently assaulted in connection to their work in Russia, according to CPJ research. Victims include internationally known figures like *Forbes Russia* editor Paul Klebnikov, but many are like Maksimov who report on local corruption, crime, and human rights abuses. Worldwide, Russia ranks ninth-worst on CPJ's Impunity Index, which calculates the number of unsolved journalist murders as a percentage of each country's population.

Despite pledges from Russian leadership to address the climate of impunity, there has been little substantial progress. In the 2006 murder of investigative journalist Anna Politkovskaya, authorities took promising steps, arresting and indicting several suspects, only to let the case stagnate again. "At least with regards to this case the investigative community does something," said Galina Arapova, director of Russia's Mass Media Defence Centre, which offers legal defense to journalists and has brought defamation-related cases to the ECHR. "They don't have political will to really finish the case but they feed society with little seeds. For the others, they simply just don't do anything; or they do a little bit and then close the case and say they haven't found any evidence or suspect to bring to the court."

Arapova said the problem is not one of capability; murder investigations are often effective in Russia. Investigative Committee chief Aleksandr Bastrykin once boasted that perpetrators are caught in four out of five cases. "Interestingly that doesn't apply to cases of journalists," Arapova said. "When it comes to murder of journalists, then you have 10 years of investigation that ends with nothing. Families are trying to struggle with the Russian law enforcement system and they just lose their faith in the result."

This was nearly so for Maksimova, who in a 2010 meeting with CPJ's European and Central Asia Program Coordinator Nina Ognianova expressed her desperation to find new avenues to justice. They discussed the European Court as an option. Under the Council of Europe, the court hears complaints that signatory states have violated the European Convention on Human Rights if applicants can prove they have exhausted all domestic remedies. CPJ approached the EHRAC. Now, EHRAC lawyers Leach, Joanna Evans, and Bill Bowring represent Maksimova, as does Mark Stephens, a lawyer working in coordination with CPJ.

Maksimova v. Russia argues, among other points, that the authorities failed to conduct an effective investigation into Maksimov's death, a violation of Article 2 of the European Convention's right-to-life guarantee, which includes the obligation to investigate suspicious deaths. It also contends that the state is directly responsible for Maksimov's demise and that his disappearance is a case of unlawful detention—the argument being that evidence suggests he was abducted and murdered by parties from the police force—adding another violation of Article 2 and a violation of Article 5, which guarantees the right to liberty and security. Russian investigators also violated Article 3, the resolution addressing torture, in their disregard for Maksimov's well-being and rights, the suit argues.

The 52-page submission goes further to posit that because the case is one of a murder motivated by journalistic activity, and the journalism sought to expose official corruption, it is representative of "a systematic failure by the Russian state to protect the lives and well-being of journalists within its jurisdiction and/or to ensure the effective investigation and prosecution of those responsible for the harassment, harm, and killing of journalists within Russia (particularly those investigating and reporting upon areas of sensitivity)." By this reasoning, the applicant charges, Russia is guilty of a separate violation of Article 2 and a violation of Article 10's guarantee of freedom of expression.

■ ■ ■

A suit alleging that Russia violated Article 2 in the case of Politkovskaya was filed to Strasbourg in 2007; the court has not yet admitted it. But, according to Leach, *Maksimova v. Russia* is the first attempt to seek a judgment identifying a state pattern in which the authorities fail to effectively investigate murders of journalists and declaring that this behavior has a chilling effect on freedom of expression. In the 2007 murder of journalist Hrant Dink, the court ruled the Turkish state had violated freedom of expression by failing to protect Dink and convict all his killers, but it did not look at this link in a broader context. "It would be extremely significant if the court were to make a decision to the effect that these attacks on journalists or the authorities' failures in relation to the attacks on journalists are systemic," Leach said.

Though the court has been friendly to freedom-of-expression cases, it has mainly favored journalists in cases involving defamation, Arapova said. "We hope that cases from Russia relating to noninvestigated murders of journalists will be considered in light of Article 10 and not only Article 2," she said. "We would like to bring attention to violation of other rights when the murder of a person takes place—especially if it is connected to his professional work as a journalist."

But any important precedents that the Maksimov case may set are a long way off. Because of Maksimova's age and cancer diagnosis, the representing team requested that the matter be expedited, but more than a year has passed since the court acknowledged it received the case submission. In late 2012, there had been no word on whether the case meets Strasbourg's criteria and the court will initiate proceedings. "It could be weeks, or months," said Leach.

Complaints of lengthy delays and backlogs are common in connection with the court, which in March 2012 had 150,000 cases pending. About a quarter of these hail from Russia. Last year the United Kingdom led a charge to reform the court, calling for shorter filing windows and restrictions on eligibility—and alarming human rights groups concerned that the move would curb the court's power rather than address inefficiencies.

Strasbourg decisions are binding, but member states often don't comply in full. Russia, for example, said Leach, will typically implement recommendations for financial compensation to victims, but is less amenable when it comes to politically sensitive recommendations like legislative reform. Still, Christof Heyns, U.N. special rapporteur on extrajudicial, summary, or arbitrary executions, believes the ECHR has much to offer other regions as a model. "The European system has a very high level of compliance, and its jurisprudence—in respect of accountability—is sophisticated," he told CPJ in an interview.

Past court decisions in cases where journalists have been killed, though favorable to the applicant, have had varied impact. In 2012, lawyers representing the Dink family wrote to the Committee of Ministers of the Council of Europe excoriating Turkey for failing to execute Strasbourg's verdict and punish all of Dink's killers. Separately, Ukraine did not abide by the court's 2005 ruling that it pay damages for failing to protect the life of journalist Gregory Gongadze or investigate his death, although his widow, Myroslava Gongadze, told CPJ that Strasbourg's pressure on Ukraine kept the case alive in domestic courts. In 2012, she said she would launch new ECHR proceedings to appeal Ukraine's decision not to prosecute former President Leonid Kuchma for his alleged involvement in the murder.

Given her frail state of health, there is a good chance Rimma Maksimova may not live to learn what happened to her son, or to see if the case she has set in motion will change the way Russian authorities respond when journalists are threatened or attacked. She has named Maksimov's cousin, Sergei Kapustin, as the second applicant, to carry on the case in her absence. Regardless of the outcome, Maksimova has broken new ground in the fight against impunity. Journalists in Russia and elsewhere are indebted to her.

Elisabeth Witchel, CPJ's London-based consultant, served for many years as the organization's journalist assistance coordinator. She also launched CPJ's Global Campaign Against Impunity.

5

POLITICAL
TRANSITIONS

In Iran, Specter of One Election Looms Over the Next

By D. Parvaz

As Iran's June 2013 presidential election approaches, the media landscape is extremely bleak. At the last election, in 2009, journalists took advantage of a slight loosening of the country's traditionally stringent media controls to push against the boundaries, bringing the world news of alleged voting irregularities, public anger, protests, and the ensuing crackdown by the hard-line leadership.

That crackdown, however, hit the media sector as hard as any. The authorities have used imprisonment, the closing of news outlets, the intimidation of reporters and sources, and suffocating Internet surveillance to silence the independent media. Scores of journalists have fled into exile. With only a handful of severely weakened reformist media outlets now operating in Iran, and with most working journalists in fear of the revolving door to the country's courts and prisons, a repeat of 2009 seems unlikely. Without any kind of free or healthy press, and with reformist leaders under house arrest, political discourse has been quashed.

"We've never had any press freedoms in Iran; we censored ourselves and we were able to report within those confines. But it's become much worse," said exiled journalist Delbar Tavakoli, who wrote for *Etemad-e-Melli* and the now-banned *Sarmayeh*. "Many of our best journalists have had to quit their jobs and change their professions—perhaps going into the arts or [becoming] taxi drivers," said Tavakoli, who now lives in France and works for the Farsi branch of Radio France Internationale. "The people we have in Iran—with all the talent and ability they have—they can't work."

One journalist and media analyst working in Tehran said that "we don't see any signs of things improving—never mind that. We get regular government directives that place new limitations on what we can report, ones well beyond political reporting." The journalist, who did not want to be named for safety reasons, added, "Now the issue is topics such as the price of chicken, the rising rate of the U.S. dollar" against the rial. "This sort of thing just pushes us further away from being able to effectively report important political issues, such as elections."

■ ■ ■

And yet Iran is under intense international pressure over its nuclear ambitions and its economy is staggering. The country's ever-shifting internal political rifts and alliances are difficult for even close observers to grasp. All this makes it impossible to know how media coverage of the election will play out. Despite Iran's long history of censorship, journalists have a tradition of seizing on any opportunity to report, even when a harsh reaction looms.

Under the constitution, President Mahmoud Ahmadinejad cannot stand for re-election to a third term, leaving the 2013 vote a contest between his supporters and the conservative backers of Supreme Leader Ayatollah Ali Khamenei. Ahmadinejad, once part of the conservative establishment himself, fell out of favor with Khamenei as he struggled to form his own power base. Among the early front-runners in the establishment camp were Parliament Speaker Ali Larijani and Mohamad-Bagher Ghalibaf, the mayor of Tehran. In October, as Iran's currency tumbled, Larijani and Ahmadinejad publicly traded barbs over the latter's management of the economy.

Elections in Iran are usually tightly managed, with the choice of presidential and parliamentary candidates limited to those pre-approved by the establishment. The results are often locked up before polls even open. Three and a half years ago, Iranian authorities appeared highly confident that Ahmadinejad would win his second term in office. Amid this hubris, the regime seemed to allow a small window for the tightly controlled media to dispatch articles, interviews, and sound bites in the run-up to the vote.

"Things were pretty open—people were pretty confident before the elections," said Golnoush Niknejad, editor-in-chief and founder of *Tehran Bureau*, a website dedicated to covering Iran from within, using Iranian journalists whenever possible. "The campaign seemed different. The government allowed for live, televised debates and wanted to make it seem like people, especially young people, were participating in the elections," said Niknejad, who is based in Boston. "Before 2009, we didn't even have people using pseudonyms. People thought if they were doing a fair job of reporting, then they didn't have anything to worry about."

But the small freedoms that are allowed in Iran are calculated, with the aims of presenting the country as a functioning democracy and getting a read on who will report what. By allowing such leeway from time to time, Tavakoli said, the government can get "the full measure of their opponents," which include the nonstate media as well as the opposition. She likened Tehran's control of the press to flying a kite. "Sometimes you give more string, sometimes you pull back—but you keep enough tension to keep the kite afloat," she said.

When Ahmadinejad was declared the 2009 election winner, millions who had supported reformist candidates Mir Hossein Mousavi and Mehdi Karroubi took to the streets to protest, and the uproar appeared to take the regime by surprise. The Green Movement, as reformers called it, flowed through the veins of Iran's cities, filling squares and major thoroughfares. As protesters clashed with security forces, violence spread through streets and neighborhoods. Homes were raided and activists, politicians, and journalists alike were targeted by the regime. Tweet-by-tweet reporting had proved more than the government would tolerate.

"What happened on the 22nd of Khordad [Election Day on the Iranian calendar] was a destructive tsunami," said the journalist in Tehran. In the weeks after the vote, journalists faced unprecedented levels of censorship, threats, and arrests.

"Every day, it seemed, there were fewer of us at editorial meetings, and this went on not just for a month or three months, but for a year," the journalist said. "Every day, we'd hear that more of our colleagues had been arrested."

State agents were busy identifying reporters at the scenes of demonstrations. "In the first days after the elections, we saw these guys filming us and we asked, 'What are you getting footage for?'" Tavakoli said. "And they just smiled and said, 'You'll see.'"

The August 2009 raid on the Tehran offices of the Association of Iranian Journalists signaled a sea change. "It was something like a coup," said Ali Mazrooei, who was the director of the association at the time. The group's offices remain closed. Mazrooei now runs the reformist news site *Razhesabz* from Belgium. "The situation is getting worse than before," Mazrooei said. "There's no freedom for reporters and for press."

CPJ surveys over the past three years have found that Iran imprisons at least 40 to 50 journalists at any given time, making the country one of the worst jailers of journalists worldwide. Most are held on anti-state charges. Throughout this period, the authorities have maintained a revolving prison door, freeing some detainees on furloughs even as they arrest others. Freed prisoners are called back seemingly at random, sometimes repeatedly.

Zhila Bani-Yaghoub, who worked for a number of nonstate media outlets, began serving a one-year sentence in September 2012 for "insulting" Ahmadinejad and "spreading propaganda." But her time served will be only a beginning—she's also been banned from practicing journalism for 30 years. Bani-Yaghoub's ban is a particularly lengthy court-imposed sanction, but the government can also simply refuse to renew a journalist's work permit, achieving the same effect in a less blatant way.

CPJ has documented that at least 68 Iranian journalists have fled into exile over the past five years, although some Iranians believe the actual numbers to be much higher. Mazrooei estimates that about 160 journalists have gone into exile since the 2009 elections and that an equal number are in jail. Masih Alinejad, a prominent exiled journalist who lives in the United Kingdom, said in a 2010 interview that international records do not take into account lesser-known reporters working for small outlets in small towns. Tavakoli also said the government is no longer arresting only key media figures. "There used to be the case that only high-profile targets were arrested," she said. "Now, they can't tolerate any noise."

News outlets, too, are subject to bans—some permanent and others intermittent. A handful of reformist outlets still operate inside the country, but they are vulnerable to the whims of the hard-liners. For example, *Shargh*, a reformist newspaper, has been ordered to cease publishing four times in eight years. In September 2012, the government suspended *Shargh* after the paper published a cartoon that some interpreted as insulting the Basij militia. An arrest order for its editor, Mehdi Rahmanian, was also issued.

The reformist movement now largely counts on foreign-based sites more than domestic ones for news—such as Mousavi's August 2012 trip to the hospital under tight security, which went unreported by official news agencies. Online reformist publications operating from abroad, such as Mazrooei's *Razhesabz*, are intermittently blocked for Iranian users.

Indeed, censorship of the Internet and other telecommunications has been at the heart of the regime's strategy of control. Iran has invested heavily in technology and personnel with the explicit intent of restricting Web access. Iranians face frequent slowdowns in Internet service; Twitter is periodically blocked; and while Google's Gmail service was once considered safe, Google revealed in 2011 that the Iranian government had been intercepting Gmail messages. Most Iranians assume that landlines or mobile phones are monitored, although some are comfortable using voice-over-Internet-protocol such as Skype.

When discussing countries that pose threats to global cybersecurity, Eric Schmidt, Google's executive chairman, told CNN in December 2011 that Iranian authorities are "unusually talented" in cyberwar. "You always worry that the Iranians have somehow broken into some of the encrypted software that's used to control things," he said.

■ ■ ■

Even if journalists dared to report in this climate of fear, it's unlikely that sources would speak to them. Trust between reporters and their sources, fundamental to newsgathering everywhere, is critical in a place like Iran. The country's interrogators are practiced at drawing confessions, sometimes creating informants out of their terrified subjects. Under duress in detention, the prominent journalists Roxana Saberi and Maziar Bahari both confessed to acting against the Islamic Republic. Tavakoli said that she fled into exile not because she feared for herself, but because of the threat that her arrest could pose to others.

Given Iran's lack of transparency concerning public records, most reporting is done on the streets. But reformists are not given permits to gather; since 2010, the few reformist demonstrations of note have been silent protests, as any chanting would prompt an attack from the Basijis, the state militia often seen charging crowds on motorcycles, wielding batons. With no events to report on the street, the story of Iran's dissent remains hidden—difficult and risky for reporters to dig up and present. Even when mass arrests of journalists are not happening, tight surveillance and random punishment still have a chilling effect, something Niknejad describes as "psychological warfare."

"There won't be any chance for any coverage," Mazrooei said of the coming elections. Reporters "prefer to be silent to see what is going on with the country. They are waiting."

Niknejad is almost certain that she will not have access to a wealth of journalists in Iran by election time. "I don't think that the environment is going to be there," she said. "So much can happen between now and the election. At the end of the day, they will make sure that the situation [in 2009] does not happen again."

Tavakoli described the current practice of journalism in Iran as "a radical act" mostly because so few dare to do it. "With this regime," she said, "the future of journalism grows darker by the day."

Still, Iran remains an enigma, even to those who cover the country from within and have intimate knowledge of the government's workings—including close encounters with the regime's interrogators and prisons. Potential shifts in the country's internal power structure could shape what happens on the streets and how the media cover it.

Mazrooei acknowledges that things could change rapidly before the election. "We don't even know what's going to happen next week, let alone by then."

D. Parvaz, a journalist and Middle East analyst, works for Al-Jazeera and is based in Doha, Qatar.

Disdain for Foreign Press Undercuts China's Global Ambition

By Madeline Earp

C hina's new leaders have an opportunity to transform international media relations when they assume power in 2013. But their predecessors spent the previous year ensuring that reforms would take years to manifest—even if the new generation shows the political will to implement them.

In 2012, Chinese leaders appeared less concerned than they had in some time with how their treatment of the foreign press corps was perceived internationally. The government forced a foreign correspondent out of the country for the first time since 1998 and allowed anti-foreign popular sentiment to flourish, to the detriment of international correspondents. Obstruction of reporting seemed particularly stark when looking back to the 2008 Beijing Olympics, when leaders tried to appease international media companies concerned about lack of access. The restrictive measures on the mainland came even as the

Chinese Communist Party pushed an unprecedented expansion of its own news media into global markets.

In November, seven new members of the party's leading Politburo Standing Committee were selected at the 18th Party Congress, completing the long-planned ascension of Vice President Xi Jinping to the head of the party and positioning him to take the presidency at the March 2013 legislative session. Liu Yunshan, longtime leader of the propaganda department, was among the new lineup, which analysts described as conservative.

"Nothing should be ruled out," Robert J. Barnett, who watches China as the director of the Modern Tibet Studies Program at Columbia University in New York, told CPJ. "This is a new leadership, going through an unprecedented transition upheaval, facing unparalleled challenges from social and economic tensions in China."

■ ■ ■

But the press received little encouragement to chart these upheavals, with restrictions on visas and accreditations tightened ahead of the Congress and hotel owners instructed to report guests whose resident permits identify them as journalists, according to the translation of a notice by the California-based *China Digital Times*. It wasn't clear how Xi and his cohort might transition from this dismal beginning. To make the media globally competitive and functional as a domestic watchdog—especially as economic growth slows and wealth discrepancies continue to reverberate—reforming media policies in line with international norms is a necessity. Though many observers believe the new leadership recognizes the need for change, there's little hope this can be achieved within existing frameworks or with any urgency.

"Many people are hoping the new team will move towards greater transparency and a deeper commitment to freedom of the press, but it's premature to say if this is likely anytime soon," Melinda Liu, Beijing bureau chief of *Newsweek/Daily Beast* and a former president of the Foreign Correspondents Club of China, told CPJ.

A significant marker in 2012 came when the Ministry of Foreign Affairs declined to renew the accreditation of Al-Jazeera English correspondent Melissa Chan, forcing her to leave Beijing after five years.

Delaying and denying visas—or threatening to revoke them—is a long-standing technique for discouraging critical reporters. But this de facto expulsion was the most egregious example CPJ had documented since the 1990s, and it cast a chill over the entire press corps because the motivation was unknown. When correspondents pressed spokesman Hong Lei for more information about the decision at a Foreign Ministry press briefing, he said, "With regard to the relevant issue, I think relevant media and journalists are clear about that." They weren't. Chan told CPJ she remains unclear why the government would not renew her credentials. "The Chinese have not been entirely forthcoming," she told CPJ. "I guess we just won't be able to know." Under relatively unknown new leaders, foreign journalists will need to continue to guess which lines cannot be crossed.

Those who retained permission to work found their access eroded. In May, security officials summoned for questioning a dozen journalists covering the treatment of blind legal activist Chen Guangcheng in a Beijing hospital. At least two journalists' press cards were temporarily confiscated because the hospital parking lot was supposedly off-limits to reporters. Similarly, in 2011, police told international reporters seeking to cover anti-government protests—the Jasmine uprising that was crushed before it began—that they required advanced authorization to report, even though they were in one of the busiest shopping districts in the capital.

Nor were journalists able to get substantive information through official channels. In the digital media age, Foreign Ministry news conferences appeared particularly archaic. After Chen garnered global media attention for fleeing house arrest for the sanctuary of the U.S. Embassy in Beijing, Chinese Vice Foreign Minister Cui Tiankai told reporters he had "no information" on the case. In September, Xi Jinping's absence from public events prompted speculation about his health, with one journalist asking at a regular ministry news conference whether the official had died unexpectedly. "I hope you can ask a serious question," was Hong's response.

Officials' interactions with journalists on overseas trips were also characterized by suspicion. President Hu Jintao's refusal to schedule news conferences overseas drew strong criticism on a June trip to Denmark. Organizers of a September EU–China summit in Brussels canceled the post-meeting news conference, an established tradition at the event, after Chinese participants tried to vet attendees and limit the number of questions, according to the Associated Press. On a high-profile visit to the United States in February 2012, future president Xi didn't hold any news conferences, which may be an indication of the approach he will take in office.

This was "especially disappointing" to Liu, who headed the Foreign Correspondents Club of China during a window of openness shortly before the start of the Olympics in 2008. After the Sichuan earthquake in 2008, Liu said, "Premier Wen Jiabao held a press conference for foreign media near the epicenter of the quake where unscripted questions were asked and answered." International diplomacy also had some effect in promoting openness at the time. "During the year before the Games, the Foreign Correspondents Club of China had regular liaison with foreign embassies in Beijing to brief diplomats on changing regulations and events on the ground. It helped when foreign governments raised their concerns about press freedoms to the Chinese Foreign Ministry. And the ministry itself wanted to appear responsive to foreign journalists' concerns," Liu said. "However, the pendulum swung back toward greater restriction of media access."

■ ■ ■

The Foreign Correspondents Club of China faces its own share of restrictions. In August 2012, it issued a statement condemning four attacks against international reporters, but its activity was muted in comparison to past years. Though the group formerly logged incidents involving foreign correspondents on its website, the information has been circulated to a members-only list since mid-2010. A Foreign Ministry official threatened the organization with "serious consequences" should it continue to post such material, said Peter Ford, the club's president. He said the group interpreted the "vague and ambiguous threat" to mean that the authorities might close the club, officially an illegal organization, or make it hard for its leaders to work in China.

Foreign officials appeared to have limited ability to influence press conditions. Twenty-six German correspondents working in China wrote to Chancellor Angela Merkel asking her to intervene on their behalf during a visit scheduled in August. Some reports said she raised the issue privately, but there was no public result. CPJ appealed to U.S. Secretary of State Hillary Rodham Clinton and Danish Prime Minister Helle Thorning-Schmidt to raise the issue in their travels to Beijing, but the effort met with no apparent success. It's unclear if new leaders wanting to start off international relations on a fresh footing will be any more approachable.

Broad censorship of foreign news reports remained in place in 2012; international satellite channels, for example, were largely unavailable to the public. *China Digital Times* published a government listing, circulated in advance of the November Congress, that said 33 such channels were permitted in "domestic hotels serving foreigners rated three stars and above." Encoded signals from the channels are under the sole control of the state-owned China International Television Corporation. The government's notice said that no other venue could broadcast the signals without approval, according to *China Digital Times*.

The authorities blocked a June report by the U.S.-based Bloomberg news agency that examined the financial assets held by Xi Jinping's family and associates. Just months ahead of Xi's expected designation as the next president, this was an especially sensitive report. Bloomberg's terminal service, which provides real-time financial data, was unaffected by the censorship, although Hong Kong's *South China Morning Post* reported in September that the Chinese market for the service shrank in the aftermath of the report. In October, the website of *The New York Times* was blocked within an hour of the paper's publication of an exposé on the family wealth of outgoing Prime Minister Wen Jiabao. Earlier in the year, the *Times* reported that a Sina Weibo microblog account linked to its newly launched Chinese-language edition was censored within a week of being activated. Tight restrictions applied to Chinese journalists, too: Jian Guangzhou, who broke the story of contaminated Sanlu milk formula for the Shanghai-based *Oriental Morning Post* in 2008, quit the paper in October. "I definitely couldn't do [that investigation] today," Jian told the McClatchy news service.

Censorship and obstruction were accompanied by a rise in antiforeign sentiment, as the party used state media to manipulate public anger. As the dispute with Japan over the Diaoyu or Senkaku islands in the East China Sea intensified in mid-September, propaganda officials withheld the habitual orders to suppress reporting on "mass incidents," the party's phrase for public disturbances. Violent anti-Japanese protesters took to the streets across major Chinese cities, encouraged by saturation media coverage. The repercussions were severe: Several Japanese companies temporarily halted production in China as thousands looted factories, and one man was beaten and partially paralyzed while driving his Toyota Corolla, news reports said. When police in southern Guangzhou resorted to tear gas to contain protesters, domestic media changed course and urged restraint. Censors blocked videos and search terms related to the demonstrations, according to the Associated Press. The Tokyo-based Overseas Courier Service Co. told the English-language *Japan Times* that Chinese customs officials seized at least two entire October issues of Japanese newspapers delivered by air for distribution in China, because they contained reports on the developing dispute. The report did not identify the newspapers by name.

■ ■ ■

If Xi Jinping and other new Communist leaders persist in this attitude toward foreign correspondents on home soil, they may find other states unwilling to cooperate with Chinese media expansion around the world. The conflict with Japan provided a small illustration when China protested the Japanese coast guard's detention of two journalists who had accompanied Chinese activists planting flags on the unoccupied islands—a rare instance of a foreign government obstructing the Chinese press. Japan promptly released the two reporters.

In June, a U.S. Congressional subcommittee on immigration met to consider the proposed Chinese Media Reciprocity Act of 2011, which would restrict the number of U.S. visas granted to journalists working for Chinese state media. The bill was based on a faulty analogy between American news outlets with state backing, like Voice of America, and the complex system of licensing in China that mandates some level of state sponsorship for all media. The bill's drafters identified only 13 state outlets, and hoped that China's fear of limited access for those outlets would prompt Beijing to offer more visas to their U.S. counterparts. CPJ opposed the act, which had not been passed by late

2012, on grounds that it would likely goad China into retaliation, not reciprocity, at the expense of journalists in both countries. But the bill served as a measure of the resistance Chinese journalists might encounter if their leaders refused to grant them independence.

An episode in Canada bodes ill for China's effort to create global media networks. Mark Bourrie, a 55-year-old Canadian who worked for the Xinhua news agency, publicly resigned in April after his employer asked him to report an event involving the Dalai Lama as an internal briefing, not as public news. Bourrie also said he had been told to gather names and addresses of anti-China protesters in Canada. Xinhua's Ottawa bureau chief denied his account, according to the Canadian Press, but the details rang true for analysts familiar with Xinhua's two-tier domestic publication system, which reserves sensitive content for government-only distribution. Linda Jakobson, East Asia program director of Australia's Lowy Institute for International Policy, highlighted another concern on the organization's blog in October, saying a Xinhua reporter had misquoted her as praising China's role in facilitating talks with North Korea. She had actually commented critically on China's involvement more than a year earlier, she wrote. "The official media continues to either censor or intentionally misconstrue any stance which does not conform to what the propaganda officials have deemed as the correct interpretation," Jakobson said.

Other factors undermine China's effort to find a global audience for its state media, such as the behavior of Yang Rui, the high-profile host of "Dialogue," a CCTV English-language talk show structured around debate with international guests. Encouraged by viral media stories about badly behaved foreign nationals and the launch of an official public campaign to tighten visa checks, Yang published a series of comments about "foreign trash" on his personal microblog, culminating in a reference to Melissa Chan's dismissal. "We kicked out that foreign bitch and closed Al-Jazeera's Beijing bureau," Yang wrote in May, according to a *Wall Street Journal* translation. After foreign guests boycotted his show, Yang grudgingly conceded that his choice of wording was "incautious." Select posts from his microblog archive— including one saying that U.S. journalists are "afraid of getting fired by their Jewish bosses"—were deleted, according to the *Shanghaiist* website, which published them in translation. Even in his belated October apology, Yang stressed that "foreign correspondents in China united" against him, which "proves the influence of our program."

Though Yang's language prompted widespread debate, the offensive post about Chan went unrebuked by propaganda officials. In fact, state media amplified it: The *Global Times* reprinted the language in a special section titled, "Foreign Devils or Angels?" This was particularly troubling since, like "Dialogue," the *Times* is geared to an English-speaking audience perfectly positioned to mediate between the Chinese state and the world. If these outlets continue to adhere to the state's disdain for their audience, they are unlikely to achieve commercial success. Blogger Charles Custer, who was based in Beijing at the time, described Yang as "one of the faces of China's soft power push" on his site, *China Geeks*. "The fact that [Dialogue's] host is apparently a racist xenophobe is probably indicative of how successful China's soft power push is likely to be," Custer wrote.

It apparently has not occurred to outgoing Chinese authorities that courting international journalists at home would be the surest way to kick-start soft power. If new leaders have a different view, it has yet to manifest. Even the announcement of the date for the Congress just before the National Day holiday seemed intended to elude, or at least annoy, the foreign press. "Announcement of . . . Nov 8 Party Congress date is Chinese equivalent of the Friday afternoon document dump, before a weeklong holiday," *The Washington Post*'s Keith Richburg complained on Twitter, one of 13 similar reactions compiled by the China-based blog, *Beijing Cream*.

Also slipped quietly into the news cycle that Friday was the announcement that Bo Xilai, the ousted Chongqing Communist Party leader, would be prosecuted for abuse of power and other crimes related to the 2011 fatal poisoning of British citizen Neil Heywood over an alleged "economic dispute" with the erstwhile anti-corruption czar's family. Bo's wife, Gu Kailai, was given a suspended death sentence for that murder in August, though at least one Chinese forensic expert has disputed the evidence used in her trial, according to *The Wall Street Journal*. The story, and the corruption allegations surrounding it, rocked the nation when they were exposed earlier in the year—thanks in good part to a push by highly motivated international correspondents. Local journalists had long been stymied in their own efforts to reveal Bo's wrongdoing. A former CPJ award winner, Jiang Weiping, served six years in jail for anti-graft reports published in Hong Kong that implicated Bo when he was governor of Liaoning Province. A Chongqing freelancer, Gao Yingpu, was handed a three-year sentence in a closed-door trial in 2010 after criticizing Bo on his personal blog. The decision to charge Bo was a victory for all those whose relentless pursuit of the story forced the party to investigate one of their own.

Yet announcing the charge in a way intended to minimize overseas news coverage implied that his prosecution would take place on the party's terms, and not to appease critics of China's entrenched political corruption. It also underscored the ambivalence leaders have toward the foreign press corps, a community they still treat as agents of hostile powers, regardless of their essential role in the country's information culture. On November 1, *China Digital Times* reported that Chinese environmental protesters in southwestern Ningbo applauded international correspondents as "family" after domestic media refused to cover their concerns, clustering around reporters to protect them from police and spontaneously hoisting a cameraman above the crowd for a better perspective. China's new leaders might take heed.

Madeline Earp is senior researcher for CPJ's Asia Program. She has studied Mandarin in China and Taiwan, and graduated with a master's in East Asian studies from Harvard. She is the author of the 2010 CPJ report, "In China, a Debate on Press Rights."

6

BEHIND BARS

Under Cover
Of Security, Governments
Jail Journalists

By Monica Campbell

Along an isolated stretch of Ethiopian desert, under a gray July sky, soldiers dragged journalist Martin Schibbye from a truck, stood him up, raised their Kalashnikovs, and fired. The shots whistled by his head. "I thought, just get it over with," Schibbye said. "I'd given up." By that time, he thought his colleague, photojournalist Johan Persson, was already dead. Soldiers had dragged Persson in a different direction and fired repeatedly. Those shots turned out to be near-misses as well, intended to intimidate and instill fear.

The two Swedish journalists were allowed to live that day, but they were not allowed their freedom. For more than 400 days, they were jailed in Addis Ababa, shuttled from solitary cells to rat-infested rooms crowded with prisoners, some with tuberculosis.

The ordeal ended as the two journalists, fearing years in prison, finally relented. Yes, we collaborated with terrorists. That is why we were jailed. Yes, they told Ethiopian state television, we respect the court. All lies, of course, Schibbye and Persson said after they were freed in September 2012 on a pardon. "It was humiliating, but we felt forced to say those things," Schibbye told CPJ. "We were still unsure they'd actually let us go."

More than a year earlier, in June 2011, the two journalists had crossed into eastern Ethiopia from Somalia and embedded with members of the separatist Ogaden National Liberation Front, or ONLF. "We'd heard about rapes, executions, and an exodus from the Ogaden region, and that a Swedish oil company had operations there," said Persson, who went to Ethiopia with Schibbye, a freelance writer, to report a story for the Swedish magazine *Filter.* "We wanted to go and see what was happening at the source." Ethiopian security forces seized the journalists during a raid on the separatist group. But unlike the cases of other foreign journalists who were expelled for covering issues Ethiopian authorities wanted to keep secret, the prime minister at the time, Meles Zenawi, called the Swedes "messenger boys of a terrorist organization" and authorized their prosecution under the country's anti-terrorism law. Ethiopian officials forced the journalists at gunpoint to participate in films re-creating their arrests—cartoonish skits with civilian actors playing ONLF members and the journalists cast as accomplices. "It was a circus," Schibbye said, "and we feared for our lives throughout."

Now, back in Stockholm, the journalists are troubled most by the six journalists still behind bars in Ethiopia, including the award-winning editor and blogger Eskinder Nega. "When we left the cell for the last time, everyone cheered," Schibbye said. "They said, 'Tell the world about us. Tell them what's happening.'"

■ ■ ■

CPJ research has tracked a significant rise in journalist imprisonments since 2000, a year before the September 11 terrorist attacks on the United States fueled the expansion of anti-terrorism and national security laws worldwide. The number of journalists jailed worldwide hit 232 in 2012, 132 of whom were held on anti-terror or other national security charges. Both are records in the 22 years CPJ has documented imprisonments. CPJ's analysis has found that governments have exploited these laws to silence critical journalists covering sensitive issues such as insurgencies, political opposition parties, and ethnic minorities.

The past decade has seen waves of mass arrests on such charges, beginning in countries like Eritrea and Cuba and followed more recently in Turkey and Vietnam. The United States helped legitimize the tactic by imprisoning at least 14 journalists in Iraq, Afghanistan, and Guantánamo Bay throughout the past decade. Although most were never formally charged, all were broadly accused by U.S. officials of having committed security or terror-related offenses. U.S. officials never substantiated any of the allegations.

Throughout the world, CPJ research has found, the vague wording of national security and terror laws has allowed the authorities wide latitude to retaliate against reporters covering sensitive issues. In China, for example, Article 103 of the penal code criminalizes "undermining the unity of the country," allowing the prosecution of journalists covering minorities like Tibetans and Uighurs who have grievances with official policies. Journalists in China can also be charged under the broad provisions of Article 105, which states: "Whoever incites others by spreading rumors or slanders or any other means to subvert the State power or overthrow the socialist system shall be sentenced to fixed-term imprisonment of not more than five years, criminal detention, public surveillance, or deprivation of political rights."

In 2009, Ethiopia passed new anti-terrorism legislation that includes ambiguous language that could permit a journalist to be jailed for anything from covering a protest to working with a foreign news service. It criminalizes coverage of any group the government deems to be terrorist, a list that includes not only the ONLF separatists but opposition political parties. Article 6 states: "Whosoever publishes or causes the publication of a statement that is likely to be understood by some or all of the members of the public to whom it is published as a direct or indirect encouragement or other inducement to them to the commission or preparation or instigation of an act of terrorism . . . is punishable with rigorous imprisonment from 10 to 20 years." The law also prohibits "the use of any telecommunications network or apparatus to disseminate any terrorizing message" or "obscene message," subjecting violations to a prison penalty of up to eight years.

In Ethiopia, at least 11 reporters have been jailed since the 2009 anti-terrorism law took effect. One of the best-known cases involves Eskinder, a journalist who lived in Washington before returning to his native Ethiopia in the 1990s to start an independent newspaper. Officials have long targeted Eskinder, shutting his newspapers and jailing him previously on anti-state charges. His wife, journalist Serkalem Fasil, gave birth to the couple's son while she was imprisoned several years ago.

The most recent case against Eskinder stemmed from a 2011 column in which he challenged the government's claim that imprisoned journalists and activists were actually terrorists. Officials said that Eskinder's commentary provided "moral support" to outlawed individuals and groups and charged him with terrorism. After his arrest, Eskinder was further charged with having links to Ginbot 7, a banned political party based in the United States, and with receiving weapons from Eritrea. Eskinder denied the charges, and prosecutors presented no evidence tying him to arms trafficking or any other terrorist activity. In July, a judge sentenced Eskinder to 18 years in prison.

"His story is a powerful symbol of the dramatic repression of freedom of speech in Ethiopia," said Jason McLure, a former Bloomberg correspondent in Ethiopia who worked with Eskinder and runs a blog called FreeEskinderNega.com. "He won't fold, and he's willing to pay a high price for that."

Although the greatest cost is borne by those in prison, the public suffers as well. In Ethiopia and other nations, CPJ research shows, national security prosecutions have forced many journalists into silence. One Ethiopian reporter, who spoke on condition of anonymity for fear of reprisal, said he was detained on anti-terrorism charges after covering protests by Muslims opposing government policies seen as curtailing religious freedom. Fearing he could be swept into a legal vortex, he abandoned reporting on Muslim activities in the country. "It is very difficult to be a journalist and exercise the profession without fear of getting charged under the new anti-terrorism law," he told CPJ.

■ ■ ■

Iranian authorities also use national security laws as a club to intimidate journalists, particularly since the disputed 2009 presidential election. CPJ surveys since that time have found 40 to 50 journalists imprisoned at any given time, many of them serving lengthy terms in inhumane conditions. The prosecutions, typically on charges such as "propagating against the regime" and "acting against national security," have chilled news coverage within Iran and driven vulnerable writers and editors into exile. At least 68 Iranian journalists have fled the country since 2007, CPJ research shows.

Crackdowns often precede elections or other events that Iranian authorities see as sensitive. In January 2012, ahead of the country's parliamentary election, police arrested at least a half dozen journalists associated with reformist papers. Illustrating the far-reaching application of national security laws to spread fear, the authorities detained the well-known writer Marzieh Rasouli, who covered arts and culture for reformist newspapers but was not known for her political coverage. She was accused of "acting against national security."

Hadi Ghaemi, director of the New York–based International Campaign for Human Rights in Iran, said the vague language of the laws allows for blanket arrests of those seen as political opponents. "And it might get worse," Ghaemi said. "As international tension over Iran's nuclear program grows, along with political infighting and next June's presidential election, the effort to control the press through anti-state laws is set to increase."

Although local reporters constitute the majority of those targeted by national security laws, the local news bureaus of foreign agencies can also be vulnerable. In Iran, the Reuters news agency saw its accreditation pulled in October on charges of "propagating against the regime" after a video report about a martial arts group in Tehran mistakenly called the participants "assassins." Reuters issued a correction and clarified that the Tehran bureau chief, Parisa Hafezi, an Iranian, had not been involved in the editing of the video script. But officials also pursued a criminal case against Hafezi and, in September, a jury found her guilty of anti-state charges. The use of anti-state charges against the local news bureau of an international outlet, Ghaemi said, reflected a disturbing shift in tactics by Iranian authorities.

China, one of the world's worst jailers of the press, has used national security laws to enforce compliance with the views officially approved by the country's propaganda department. Journalists challenging that authority are at risk. Newspaper editor Shi Tao, for example, has been jailed since 2004 for emailing to an overseas news outlet a propaganda department directive on how to cover the anniversary of the Tiananmen Square protests. The directive, an unremarkable set of instructions that called for news media to convey the official stance on Tiananmen, was retroactively classified a state secret, and Shi was convicted of disclosing information that harmed national security.

In 2008, Chinese authorities began turning to national security laws to silence journalists covering marginalized ethnic groups. In December 2012, when CPJ conducted its most recent census of imprisoned journalists, more than half of the 32 journalists imprisoned in China were Tibetan and Uighur journalists who had covered ethnic unrest, a topic the central government has worked hard to suppress. In those cases and others, the authorities typically filed charges of inciting subversion, subverting state authority, or promoting disunity; in most of the cases, published articles constituted the primary evidence. "If you're arrested and charges are filed—if it gets that far—chances are very good that you'll be convicted," said Victor Clemens, a San Francisco–based researcher at Chinese Human Rights Defenders, an online network of human rights activists. "We'll see a blogger [arrested] for writing about land issues or a religious group and slapped with charges that are barely defined and for crimes that are rarely even described beyond a few words. It's ruthless."

In Vietnam, the authorities have used anti-state charges in an ever-widening crackdown on critical coverage of land seizures and the country's relations with China. Online journalists are heavily targeted: all but one of the 14 journalists in prison in late 2012 worked on digital platforms not easily controlled by the state's extensive censorship regime. "It's more than the mere growth of online media," said Peter Noorlander, executive director of the London-based Media Defense League Initiative, which helps pay defense costs and trains lawyers in media law worldwide, including Vietnam. "What we're seeing is increasing nervousness on the part of the government about threats to its existence." In September, three bloggers who co-founded the Free Journalists Club, a website that carried stories critical of Vietnam's relations with China, were sentenced to prison terms ranging from four to 12 years on anti-state charges related to their journalism.

Four contributors to the online news outlet *Redemptorist News* have been jailed for more than a year, three of them charged under Article 79 of the penal code with engaging in activities aimed at overthrowing the government. *Redemptorist News*, which is run by the Congregation of the Most Holy Redeemer, reports on the country's persecuted Catholic minority, land disputes between the government and grass-roots communities, and other social issues. "We have our own report-ers, but we also publish information from the people if we feel we can say something on their behalf," Dinh Huu Thoai, a priest who helps edit the site, told CPJ in a 2012 interview. "We stand for the people who have no voices."

■ ■ ■

Although the government of Turkish Prime Minister Recep Tayyip Erdoğan has won accolades for building the country's economy and raising its international image, it constrains journalists from covering the Kurdish issue or addressing other sensitive political topics. In an extensive August 2012 survey, CPJ found 76 journalists jailed in Turkey, at least 61 in direct relation to their work. Nearly all of those jailed faced national security-related charges. More than three-quarters of the imprisoned journalists had yet to be convicted of a crime and were held as they awaited resolution of their cases.

Of those imprisoned in Turkey, about two-thirds were Kurdish journalists charged with aiding terrorist organizations by covering the viewpoints and activities of the banned Kurdistan Workers Party, or PKK. Nearly all of the other jailed journalists faced allegations that they took part in anti-government plots or were members of banned political movements. In a June 2012 letter to CPJ, Justice Minister Sadullah Ergin justified the criminal prosecution of journalists, saying that Turkey must balance the protection of free expression against the need to bar "the praising of violence and terrorist propaganda." But in numerous cases, CPJ's analysis found, Turkish authorities conflated the coverage of banned groups and the investigation of sensitive topics with outright terrorism or other anti-state activity.

"Journalists are not preaching terrorism. They are not telling their readers to get a bomb and kill," said Mehmet Ali Birand, a veteran broadcast journalist and columnist in Turkey. "Still, with any story we do on Kurdish or separatist groups, we face enormous government pressure to cast them as terrorists. If not, you'll have a minister or top official that night on television singling you out for not doing enough to help the country's security forces."

The cases against two prominent investigative reporters, Nedim Şener and Ahmet Şık, illustrate the overreaching nature of the Turkish prosecutions. Both spent more than 12 months in detention on charges that they aided an anti-government conspiracy by writing or contributing to books about the influence of the Islamic Fethullah Gülen movement on Turkish public affairs. The cases, still pending in late 2012, were filled with irregularities and illogic. The charges, for example, were based almost entirely on computer documents whose authenticity has been disputed. Şener said he never contributed to any book about the Gülen movement, although he has long faced government harassment for other critical reporting. Most notable is that Turkish authorities have not fully explained why writing about a group's political influence would constitute a crime against national security.

International outcry prompted the government to free Şener and Şık while their cases continued through the court system. "But being released from jail doesn't mean you are free," said Necati Abay, an Istanbul-based journalist and spokesman for Turkey's Platform for Solidarity With Arrested Journalists, a small network that tracks jailed journalists and coordinates visits and other forms of support for imprisoned journalists. "The threat is there that you could easily be sent back to jail." Abay has been arrested several times for his work, including in 2003 when he was accused of belonging to a banned Marxist group, an allegation he denies. He said his arrest was just one example of a long official clampdown on the socialist weekly, *Atılım*, where Abay has worked as an editor. The government has closed the paper at times and regularly labeled its staff as dangerous Marxists.

Press freedom advocates are intensifying their calls on governments to follow international standards in the application of national security laws, invoking Article 19 of the Universal Declaration of Human Rights, which guarantees the right to seek, receive, and impart information. When he was commissioner for human rights for the Council of Europe, Thomas Hammarberg issued two detailed reports that identified deficiencies in Turkey's criminal justice system, including its broad definition of terrorism offenses and the excessive length of its criminal proceedings. Turkey made modest reforms in 2012, reducing some penalties and altering the system that adjudicates terrorism cases. But the measure did not fundamentally change the anti-terror law to rid it of the broad, ambiguous language used to silence critical news and opinion.

Mats Johansson, a member of Sweden's parliament and the rapporteur on press freedom for the Council of Europe, found in his own 2012 report that there was deterioration in Turkish democracy that was "mirrored by a retreat of press freedom." In an interview with CPJ, Johansson said international pressure requires great persistence. Turkish politicians, after all, have used his critiques to bolster their own arguments that foreigners should not meddle in national affairs. "We cannot force Turkey to reform its laws," Johansson said. "What we can hope for, however, is incremental change as pressure builds over time. It's very patient work."

The price of not exerting pressure is enormous. In Ethiopia today, a reporter told CPJ, "journalists, editors, media owners—they all censor themselves. Any political news, if it's not liked by the government, can get a journalist charged with treason." As did many others, he spoke only on condition of anonymity. He feared a government reprisal.

Monica Campbell is a San Francisco–based journalist who reports for Public Radio International's "The World." Campbell has reported for CPJ from Mexico, Cuba, and Venezuela.

Torture and Injustice
In a Small Town

By Muzaffar Suleymanov

Ethnically motivated beatings, arsons, and killings were sweeping through southern Kyrgyzstan, and Azimjon Askarov was exhausted. It was early on June 13, 2010, and Askarov, a prominent reporter and human rights defender, had been up all night documenting the unrest that pitted ethnic Kyrgyz and Uzbeks against one another, a conflagration that ignited three days before in Osh and was now racing through his village of Bazar-Korgon.

At 5 a.m., unable to stay awake, Askarov asked a companion to drive him home. About four hours later, Askarov recounted in a recent interview for CPJ, his wife awakened him with news: A police officer had just been killed. Askarov roused himself, grabbed his camera, and headed out, going first to his office and then to the scene of the killing on the nearby Bishkek-to-Osh highway, a mountainous four-lane thoroughfare where hundreds of ethnic Uzbeks had massed in an effort to block what they perceived to be Kyrgyz efforts to move aggressors and weapons into the region.

The situation was tense as he arrived, Askarov recalls, as police were firing into the crowd and a civilian, bleeding, dropped to the ground in front of him. In all, three civilians were killed in the village that day along with the officer, the human rights group Kylym Shamy said. By the time the violence subsided in Bazar-Korgon on June 15, at least 19 were dead, more than 130 were injured, and more than 400 buildings had been torched, according to accounts from the government, news outlets, and human rights groups. Askarov was among those keeping a close tally, visiting the morgue to identify bodies, interviewing local residents and officials, keeping a diary with his extensive notes, shooting videos, and taking photographs.

But two days after the confrontation on the highway, Askarov was himself in police custody, where he would endure prolonged brutality during which officers "beat me like a soccer ball." Today, nearly three years later, Askarov, a 61-year-old Bazar-Korgon native of Uzbek descent, is serving a life prison term on charges that he was complicit in the officer's murder and had committed a series of other anti-state crimes. The conviction has been challenged by the government's own ombudsman's office, and Askarov's lawyers are pursuing a complaint with the U.N. Human Rights Committee.

■ ■ ■

The case against Askarov boils down to three broad allegations: that he incited the crowd gathered on the highway to kill Myktybek Sulaimanov, a police officer, sometime after 8 a.m. on June 13, 2010; that, a day earlier, he fired up another crowd to take a local mayor hostage, a crime that did not actually take place; and that he possessed 10 bullets, which were found in his home during a police raid marked by irregularities.

By September 2010, Askarov had been convicted on the thinnest of evidence, the testimony of self-interested police and public officials who claimed he made remarks to incite crowds to violence. Yet Askarov was not observed participating in any act of violence and, aside from the disputed bullets, was not linked to any crime by any other evidence. His trial was conducted in an atmosphere of intense intimidation of the defense—Askarov and his lawyer were assaulted during the

proceedings—and a general climate of fear among the Uzbek population, all of which served to deter would-be defense witnesses. People
who could have provided exculpatory testimony—including Askarov's
wife and neighbors, whose accounts contradicted those of police—were
ignored by authorities and too frightened to testify.

Police and prosecutors had plenty of reason to target Askarov.
During years of investigative reporting on law enforcement corruption
and human rights abuses in southern Kyrgyzstan, Askarov had ended
careers and embarrassed local officials time and again. His reporting on
the June 2010 ethnic unrest, which included photos and videos, provided yet another reason for authorities to fear him.

"Certainly Bazar-Korgon police and prosecutors benefited from
my imprisonment—they're the most criminal among Kyrgyzstan's
law enforcement agencies," Askarov said from Penal Colony 47 outside Bishkek in comments recorded for CPJ by his lawyer, Yevgeniya
Krapivina. "I always obstructed their corrupt work. . . . They hated me."

Askarov was an artist by training, specializing in landscape paint-
ing, but he was far better known for his work in human rights and
investigative journalism. He founded the human rights group, Vozdukh
(Air), and in articles published in his group's bulletin, *Pravo Dlya Vsekh*
(Justice for All), and on the regional news websites *Golos Svobody*
(Voice of Freedom) and *Ferghana News*, he exposed abuses and got
results.

In 2003, Askarov's reporting led to the release of a local woman
who was repeatedly raped by police and male detainees during her
seven-month-long pretrial detention. More muckraking reports followed. In 2004, for example, Askarov investigated the case of a local
man who died after being beaten in police custody, local journalists
reported. Most notably, in 2007, he derailed the prosecution of a local
couple charged in the murder of a woman named Mairam Zairova.
Askarov tracked down Zairova in Uzbekistan, where she was very
much alive, and produced her in court. With the corpse misidentified,
the prosecution's theory collapsed and the couple was cleared. The
regional prosecutor was sacked because of the botched case, another
in a series of disciplinary actions and dismissals of police officials and
prosecutors stemming directly from Askarov's investigative reporting,
Daniil Kislov, editor of *Ferghana News*, told CPJ.

"I believe it was his work on Zairova's case that prompted the police to seek revenge," said Nurbek Toktakunov, another of Askarov's lawyers. And spring–summer 2010 was, according to two independent investigations, a time when law enforcement standards had broken down in southern Kyrgyzstan. The investigations, conducted by the New York–based Human Rights Watch and a commission sanctioned by the United Nations and the Organization for Security and Co-operation in Europe, each found a pattern of prejudicial law enforcement in the aftermath of the unrest, with ethnic Uzbeks disproportionately targeted for arrest and imprisonment.

■ ■ ■

Throughout southern Kyrgyzstan, the June 2010 ethnic unrest claimed the lives of at least 470 people and displaced thousands of others. Although a June 10 ethnic brawl in an Osh casino marked the beginning of the violence, tensions had been high since the April 2010 ouster of President Kurmanbek Bakiyev. Jockeying for power in the ensuing vacuum, Kyrgyz politicians had courted the support of ethnic Uzbeks, a traditionally apolitical but economically thriving bloc concentrated in the south. Ethnic Kyrgyz, who hold most governmental and law enforcement positions in the south, as they do elsewhere in the country, grew fearful at what they perceived to be the Uzbeks' newly elevated political position. In particular, Kyrgyz residents perceived Uzbek-organized rallies against Bakiyev as calls for southern autonomy.

Ethnic Uzbeks bore a heavier toll during the June violence, both as victims of violence and detainees held on allegations of committing the violence, Human Rights Watch reported. "Ethnic Uzbeks constituted the large majority of victims of the June violence, sustaining most of the casualties and destroyed homes, but most detainees and defendants—almost 85 percent—were also ethnic Uzbek," Human Rights Watch found. "Of 124 people detained on murder charges, 115 were Uzbek. Taken together with statements from victims describing law enforcement personnel's use of ethnic slurs and focus on the ethnicity of alleged perpetrators and victims during detention, these statistics raise serious questions about ethnic bias in the investigation and prosecution of crimes during the June violence."

No other crime committed in Bazar-Korgon during the June 10–15 unrest was successfully prosecuted, according to accounts from Toktakunov and local human rights defenders.

CPJ's research has found that the once-vibrant Uzbek-language media in southern Kyrgyzstan was virtually erased in the aftermath of the violence. The morning after clashes erupted in Osh, the regional government ordered Osh TV and Mezon TV, independent stations with Uzbek owners, to cease their broadcasts. Authorities alleged the stations had incited violence; CPJ's review found they had covered rallies by ethnic Uzbeks but had not orchestrated calls for violence. Both stations suffered heavy damage from unidentified vandals, and Mezon TV never returned to the air. While Osh TV did resume broadcasting, it was ultimately transferred to ethnic Kyrgyz ownership after it faced a series of official raids, seizures, and detentions.

Despite its declared commitment to press freedom and the rule of law, the national government has effectively turned its back on repression in the south and the reported abuses in the Askarov prosecution. Former President Roza Otunbayeva, who said publicly in May 2011 that Kyrgyzstan had no persecuted reporters, did not respond during her tenure to CPJ letters seeking intervention. Her successor, Almazbek Atambayev, has not responded to renewed calls for Askarov's release. Kyrgyzstan's Prosecutor General Aida Salyanova, the country's top law enforcement official, did not respond to written questions submitted by CPJ about the case, among them whether her office has examined reports of police brutality against Askarov.

■ ■ ■

Askarov would be arrested on June 15, 2010. He had spent the two days since the highway confrontation visiting the local hospital, scouring the streets of Bazar-Korgon, interviewing the wounded, and sharing information with Moscow- and Bishkek-based journalists and human rights defenders, including those with the OSCE's Kyrgyzstan office. Askarov said his dispatches included details on the movement of arms in the region, and police abuses that included at least two shootings that he had witnessed. His work was commonly known. Askarov recalls a local judge, Daniyar Bagishev, encountering him on the street on June 15 and warning him to stop gathering information on the crisis. "You are venal and sell these materials for U.S. dollars. But this information is a state secret and nobody should learn about it," Askarov remembers the judge saying. Contacted by CPJ, Bagishev declined to comment.

A half-hour later, a police cruiser arrived at Askarov's house: "You need to come with us," he was told.

Before leaving with police, Askarov said, he managed to slip his digital camera, with its stored images, into a folder he gave to an acquaintance. Fearing what might happen to Askarov, local human rights defenders then scrambled to hide his other reporting files and move the journalist's wife and other family members to safety. His family ultimately left the region.

Once at the local precinct—the same station where Sulaimanov, the slain police officer, had worked—officials asked for Askarov's help in building criminal cases against leaders of the Uzbek community. "Tell us who of them had guns," officers demanded, and he refused. They asked him for his camera and reporting materials, and he lied about their location. Officials soon took Askarov into custody. "Blame yourself," Askarov recalls being told. Thus began an ordeal in which police officers repeatedly beat Askarov and told him they would rape his wife and daughter if he refused to hand over his reporting materials. His brother, who came looking for him, was himself beaten badly, Askarov said.

For Askarov, the beatings would continue for the next three days, during which he was denied access to a lawyer. The journalist told CPJ that officers beat him with a gun, baton, and a water-filled plastic bottle. Once, he recalled, he was beaten so badly that he fell unconscious. "After I stood up, they made me sing the Kyrgyz anthem even though I was barely alive. Next, they took me to an investigator's room, where a police agent named Nurbek hit me with his gun handle in the head. My head was bleeding like a slaughtered chicken," Askarov told CPJ.

After Toktakunov, the defense lawyer, was finally allowed to see his client, he took a statement in which Askarov said he had been beaten by police and needed medical treatment. But the journalist was soon coerced into recanting. "Police threatened to strangle me with a pillow at night if I did not withdraw my request for a medical exam," Askarov told CPJ. "I had no other choice." Questioned about the abuse by a CPJ representative at a May 2011 meeting in New York, Kyrgyzstan diplomatic officials and presidential aides asserted that Askavov had been beaten by a cellmate. Police would hold Askarov in the local precinct, among Sulaimanov's inflamed colleagues, for more than a month, contrary to a law that requires detainees to be moved to a Ministry of Justice facility within 10 days.

According to Human Rights Watch and Askarov's own account, the beatings continued even as trial proceedings began in September 2010. In one instance, Askarov told CPJ, "three policemen beat me like a soccer ball outside the courtroom, saying that I was too intelligent and was not letting them prosecute me." Toktakunov was himself assaulted—in the presence of court officials—by relatives of the slain police officer. Human Rights Watch said the judge called for order in the courtroom but "did not warn or discipline any of the abusive spectators."

Askarov has suffered "severe and lasting" effects from the brutality, according to Sondra S. Crosby, a physician whose clinical practice at Boston University School of Medicine focuses on torture. Crosby, hired by the Open Society Justice Initiative, which helped prepare Askarov's U.N. complaint, examined Askarov in jail in December 2011, more than a year after most of the abuse occurred. She found that he "appears to have suffered severe and lasting physical injuries as a result of his arrest and incarceration. His description of acute symptoms, as well as chronic physical and psychological symptoms, his physical examination, and his psychological evaluation, are all highly consistent with his allegations of trauma."

■ ■ ■

The trial would bring no relief for Askarov. As proceedings were getting under way, a regional prosecutor told the journalist he should forget about the due process he often cited in his news reports, Askarov told CPJ. "We will prosecute you according to other laws," the prosecutor said.

Askarov was tried in Bazar-Korgon District Court alongside seven co-defendants. All faced charges of inciting disorder; four were directly charged with Sulaimanov's murder. All would be found guilty, including Askarov, who was convicted of complicity to murder, attempted hostage-taking, incitement to ethnic hatred, participation in mass disorder, and possession of ammunition. Although some co-defendants had made self-incriminating statements, none implicated Askarov in any wrongdoing.

The murder-complicity case against Askarov was based on testimony from Sulaimanov's fellow officers who were dispatched to clear the highway of protesters at about 8 a.m. on June 13, 2010. Confronted by an angry crowd that was several hundred strong, the officers quickly retreated but Sulaimanov was not among them. Assailants stabbed him several times and burned his body with a Molotov cocktail, the verdict said. No police officer testified as having witnessed the killing, which was believed to have occurred at about 8:30 a.m.

But seven officers, including the Bazar-Korgon police chief, told the court they saw Askarov in the crowd beforehand calling on the protesters to "kidnap the police chief and kill the others." Six other police officers testified against the co-defendants, but they either did not place Askarov at the scene or told the court that another man had made calls to violence, the verdict said.

By his own account, Askarov said he showed up at the highway well after the crime was committed. An investigation commissioned by the government's ombudsman's office, which oversees human rights issues, concluded that Askarov was not at the scene prior to the murder and played no role in the officer's killing. The ombudsman's office said it reached its conclusion after interviewing witnesses and local officials, and reviewing investigative reports.

The attempted hostage case was built on the accusation of the local mayor, who said the alleged crime took place on June 12, 2010, near the Uzbekistan border, as the official was trying to stop ethnic Uzbek residents of Bazar-Korgon from seeking refuge in the neighboring country. Mayor Kubatbek Artykov alleged that Askarov called on "unidentified" people in the crowd to take him hostage, an account that only two mayoral aides could corroborate. No actual hostage-taking attempt took place, according to the verdict. Askarov confirmed that he talked to the mayor that day, but only to ask if the official could guarantee the safety of the Uzbek villagers. He said the mayor refused.

The defense also disputes the reported search of Askarov's home, during which investigators claimed to have found 10 bullets for a

Makarov pistol. Investigators failed to produce in court any witnesses to the seizure, a step required under Kyrgyz law, and they failed to seal the bullets as evidence, which is also required. No pistol was found. "They made up that police report to lock him up longer," Toktakunov told CPJ.

■ ■ ■

The defense has argued that investigators failed to take statements from any witness who would have spoken on Askarov's behalf, including neighbors who witnessed him at home during the time the police officer was killed, and a mullah who witnessed the journalist's encounter with the mayor. The overall climate of fear and intimidation, coupled with authorities' inaction in response to attacks against the defendants and their lawyers, made it impossible for defense witnesses to testify on their own initiative, Toktakunov told CPJ. "Authorities refused to guarantee any protection for the witnesses, and I could not risk bringing anyone to court," he said. One potential character witness considered testifying despite the risk, he said, but dropped out after receiving threats against her family.

In an appeal to the Kyrgyzstan Supreme Court, Toktakunov cited a "lack of impartiality" at trial. He noted that his request for a change in venue for the trial was rebuffed despite the widespread ethnic hostilities in southern Kyrgyzstan at the time. Judge Nurgazy Alimkulov failed to inquire about the evident bruising on Askarov's face, and did not discipline those in the courtroom who attacked and threatened the defendants, Toktakunov noted. The atmosphere prevented Askarov from getting a fair trial, he wrote. "In conditions of fierce moral and psychological pressure, defense lawyers in the case had to fulfill their duties with great caution, at times declining to use certain resources. For example, all of the defendants' lawyers decided not to bring defense witnesses to court because the court authorities could not guarantee their safety."

Kyrgyzstan's Supreme Court rejected Askarov's appeal following a hearing that the defendant was not allowed to attend.

Domestic appeals exhausted, defense lawyers are pursuing a complaint with the U.N. Human Rights Committee, arguing that

Kyrgyzstan violated Askarov's rights under the International Covenant on Civil and Political Rights—in particular, his right to liberty and security, his right to a fair trial, and his right not to be subjected to torture. Among the complaint's central points: Police tortured Askarov in custody; authorities failed to investigate the abuse or grant Askarov independent medical treatment; authorities denied Askarov access to an attorney and failed to provide him sufficient time to prepare a defense. The complaint asks the U.N. body to recognize the injustices Askarov suffered, call for his immediate release, and seek an investigation into the abuse that would lead to the punishment of those responsible. In addition, the lawyers are asking the Human Rights Committee to demand that Kyrgyzstan introduce systemic safeguards to prevent similar violations from happening in the future.

Askarov and his lawyers also hope that Kyrgyz authorities will, on their own, revisit the case based on statements from numerous witnesses who have agreed to testify if their safety can be ensured. In statements collected by defense lawyers and made available to CPJ, at least five people said they saw the journalist at home at the time of the police officer's killing. Askarov's lawyers are collecting statements from witnesses who dispute the other allegations.

"He is imprisoned," one neighbor's statement said, "for nothing."

Muzaffar Suleymanov is the research associate for CPJ's Europe and Central Asia program. He was a contributor to CPJ's 2009 report, "Anatomy of Injustice," an examination of unsolved journalist murders in Russia.

In Eskinder's Story,
A Nation's Disappointment

By Charlayne Hunter-Gault

The police bundled Eskinder Nega into a car moments after he stepped out of an Internet café in Addis Ababa. Being questioned was nothing new for the veteran journalist, long a critic of Prime Minister Meles Zenawi's government. But this time Eskinder was driven straight to the office of the deputy national police commissioner.

"Do you know why you're wanted here?" the deputy commissioner, Girma Kassa, demanded, according to an account Eskinder wrote shortly after the February 2011 episode. There was little doubt as to the reason. Eskinder's articles, including one about the uprisings sweeping the Arab world, were spread across the official's desk. As recounted by Eskinder, the official had a warning: "Let me tell you what will happen if the Arab Spring comes to Ethiopia as you dream of. We won't kill citizens. First, we will come to you and your likes. Are you listening? We are tired of arresting you. We will take serious measures. Are you listening? We are tired of you! We have already decided!"

Within months, security forces had jailed Eskinder on vague accusations of involvement in a terrorist plot. Ethiopia, despite its reputation in many Western capitals as a model for economic development, is one of Africa's most repressive countries. Dozens of journalists have been imprisoned for their work or have fled the country in fear of reprisal, CPJ research shows. And anyone who thought Meles' death in August 2012 might lead to an easing of media restrictions has so far been disappointed.

■ ■ ■

When I visited Ethiopia in June 2012 with colleagues from the Committee to Protect Journalists and the African Media Initiative, the atmosphere was tense. Independent journalists asked to meet with us discreetly, at a low-profile hotel, in hopes of eluding government surveillance. Speaking quietly but urgently, they told us that the anti-terrorism law enacted in 2009, the one used to charge Eskinder, was "a game-changer."

Constitutional protections for freedom of speech, previously under threat, were effectively dead, they said. The vague terror legislation makes it a crime to cover groups the government considers to be terrorists, a category that includes opposition parties. Most journalists were treading softly, but Eskinder, a 44-year-old blogger and former newspaper editor, had been among the very few defiantly plugging away.

At the time of our visit, three Ethiopian journalists and two Swedish reporters had already been convicted under the terrorism law and sentenced to lengthy prison terms, while Eskinder and five exiled journalists who had been tried in absentia awaited sentencing. The evidence in the cases did not match the severity of the charges: The prosecution cited the journalists' communications with critical Ethiopian diaspora news sites, for example, or their articles covering the activities of the banned U.S.-based opposition group Ginbot 7. During Eskinder's trial, prosecutors showed a grainy video of a town hall–style meeting during which he discussed whether an Arab Spring would ever come to Ethiopia. No evidence tied him to any actual terrorism activity.

We arrived in Ethiopia determined to gather information, meet with government officials, and advocate on behalf of the detained journalists. Eskinder would soon be sentenced to 18 years in prison, although our visit and other international advocacy efforts may have spared him the life term that a terrorism conviction could have brought.

Our visit had sad echoes from the past. I had made a similar trip with a CPJ delegation in 2006, when 15 journalists were in jail for their work. Back then, we secured a meeting with Meles, who allowed us to visit the detainees and bring them reading material. We had been mildly encouraged by the meeting, even getting the prime minister to acknowledge that his inaccessibility to independent media might have led to the news coverage he saw as negative.

Eskinder was in prison that time as well, one of nine detentions in all that he has endured during his career. We met him at Kality Prison, along with several other detainees, including his wife, Serkalem Fasil, a journalist and publisher who was a few months pregnant. She seemed very fragile at the time, although she is anything but. Serkalem, denied proper prenatal care and nutritious food, gave birth in prison to a son, Nafkot, who has had to overcome a lot.

Each of the detained journalists spoke with us that day. Eskinder, who had been educated in the United States, was the most fluent in English and made a strong case on behalf of them all. The journalists faced anti-state charges based on editorials in their newspapers criticizing the government's brutal crackdown on peaceful protests after a disputed general election in mid-2005. Many obtained pardons but only if they pleaded guilty and waived their defense. Eskinder and Serkalem took their cases to trial and won acquittals, but the government still banned their newspapers and slapped Serkalem's publishing house with a heavy fine.

From that time until his 2011 imprisonment, Eskinder had been turning out thoughtful, analytical columns on a range of topics, including the U.S. diplomatic cables on Ethiopia released by WikiLeaks, the role of ethnicity in local politics, public corruption, and the rule of law. Most of the pieces were published on U.S.-based, exile-run news sites. In a January 2011 column, Eskinder expressed admiration for the American Civil Liberties Union's principled "defense of the First Amendment rights of white supremacists KKK and neo-Nazis," to explain his support for the rights of former regime officials facing trial. With the outbreak of the Arab Spring, Eskinder also wrote about the domestic implications of the uprisings.

The protests in the Middle East and North Africa clearly unnerved the Meles regime, which had itself taken power after a rebellion. The government was using the terror law and other anti-state statutes in a renewed effort to silence dissent. Eskinder wrote about the improbability of the case against one newly charged terror suspect—Debebe Eshetu, a prominent 72-year-old actor—and criticized the government's misuse of the law. Five days later, on September 9, 2011, Eskinder was jailed.

■ ■ ■

Prospects for Ethiopian freedom seemed so different back in 1991. After a 17-year rebellion, Meles and his Ethiopian People's Revolutionary Democratic Front (EPRDF) had forced dictator Mengistu Haile Mariam into exile. "Now is the beginning of a new chapter. It is an era of unfettered freedom," Meles promised Ethiopians in one of his first speeches as victorious rebel leader.

The new constitution guaranteed freedom of the press for the first time in Ethiopia's long history. But when the first independent newspapers, including Eskinder's weekly, *Ethiopis*, began criticizing the country's new rulers, the EPRDF was quick to confiscate the freedoms it had proclaimed. In a 1995 report, CPJ noted that the EPRDF had "substantially increased press freedom and improved the human rights situation shortly after coming to power" but later "detained, imprisoned, and fined dozens of journalists" to silence critical reporting.

Today, the EPRDF remains the dominant political party in Ethiopia, solidifying its power by using the law to gag critics, eviscerate independent rights groups, and restrict the free use of telecommunications. In 2010, the EPRDF and affiliated parties faced virtually no opposition as they swept 545 of 547 seats in elections criticized by the U.S. State Department. Government pressure forced at least 72 independent newspapers to shut down during Meles' 21 years in power, CPJ research shows.

We were unable to meet with Meles during our visit in June 2012. As it turned out, the prime minister was suffering from cancer and was in the last weeks of his life. Yet even that sort of basic information was withheld from the public by a government that kept asserting that Meles was fine up until the day he died. (I learned of Meles' illness from an Ethiopian cab driver in Washington before it was publicly reported.) While in Addis Ababa, we had a cordial meeting with Communications Minister Bereket Simon, but he insisted that the journalists in prison were there for reasons other than their work and that the government was simply enforcing the law.

The work of journalists like Eskinder is especially vital in a country where citizens have little to no ability to hold rulers to account over public spending, or aid from Western governments. "How poor or rich [former first lady] Azeb and Meles exactly are may never be satisfactorily answered," Eskinder wrote in an April 2011 column discussing Azeb Mesfin's denial of Spanish media reports of a shopping spree in Spain. "What could rather be satisfactorily explained is why people, including passionate EPRDF supporters, are more inclined to believe than disbelieve the stories about hidden riches. In the absence of the checks and balances of a democracy, a despot is at liberty to take at will."

The United States has been among Western governments providing humanitarian assistance to the country, as well as funds to help the government maintain its position as a bulwark against Al-Qaeda–affiliated terrorists in a highly unstable region. Yet the U.S. State Department's human rights report for 2011 also notes the arrests of "more than 100 persons between March and September, including opposition political figures, activists, journalists and bloggers." It said "the government charged several of those arrested with terrorist or seditious activity but observers found the evidence presented at trials to be either open to interpretation or indicative of acts of a political nature rather than linked to terrorism."

For now, there's little evidence the Ethiopian government is listening to anybody but itself. That's a pity for a country that has such a rich history as the oldest independent nation in Africa and as home to the first human ancestors. Ethiopia could be a positive role model for other countries on the continent, as they, too, struggle with fulfilling the promise of democracy and freedom of speech.

The Ethiopian government has only to remember its own promises. Despite all odds, Eskinder is optimistic. "Inevitably," he said during an April 2012 court hearing, "freedom will overwhelm Ethiopia."

Charlayne Hunter-Gault, a CPJ board member, is an author and a former correspondent for National Public Radio and the Public Broadcasting Service. She covered Africa for many years. CPJ's Mohamed Keita contributed to this piece.

7

RISK AND REWARD

The Spy in Your Pocket: Mobile Journalism's Risk

By Danny O'Brien

I n the days after Marie Colvin and Rémi Ochlik died in the Syrian city of Homs in 2012, fellow conflict reporters speculated on the role that satellite phones might have played. Colvin and Ochlik were working from a makeshift media center that was precisely targeted by rockets. Had the killers hunted them down using signals from the very phones with which the journalists reported their stories?

The risks of working in a war zone were familiar, but the apparent dangers of using a telecommunications device common among foreign correspondents represented a new uncertainty. Experienced journalists struggled to understand what the technology could reveal about their locations, and to grasp the possibility—raised by *Libération* journalist Jean-Pierre Perrin, who had been with Colvin in Homs—that Colvin and Ochlik were singled out by the Syrian army precisely for their ability to transmit news from a city deliberately denied communication links. Journalists' phones were being used to broadcast the atrocities taking place in the city, and for that reason, the authorities might have sought to trace and eliminate those transmissions at the source.

Although not every journalist is an international war correspondent, every journalist's cellphone is untrustworthy. Mobile phones, and in particular Internet-enabled smartphones, are used by reporters around the world to gather and transmit news. But mobile phones also make journalists easier to locate and intimidate, and confidential sources easier to uncover. Cellular systems can pinpoint individual users within a few meters, and cellphone providers record months, even years, of individual movements and calls. Western cellphone companies like TeliaSonera and France Telecom have been accused by investigative journalists in their home countries of complicity in tracking reporters, while mobile spying tools built for law enforcement in Western countries have, according to computer security researchers working with human rights activists, been exported for use against journalists working under repressive regimes in Ethiopia, Bahrain, and elsewhere.

"Reporters need to understand that mobile communications are inherently insecure and expose you to risks that are not easy to detect or overcome," says Katrin Verclas of the National Democratic Institute. Activists such as Verclas have been working on sites like SaferMobile .org, which give basic advice for journalists to protect themselves. CPJ recently published a security guide that addresses the use of satellite phones and digital mobile technologies. But repressive governments don't need to keep up with all the tricks of mobile computing; they can merely set aside budget and strip away privacy laws to get all the power they need. Unless regulators, technology companies, and media personnel step up their own defenses of press freedom, the cellphone will become journalists' most treacherous tool.

■ ■ ■

To examine the center of the mobile phone revolution, one must go not to the labs of Silicon Valley or the iPhone factories of China, but to the Kenyan capital, Nairobi. Kenya's economic and political stability has grown hand in hand with its cellphone infrastructure. The World Bank reported in 2011 that the country's information and communications sector was contributing nearly a full percentage point to economic growth, driven by cellphone ownership that went from a fraction of one percent of the population in 1999 to more than 64 percent in 2011. The number using cellphones quickly leapfrogged those using traditional wired telephone and Internet connections, and the country is now held as a model and testing ground for the future of mobile worldwide. Kenya is the home of M-PESA, the first ubiquitous mobile-based payment and banking system, which lets Kenyan citizens use their cellphones to carry the equivalent of a cash balance and make safe, instant purchases of a wide spectrum of items such as electricity and roadside goods. It's also home to Ushahidi, a disaster mapping system first created to let mobile users record instances of election violence in 2007.

Nairobi, with a population of almost 3.4 million, is also home to East Africa's large community of exiled journalists. Having fled oppression in Rwanda, Eritrea, Somalia, or Ethiopia, these reporters depend on Nairobi's cheap mobile phones to stay in contact with family and friends in the diaspora and at home. The phones also deliver death threats. As I sat in a Nairobi restaurant discussing digital security with an exiled Ethiopian journalist—one of more than 50 exiled for their work in the past decade—he told me how he receives texts telling him that the sender knows where he is and is going to catch him. If they can find my phone number, he asked, can they find *me*?

The answer for reporters in dangerous situations is not reassuring. Every mobile phone is a tracking device, as Peter Maass and Megha Rajagopalan, reporters on digital privacy at *ProPublica*, have noted. Phones report their approximate location to the local cellphone company as part of the process of establishing which cell tower to use. The precision of the location mapping depends on how closely those cell towers are placed; in a crowded city like Nairobi, that can resolve to just a few feet. Many exiled journalists in this city scrape a living in the slums of Kibera and Mathare. Although these shanty towns have little in the way of sewers, street lighting, or domestic electricity, cellphone towers rise above the shacks.

Location data is retained by cellphone providers; just because someone has your phone number does not mean that person can also obtain your location. But as in most countries, cellphone companies in Kenya have an intimate relationship with the government. They depend on nationally negotiated contracts for radio spectrum, and are frequently the descendants of state-owned monopolies. (The Kenyan government held a majority stake in Safaricom, the country's largest phone provider, until its initial public offering in 2008; now the government stake is 35 percent.)

Governments in other countries, especially those unfriendly to Kenya, are unlikely to get their hands on that tracking data. But within a country, be it Kenya or the United States, use of such data is remarkably unregulated. A person in Nairobi's police force, who spoke on condition of anonymity, told CPJ that cellphone data is regularly used to detect and catch street criminals. U.S. Rep. Edward Markey released data in July 2012 showing that domestic cellphone carriers in the U.S. responded to more than 1.3 million requests for subscriber information from law enforcement in 2011, many without subpoenas or warrants.

In Ethiopia, the entire telecommunications network, including mobile and Internet, is controlled directly by the government through the monopoly Ethio Telecom. Ethio Telecom is managed by France Telecom, but is required to comply with Ethiopian government orders, including the blocking of dozens of news sites (including CPJ's website). In May 2012, the country's mobile broadband system introduced deep packet inspection to identify and block users of the anti-censorship tool Tor. Ethio Telecom's chief executive at the time, Jean-Michel Latute, told *La Croix* that the decision had been made by the communications ministry, but the deep packet inspection was nonetheless "a very useful tool" for the company.

France Telecom is not the only Western mobile phone company implicated in censorship and control of journalists. In April 2012, the Swedish investigative TV program "Uppdrag Granskning" detailed how the calls, texts, and location information of Agil Khalil, a reporter for the Azerbaijani newspaper *Azadlyg*, were handed over by Azercell, a subsidiary of the Swedish company TeliaSonera, to local security services in 2008. Khalil was assaulted several times during the period of surveillance. In response to the documentary, TeliaSonera said it would overhaul its compliance process, "start a dialogue" with the authorities in Azerbaijan, and provide employees with human rights training.

The Finnish company Nokia Siemens Networks faced a lawsuit in 2010 by the family of Iranian journalist Issa Saharkhiz, alleging the company supplied equipment used to locate the journalist via his mobile phone after he went into hiding. While on the run, Saharkhiz told *Der Spiegel*, "I turn on my mobile phone only one hour each day, because they can trace me and arrest me." Just hours after that conversation, Saharkhiz was captured, his ribs and wrists were broken, and he was taken to Evin Prison, where he remained in late 2012. In public statements, Nokia said, "This capability [to locate and monitor cellphones] became a standard feature at the insistence of the United States and European nations . . . . It is unrealistic to demand, as the Saharkhiz lawsuit does, that wireless communications systems based on global technology standards be sold without that capability." The lawsuit was voluntarily withdrawn by the family after a U.S. court held that a corporation cannot be subject to liability under the Alien Tort Act, on which the case depended. Nonetheless, Nokia Siemens Networks has divested itself of its monitoring center business, and says that "with the exception of some technical contractual links," it no longer has "any involvement with it."

■ ■ ■

Though mobile phones have the built-in capacity to track a journalist's whereabouts, they can be even more lethal in undermining the privacy of reporters and their sources when coupled with malicious software.

In the first few months of 2012, Bahraini activists reported receiving unsolicited email attachments, purportedly from the Al-Jazeera reporter Melissa Chan. The fake messages contained malware aimed at taking over the activists' desktop computers, and reporting back to a central command server in Bahrain. This sort of attack on journalists is increasingly common; Chan herself was a regular target of such malware when reporting in China. Computer security researchers Bill Marczak and Morgan Marquis-Boire discovered that this spyware was a product of a program called FinFisher—commercially produced software, made by the U.K.-based company Gamma Group, supposedly for law enforcement and government agencies. This was notable because spyware targeted at journalists and their sources is usually crafted from software built by criminal fraudsters, rather than code custom-built for government.

Subsequent samples obtained by the same researchers showed variants of FinFisher, such as FinSpy, were aimed not at desktop computers, but at iPhone, Android, BlackBerry, and Nokia mobile phones. The malware was variously capable of retransmitting text messages, recording phone calls, extracting details from address books, GPS tracking, and even silently calling a mobile phone and having it pick up and transmit conversations in its vicinity. Marczak and Marquis-Boire also discovered servers designed to receive reports from FinFisher products not only in Bahrain, but in Brunei, Ethiopia, Turkmenistan, and the United Arab Emirates. Gamma denied selling to these states, and suggested the software might be pirated copies.

If governments have access to their own telecommunications infrastructure, why would they stoop to putting spyware on reporters' phones? One possibility, Marczak suggests, is to beat what protections activists and sources might already be using. "When a journalist sends emails, messages, etc., from his phone, they are encrypted over the network between his phone and the servers. If you as a government want to read these communications, you have to access them somewhere they are not encrypted. So the practical options are get a warrant or subpoena for the email provider (e.g., Gmail, Yahoo! Mail), or read them . . . on the journalist's phone. FinSpy allows you to do the latter." Other advantages include being able to spy on communications taking place outside the country. Exiled journalists or dissidents, for instance, could be tracked as easily as local reporters.

Journalists facing digital threats online have become accustomed to defending themselves with anti-virus tools and encrypting their hard drives and other communications. But mobile smartphones are not designed to permit the same degree of configurability—compared with a PC or Mac, their design is sealed against tinkering by the user, and open to control by the manufacturer and network provider. The creators of the technology argue, with some justification, that this locking down increases security for the average cellphone user. But for a reporter with security risks, such lack of control can make matters much worse. Governments can install malware like FinSpy, while the users cannot detect or remove it.

Even protective measures taken by companies can be abused by hackers. Mat Honan, a journalist with *Wired* magazine, was targeted in August 2012 by a hacker who obtained access to his online accounts, including his Apple iCloud login. The online logins permitted the hacker to take over a news site's Twitter feed; the Apple account allowed the hacker to power down his iPhone and remotely wipe it.

The reason Honan's phone was vulnerable was Apple's intimate connection with every iPhone—a capability that allows the company to find lost phones, shut down stolen devices, and update the iPhone's operating system. Phone service providers wield similar power, generally for good, but with no veto power by the end-user. Honan told CPJ last fall: "I'm completely freaked out by mobile security now in all sorts of ways that I wasn't two months ago. As reporters, our data is our most valuable asset. And while I can encrypt folders on my computer and transfer them to USB sticks, which I can then keep locked up in a safe, I can't begin to secure my phone in a similar fashion."

Companies and governments may claim that cooperation to exchange intimate information on mobile subscribers is necessary for law enforcement. But the confidential and sensitive public service performed by reporters has, until now, been protected by the processes of court order and warrants, at least in countries operating under rule of law.

Unfortunately, the laws controlling the release of phone company data have yet to be updated to take into account the far wider repositories of information now collected on users. The law that governs the handing over of this data to third parties in the United States is the Electronic Communications Privacy Act. It was written in 1996, a time when phone companies could offer either records of who called whom or audio wiretaps.

"It simply wasn't written for the mobile age," says Kevin Bankston, senior counsel at the Center for Democracy & Technology, a Washington-based Internet advocacy group. He says the authorities take advantage of the law's ambiguity to push for easier access to data. The standards for protection in the law are in great dispute, Bankston said, "and law enforcement consistently argues that the lowest standards be used." That means that location data can be obtained without a warrant in the United States because law enforcement claims it should be treated the same as billing data. Mobile phone providers in the U.S. are frequently asked to give cell tower "dumps"—mass data on subscribers who were near a certain tower during a certain period of time. That would scoop up reporters' contacts at a riot or disaster as effectively as it would scoop up data on the suspect in a crime, but the security services claim that such data is not protected by statute, and telecom companies do not, on the whole, contest such requests. Other countries largely follow the U.S. lead on such criteria.

■ ■ ■

Mobile experts say cellphones do not have to be built to act as pervasive spying devices, even when used under repressive regimes. Eric King is head of research at Privacy International, a U.K.-based advocacy organization. His group successfully lobbied the U.K. government to limit the export of FinFisher's tools to Middle Eastern countries where they might be used against journalists and dissidents. He says that the same Western technical standards—such as those developed by the European Telecommunications Standards Institute (ETSI)—that already include surveillance features could also include safeguards and limits against misuse of those features.

"Why can't ETSI standards put in explicit limits on the number of simultaneous interceptions? Vendors would only be ETSI compliant if [their networking equipment] cannot intercept more than a certain percentage of calls," King suggested. Another possibility would be for devices to create tamper-proof records whenever the surveillance features of a cellphone network are used. That would make faking telephone-related evidence against journalists harder, and leave permanent evidence of such surveillance (and who conducted it) available for future investigation by journalists or an independent judiciary.

End-user software could help, too. Mozilla, the nonprofit creator of the Firefox browser, says it is building a privacy-protective mobile phone to compete with existing Android and Apple operating systems. Phil Zimmermann, the author of the definitive encryption program for desktop computers, Pretty Good Privacy, has recently launched a new service that, he says, protects mobile phone calls from interception. Other tools, like TextSecure from Whisper Systems, offer the same protections for text messaging, provided both sides of the conversation use the same tool.

For now, while journalists can take some steps to protect themselves and their sources, they are limited by the nature of their cellphones. At a panel in May, investigative journalist Matthew Cole, who works on U.S. national security and intelligence issues, demonstrated how he conducts his work using an elaborate protocol taught to him by digital security expert Chris Soghoian. Cole uses two cellphones; they are bought anonymously; they are never used together; and one always has its battery removed, to prevent it from accidentally being activated and to ensure the two numbers are never linked.

When I mentioned this protocol to another journalist covering similar topics, Amber Lyon, she showed me her new iPhone and pointed out the flaw: Its battery couldn't be removed. We need to make sure that in the future, when all journalism will be mobile journalism, that we can find an off switch for the worst flaws of mobile security.

Danny O'Brien, CPJ's San Francisco-based Internet advocacy coordinator, has worked globally as a journalist and activist covering technology and digital rights.

Lessons From El Salvador: Security Begins With Solidarity

By Frank Smyth

N early 25 years ago, as the Berlin Wall was coming down in Europe, El Salvador's leftist guerrillas launched the largest military offensive of the nation's long civil war. The rebels took over parts of the capital and other cities from a foundering U.S.-backed Salvadoran military. After four days, the military high command decided to fight back in the way it knew best—by murdering the unarmed critics whom it had accused of being rebel sympathizers.

The slaughter started with the Jesuit priests who ran the nation's largest private university, Universidad Centroamericana, and who published and edited a weekly newsletter and monthly journal closely read by international policy makers. The priests—Ignacio Ellacuría, Ignacio Martín-Baró, and Segundo Montes—also ran select foreign stories in translation, including several of mine. Although I hadn't necessarily thought of the three as professional colleagues at the time, their journalistic role was clear. The Jesuits explained events in a way that few in the nation's press corps still dared after a string of murders targeting journalists and other critics.

"When the Jesuits were killed, their relationship to news and its distribution had much to do with their being targeted," said Anne Nelson, who served as CPJ's executive director at the time. CPJ documented the priest's deaths and called them journalists in the 1989 edition of this book. In effect, the organization concluded that the practice of journalism—not one's position or title or publication—is what makes an individual a journalist. Today, the priests' names are etched in the glass plates of the Journalists Memorial at the Newseum in Washington.

The November 1989 murders of the three priests—killed along with three other Jesuits, their housekeeper, and her daughter—came at a pivotal moment for the press corps in El Salvador. Three other journalists were murdered earlier that year, punctuating years of brutal violence against domestic reporters. It became clear that mobilizing the press in a united front would be crucial in keeping journalists alive.

■ ■ ■

By its nature, front-line journalism will never be safe. Reporters respond to conflict, photographers head toward danger. But the risk can be compounded by divisions in the press corps. In every country, there is much that can divide journalists: political perspectives, ethnicity, religion, and professional rivalries to name a few. Journalists working in new formats are sometimes shunned by those working in traditional media. Something as basic as the geographical divide between rural and urban journalists can get in the way of professional solidarity.

But as journalists learned in El Salvador and in other dangerous places such as Colombia, professional solidarity is essential in stemming reprisals. Defending a single journalist who is under attack, no matter the individual's position or perspective, ends up protecting the practice of journalism for everyone. Today, professional solidarity is being tested with mixed results in nations such as Turkey, Honduras, Mali, and Brazil.

Even as Turkey's international profile has risen, it faces severe challenges from a long-standing Kurdish insurgency, deep internal political divisions, and civil war on its doorstep in Syria. Successive governments, most recently the administration of Prime Minister

Recep Tayyip Erdoğan, have a long record of prosecuting and jailing journalists.

Historically, Kurdish journalists have borne the brunt of these prosecutions, typically on charges of aiding terrorist organizations by covering the viewpoints and activities of the banned Kurdistan Workers Party, or PKK. In 2004, left-leaning and Kurdish journalists formed the Platform in Solidarity With Arrested Journalists, complaining that Kurdish journalists were being jailed for merely interviewing rebel fighters. Other Turkish press groups, the Platform said, "were not defending those journalists at all—they were not even recognizing them as journalists."

The authorities have expanded their repressive tactics in recent years: Dozens of non-Kurdish journalists have been jailed on allegations they took part in anti-government plots or were members of banned political movements. Thousands of other criminal prosecutions have been brought against writers and editors accused of "denigrating Turkishness" by presenting unpopular views, or interfering with law enforcement proceedings by reporting too critically about government investigations. In an August 2012 television appearance, Erdoğan delivered a "message to all media" in which he instructed them to stop covering the Kurdish conflict. Any reporting on the PKK's activities, he said, amounted to propaganda.

Few Turkish media outlets or mainstream journalists have challenged the government's efforts to suppress news of the Kurdish conflict or spoken out on behalf of their jailed Kurdish colleagues. "The mainstream Turkish media have been contaminated by the discourse of war and are easily tempted to be a part of the ruling elite," Ece Temelkuran, a well-known Turkish journalist and author, told CPJ. The fractious response to the crackdown on Kurdish journalists has ultimately left the entire press corps vulnerable.

The Erdoğan government has exploited the deep-seated political and ethnic divisions among journalists to isolate critics in the press. It then pressures the politically sensitive owners of media outlets—most of them corporate entities with diverse holdings—to rein in or fire the critics. "The journalists and writers of the mainstream press don't show more solidarity with the arrested journalists and writers because they are afraid of the government," Necati Abay, a founder and spokesman for the Platform in Solidarity With Arrested Journalists, told CPJ. "The fear of losing your job reduces solidarity."

■ ■ ■

A staggering number of journalists have been killed in Honduras since the 2009 military-backed coup that ousted President Manuel Zelaya. Fourteen reporters and editors have been murdered, at least three in direct relation to their work.

Honduran journalists stepped up in May 2012 when thousands marched in Tegucigalpa and four other cities to protest the slayings, nearly all of which have been committed with impunity. One protester wore tape over her mouth with the handwritten words, "If I Speak I Die." The march was organized after the murder of a popular radio host, Ángel Alfredo Villatoro, whose body was found with two bullet wounds to the head a week after he was abducted. "This is a call for attention that we want to send to the authorities, mainly to those who handle matters of justice, that they must guarantee our right to exercise our profession without fear, murders, or threats," journalist Yessenia Torres told the marchers.

Though the Association of Journalists of Honduras, a leading professional group, had co-sponsored the march, it all but ignored the earlier string of journalist murders. "They talk about press freedom, but they don't act when journalists are attacked," said Héctor Becerra, executive director of a grassroots group called Committee for Free Expression or C-Libre. Becerra and others formed C-Libre in 2001 after concluding that the nation's largest journalism groups acted only in cases involving their own members. The Association of Journalists of Honduras did not return calls, emails, and social media messages seeking comment.

The Honduran press corps, like the country, has been polarized since the June 2009 coup that ousted the leftist Zelaya. Many of the journalists murdered since the coup were perceived as supportive of Zelaya—and many worked for local broadcast outlets outside the capital. These journalists, said Becerra, typically don't belong to any national union or professional group that can publicize the cases.

Journalists in Mali faced a similar test after two decades of democracy came to an abrupt end in March 2012. A northern insurgency fueled by arms from neighboring Libya, combined with a military coup led by junior officers and enlisted men, divided the nation and put journalists at risk from all sides. In the capital, Bamako, military authorities detained and interrogated at least eight journalists after the March coup, accusing some of having rebel ties. In the north, where ethnic Tuareg rebels allied with radical Jihadi militants, more than a dozen radio stations were attacked, journalists were dragged off the air, and severe censorship measures were imposed.

As in Honduras, journalists in Mali were initially divided over the coup, said Manak Kone, president of the Mali Press Center. The organization, established in 1995, had focused primarily on training and information services until mounting anti-press attacks forced it into an advocacy role. In July 2012, for example, eight masked gunmen stormed the offices of *L'Indépendant* after the paper ran stories critical of the new military regime, abducting publisher Saouti Labass Haïdara. He was found dumped by a roadside four hours later, with head and hand injuries. The Mali Press Center helped organize a demonstration in response, delivering a statement to the new government "to protest against aggression, intimidations, kidnappings and other bullying experienced by Malian journalists."

Journalists in the capital were less vocal, however, about attacks on their colleagues in the rural north. Malick Aliou Maïga, a prominent local radio journalist who also filed stories for the U.S. government-funded Voice of America, was beaten by Islamist rebels in the northeast in August. The press in Bamako covered the attack only after it received international attention.

Despite the slow response, Kone said, the Bamako press is becoming more aware of the plight of its northern colleagues. Reporters who have fled the rural northern areas are recounting their experiences to counterparts in the capital, he said. Solidarity may be making a difference now in Bamako. In October 2012, the transitional government of interim leader Dioncounda Traoré agreed to meet with civil society groups, including the Mali Press Center, to talk about attacks on human rights and press freedom.

■ ■ ■

Events in Brazil illustrate both the successes of professional solidarity, and the continuing challenges. After the 2002 abduction and murder of TV Globo correspondent Tim Lopes in Rio de Janeiro, journalists came together to form the Association of Brazilian Investigative Journalists, or ABRAJI. The association galvanized Brazil's news media, creating a network to spread information about attacks on the press and organize efforts to press for justice. The publicity and pressure have had results: Perpetrators have been convicted in at least five journalist slayings over the past seven years, and the authorities have won convictions against masterminds in at least two cases.

But journalist murders spiked in Brazil in 2011 and 2012, with at least seven killings coming in direct relation to victims' work. "Most of the cases happened in the countryside, or in regions where corruption is widespread among justice and police departments," said Marcelo Moreira, editor-in-chief of TV Globo and president of ABRAJI. The attacks get little attention in the national media, he said, because the press in Rio de Janeiro and São Paulo typically views provincial journalists as corrupt or politically biased. This, in turn, makes it much harder for ABRAJI and other groups to pressure police to solve the crimes, Moreira said.

Colombian journalists face similar challenges in protecting provincial colleagues, but their overall efforts to promote professional solidarity have yielded notable successes. Though the country remains a dangerous place for the press, the fatality rate has dropped significantly in the past decade. Twelve journalists have been killed for their work since 2003, CPJ research shows, about one-third the number recorded in the previous decade.

The development of what is now an extensive press freedom movement in Colombia came over decades that were marked by setbacks. The movement dates to 1986, when drug traffickers led by Pablo Escobar murdered Guillermo Cano, publisher of the newspaper *El Espectador*. His murder—the seventh work-related slaying that year—rallied the press corps into action. Broadcast and print news outlets organized a rare 24-hour news blackout to protest the murder. *El Espectador* joined with rival media outlets in a collaborative project to investigate and publish stories about drug trafficking and its devastating effect on society. The collaboration demonstrated that the Colombian press would not be intimidated by criminals and would push even harder to expose the cartels.

Still, attacks on the Colombian press abated only for a time. Journalist murders began rising again in the early 1990s. Similar to the situation in Honduras today, perceived political divisions among Colombian journalists—whether they represent the right or the left—helped undermine solidarity. Finally, in 1996, journalists of all kinds—from the writer Gabriel García Márquez to Francisco Santos Calderón, whose family owned the nation's largest daily, *El Tiempo*, and who later became the nation's vice president—came together to form the Bogotá-based Foundation for Press Freedom. The group, commonly known as FLIP, created a nationwide network of volunteer correspondents to document attacks on the press, published a field security manual, and pushed the government to provide direct assistance to journalists under threat. Media outlets undertook several collaborative investigations and agreed to general guidelines on how to cover violence without glorifying it.

"We move solidarity for big and small things," said Ignacio Gómez, a CPJ International Press Freedom Award winner and a former *El Espectador* investigative reporter who also helped found FLIP. He said FLIP enjoys wide support because it not only denounces violent attacks, but also intervenes in lesser matters such as criminal defamation cases.

■ ■ ■

The Salvador Foreign Press Corps Association was started in the 1980s with a bit of tongue-in-cheek joking: Its founders chose the acronym, SPCA, the same one used by the Society for the Prevention of Cruelty to Animals.

Although the press corps at the time seemed as polarized as the nation, the SPCA eventually became the first line of defense when a journalist was targeted. The attacks peaked during a 14-hour period on the eve of presidential elections in March 1989. Without provocation, government troops in separate cities shot and killed two Salvadoran journalists, one working for Reuters and the other for the local Channel 12 television news. During the same period, a government helicopter fired on a convoy of journalists rushing a wounded Dutch cameraman to the hospital, forcing the journalists to take cover while the cameraman bled to death.

Journalists responded with one voice. At a news conference that day, a Salvadoran reporter put military commanders on the spot: Had the soldiers who opened fire on journalists taken their cue from senior officers who openly held the press in contempt? CPJ sent a delegation to investigate, meeting with military commanders. I was elected to the leadership of SPCA on a promise to take a tough line with the Salvadoran army. Although the country remained a dangerous place for some time, Salvadoran soldiers exercised greater restraint and anti-press attacks declined.

I returned to El Salvador most recently in 2012. The spectrum of views in the press could not be broader. A former leftist guerrilla whom I knew during the war is now a columnist for a right-wing newspaper. State broadcast outlets produce quality news instead of the government propaganda spread during the war. The son of a slain guerrilla leader runs an online news outlet called *ContraPunto*. The Jesuit university teaches journalism and communications.

But solidarity is a tenuous thing. When the Salvadoran online outlet *El Faro* broke several sensitive stories in 2012, a senior government official acknowledged its journalists were at risk from criminal gangs but initially declined to provide any protection. Few in the Salvadoran press corps came to the defense of *El Faro*. Months later, when *El Faro* organized an international conference to discuss gang violence and press freedom, few rival Salvadoran journalists were asked to take part. "We were invited to cover it," one told me, "but not to participate."

When people think of journalist security, the use of encrypted files and counter-surveillance techniques often comes to mind. Those practices are important, but security is really a way of thinking, a way of approaching the job. And fostering professional solidarity is crucial to that approach. The Salvadoran journalists of the past paid a terrible price. Today's talented reporters have not been tested as severely, but they would do well to be proactive and speak as one on the issues that endanger them all.

In San Salvador, a memorial to the murdered Jesuits is a reminder of what is at stake. Visitors to the Monsignor Romero Center & Martyrs Museum can see the clothes worn by the priests when they were cut down by automatic rifle fire. The display also includes a set of clear containers. They are filled with darkened blades of grass cut from the campus lawn where the three Jesuits had spilled their blood.

Frank Smyth is CPJ's senior adviser for journalist security and the lead author of the CPJ Journalist Security Guide, *published in April 2012. Smyth has reported on armed conflicts, organized crime, and human rights in El Salvador, Guatemala, Colombia, Rwanda, Eritrea, Ethiopia, Sudan, and Iraq. Smyth is also founder and executive director of Global Journalist Security, a firm that provides consulting and training services.*

Is Covering the News Worth the Risk?

By Terry Anderson

In two decades as a journalist, much of it spent in Asia and Africa and the Middle East, I rarely asked myself why I was doing it. It wasn't for the money, which was OK but not great. It wasn't for the fame. I worked for the AP, about as anonymous (though as satisfying) a place as you can find in journalism. My stories might have appeared in 2,000 newspapers, but most often without my name, just the byline of "The Associated Press." Yes, it was exciting. Danger is exciting, if you're not the one getting hurt. When you do, it's not exciting. It's just painful.

So why? Why risk your life, your freedom, the suffering of your family, to go to the hard places of the world, the dangerous places where people are suffering and dying? It wasn't until I sat in a series of basement cells in Lebanon, held by Shia fanatics, that I had time to think about it. Seven years' worth. I tried to justify the risks I had taken, the price my family and I had paid. Was it worth it?

I had collected boxes of clippings and nearly as many war stories. Yet I could not point to a single person I could definitively say I had helped. I could not truthfully say I had solved a single problem. Indeed, I often thought that no one had ever read my stories, though they were published in thousands of newspapers.

After I came home 20 years ago, I joined the Committee to Protect Journalists to try to help other journalists. I learned of and often met hundreds of others around the world who were risking and too often losing their lives or freedom in the pursuit of the truth, journalism's only purpose. Most of them were not people Americans would recognize, not famous foreign correspondents, although there were many of those—Anthony Shadid, Daniel Pearl, Marie Colvin, to name a few. Of the nearly 1,000 journalists killed because of their work in those 20 years, the great majority had been working in their own countries, living and suffering alongside those they covered; they were subjects of the very dictatorships and oligarchies that ordered them killed, or jailed, or beaten. And for every 10 journalist deaths, only one killer was ever punished. For most of the rest, no justice was even sought.

It is those people who helped provide me with an answer, one that would satisfy the thousands of journalism students I taught at Columbia, Ohio, Kentucky, and Syracuse universities. They are the ones who know first-hand the cost of doing a journalist's job—of finding and telling the truth, as best as one can. They are people who have absorbed, in the depths of their souls, one of America's great teachings: You cannot have a free society without a free press. They believe it so much, they are willing to go to work each day, at their newspaper or radio station, or sit down at their computers, knowing the risks they are taking. And you know what? Their oppressors—those who kidnap and kill them, jail and beat them—believe it, too. They know they cannot accomplish their purpose, cannot exploit, rob, and crush their people, in the face of a free press. So they go after the journalists first.

I liked the answer given by the young freelancer Austin Tice a few weeks before he was kidnapped, probably by forces loyal to the Syrian government. "I don't have a death wish," he told those who questioned his choice to be in a war zone. "I have a life wish."

■ ■ ■

We all "know" that Americans don't care about the world, don't understand it. "I don't know the difference between Iraq and Iran," a popular, jingoistic song proclaimed a few years ago, amid the Iraq war. What a shameful thing, that we should proclaim our ignorance and be applauded. What a shaming thing for those thousands of journalists who have risked their lives to explain the difference between Iraq and Iran.

It is no longer just professional journalists who are inspired to tell the world what they are seeing. In places such as Egypt and Tunisia and now Syria, one of the most dangerous places around, citizen journalists have picked up a camera or a smartphone to record the horror around them. One of them, a Syrian-American named Amal, wrote me: "We have lost dozens of citizen journalists in this revolution. Young men who were students, employees, fathers one day became threatening targets the next day because of their cellphones, cameras, and laptops. They knew Syrians have been silent too long. Last year, they decided to never cover up Assad's crimes with silence again. And they are paying a heavy price for it. . . .

"I don't know what my dead friends would have answered to your question, 'Was it worth it?' But I do know what the ones who are alive and still film and photograph in Homs, Aleppo, Hama, Idlib, and across Syria would say to the question, 'Is it worth it to die for your camera?' They would say, 'Yes.' Because they know for the first time in their lives, their voice matters and they are doing the most important job, to tell the truth while so many are telling lies.

"Telling the truth, in a way, has become even more important than freedom. It's the road to freedom.

"I've been writing about the revolution since the beginning. I didn't expect to take on the role I now have when I began; telling my stories evolved into telling Syria's stories. I only cared about one thing: telling the truth. Sometimes it seems like an impossible task. And many times the truth hurts. But we have to keep going and hope that what's good in the people prevails over the evil."

A few days later, Amal sent me another email. A friend, also a citizen journalist, had just lost a sister to sniper fire. "She was a mother in her forties," Amal wrote. But his friend "picked up his camera the next day and continued his work: documenting the truth."

Nearly 25 years ago, we rejoiced as country after country rejected totalitarianism, as their people stood up to the police and military and demanded freedom, including the freedom to speak their minds and to hear the truth from a free press. Another wave of liberty has struck the Arab world as popular Islamic groups try to reconcile religion and democracy.

Still, in too many places, the surge toward openness is slipping away, as the forces of repression take hold again. Mexico's press is being crushed by criminal gangs. Russia is using governmental power to silence critical voices. Turkey has reclaimed the disreputable crown of the world's top jailer of journalists. In Greece, a reporter is arrested for embarrassing the rich. Even in the United States, secrecy and sycophancy are wielded in the name of "security" by a government seemingly little interested in upholding basic human rights, here or abroad.

And, as always, war claims truth as its victim. A victim that is at the heart of who we are, why we are willing to take those risks, why we would anger those in power who hide behind the lies.

I believe, like many of my colleagues, that being a journalist takes both dedication and training. It's a profession that requires preparation, and is best done with the support of a major news organization such as I had in the Associated Press, which took care of my family while I was gone and helped us greatly when I returned.

But that is becoming less and less the norm. Many young men and women, including my own daughter, are going overseas as freelancers, on their own or with only part-time jobs. Thousands of others, like Amal, are simply picking up a camera or writing a blog about what they see. Reading, seeing, and hearing their work, no one can say they are not also journalists, every bit as dedicated as any journalism school graduate.

Yes, it can be dangerous. It's also difficult and often uncomfortable, physically and psychologically. And yes, the profession is being changed by technology and economics. But it is still important that we in the rich and stable and smug places of the world support colleagues like Amal and that we send our best young people out to those distant places. That's why being a journalist, and taking risks, and telling the stories of strange people in faraway places is still a vital and satisfying job. Journalism may not directly solve problems, but without it, those problems can't be solved at all.

Terry Anderson is a former journalist, journalism teacher, writer, and business-man. He was chief Middle East correspondent of the Associated Press when he was kidnapped in Lebanon in 1985 and held for seven years by pro-Iranian militants. He is honorary chairman of the Committee to Protect Journalists, and has served as its vice chairman and executive board member.

8

MEDIA AND MONEY

Once Thriving, Afghan Media Now Endangered

By Bob Dietz

I n post-Taliban Afghanistan, Afghans and international donors both point with pride to the country's burgeoning news media. Under the austere, techno-phobic Taliban, only one state broadcaster was in operation, with a few underpowered radio stations strewn across the country. Now, estimates from the BBC and others say there are more than 400 media outlets, with newspapers and weeklies in all of the country's several languages, as well as about 150 radio stations and more than 30 television broadcasters. Though Internet penetration is incredibly low, enhanced third-generation mobile phone service is widely available, especially in the denser population centers. Literate young Afghans are embracing smartphone-based social media platforms to share information about everything from Afghanistan's chances in international cricket matches to real-time reports from the scenes of terrorist attacks.

But 2014 and the completion of the drawdown of NATO troops will be a significant milestone for Afghanistan and its press. International funding launched many of those media and then kept them alive, some for more than a decade. As the foreign military presence is vastly reduced, the international community—deep in donor fatigue and trying to cope with its own economic distress—will also withdraw much of that funding. The World Bank says international aid makes up more than 95 percent of Afghanistan's gross domestic product, but the rate of growth—which has hovered around 9 percent since 2002—is already shrinking. Although global donors meeting in Tokyo in July 2012 pledged $16 billion in continuing aid, media assistance was not at the forefront of their concerns, said Heather Barr, Human Rights Watch's Afghanistan representative, who attended the meeting. The financial viability of the country's media outlets is under threat.

"It is clear there is a direct link between the health of the Afghan economy and Afghan media," Lotfullah Najafizada, who heads the current affairs department at Tolo TV, a commercial station belonging to Moby Group, told CPJ.

But this is more than a story about the looming failure of a well-intentioned international aid effort. In addition to likely economic collapse, the political landscape will be shaky as the Karzai government hands over—or possibly does not hand over—power after the 2014 presidential elections, which might come earlier than scheduled. The ability of Afghan publishers and broadcasters to survive in even the near term looks increasingly doubtful; many might not be around to cover parliamentary elections scheduled for 2015. Meanwhile, foreign players like Iran and Pakistan—countries with less than ideal commitments to media integrity and independence—are already stepping in to fill the emerging media vacuum.

■ ■ ■

Several countries have made a point of investing heavily in Afghan media over the years, but the United States has made the largest contribution. "We're working with the most viable media organizations, trying to help them become self-sustaining," Masha Hamilton, director of communications and public diplomacy at the U.S. Embassy in Kabul, told CPJ.

Hamilton said the United States supports about 10 media organizations in one fashion or another, but the money, which comes from a wide number of sources, is rapidly disappearing. "The rebirth of Afghan media is a success story," she said. "But we know the funding that supported that growth is in a drawdown stage. The media in Afghanistan are on a glide path, and they must find a way to become sustainable."

Sustainability has become the byword for the Afghans running those news organizations as well as the funders who have thrown hundreds of millions of dollars into them over the past decade. A scramble is on to replace the rapidly evaporating international donor support with a viable commercial model relying on advertisers and, where appropriate, subscribers. But in an already shrinking economy, that pool of advertisers, never large to begin with, will not be enough to keep all the media houses alive. I consumed Afghan media for two weeks in Kabul in September 2012, and it was clear that only a handful of banks, mobile phone companies, airlines, and international aid organizations were major sources of ad revenue.

One success story had been the Pajhwok Afghan News network, a well-respected wire service launched in 2004. Danish Karokhel, the agency's director and editor-in-chief and a CPJ International Press Freedom Award winner in 2008, readily admits that staying alive will be difficult. By the time I visited Pajhwok in September, the agency had fallen on hard times, its staff was hollowed out, many of its reporters across the country unpaid for several months. Shortly before my visit, Pajhwok had received a one-year bridge loan—Karokhel said it was enough to keep the doors open, but not enough to rebuild the outlet—from the U.S. Agency for International Development (USAID). The rationale was to keep Pajhwok alive during the campaign period before the presidential elections.

Beyond that, Karokhel is struggling to find a way to keep the news agency going. A plan to invest in an office building to house other media agencies does not sit well with donors—they want to fund a news organization, not a real estate company. Even with discounting, subscriptions to Pajhwok's wire service haven't been enough to keep the agency alive, and efforts to start a news photo agency have not panned out. Banner advertising on its website is nonexistent; with Internet penetration low, advertisers do not see the value.

Karokhel is frank about his problems, and says the same issues face almost all the other media: "The cost of living, especially in major cities, continues to rise and places enormous pressure on labor costs. And to make matters worse the cost of reporting news has skyrocketed. Operational costs like rents, utilities, transportation, and communication have far outstripped most outlets' abilities to pay," he told a meeting of donor agencies.

■ ■ ■

Perhaps the most successful broadcaster in Afghanistan is the Moby Group, which runs several television channels and has branched out to broadcast regionally in Farsi. Moby is concluding an agreement with Rupert Murdoch for a Middle East channel, based in Dubai. Its commercial station in Afghanistan, Tolo TV, has been around since 2004 with stations in 14 cities, and its satellite footprint covers much of central and South Asia.

But even Moby's Afghan news operations—a 24-hour news channel and two hours of news broadcasts in Dari and Pashto on their own channels—have had to lay off staff. "A large part of our news and current affairs shows are self-sufficient, but the money available from all sources is much less than a few years ago," said Najafizada of Tolo's current affairs department. With Moby regionalizing its operations, the company's senior leadership is spending less time in Kabul, he noted, focusing on its broader, more lucrative operations across the region. Moby's founders were three brothers who had spent their exile in Australia, and the group remains committed to Afghanistan, Najafizada said. But the company is being realistic in looking outside the country to thrive.

Afghan media is surprisingly complex. The journalists with whom I spoke see a four-tiered system. There are a few truly independent media houses, largely launched by returning Afghans, usually appearing in Dari or Pashto. The government broadcaster Radio Television Afghanistan is still struggling to define itself as either a public service broadcaster or as the official voice of the government. Either way, it has not invested heavily in upgrading its broadcast facilities. A few NGO broadcasters and publications see themselves as public service entities, promoting broad human rights issues like universal education or women's rights. But the vast and growing majority of outlets are politically tied media, with a wide range of backers. The United States and other donor nations generally do not hide their role in supporting media outlets, but they are not the only players willing to fund media houses.

Many broadcasters and some radio stations are blatantly partisan in their news presentation. Disparagingly but widely called "Warlord TV," they reflect the views of the country's regional political leaders and power brokers, segmented along the lines of the civil war that followed the Soviet withdrawal in 1989. Many owners are government ministers or other high-ranking officials with deep regional and ethnic power bases. Their commitment is to cementing political influence, not to promoting open journalism.

And, increasingly, foreign players like Iran and Pakistan are gaining a media foothold in the country, with resource-starved outlets openly being recruited in an effort to form public opinion. As Tolo's Najafizada put it: "You can smell the foreign influence. It is very noticeable. And with the economic vacuum created by donors' pulling away, others are quickly moving in to fill the space."

In August, for example, Iran announced a new Afghan-centered news agency, and several TV and radio stations signed up for the service. "If no one knew who was backing those broadcasters before, their relationship to Iran was revealed," said Abdul Mujeeb Khalvatgar, executive director of NAI, an Afghan-based media training and support group.

"To a lesser extent, Pakistan is trying the same thing," Mujeeb said. He estimates that of the 30 or so television broadcasters, four are controlled by Iran. "Iran and Pakistan are emulating the Western tactics of influencing the media—they have both seen how successful that can be." In September, the government, increasingly resentful of what it sees as Islamabad's interference in its internal affairs, barred Pakistani newspapers from being imported into the country.

"Add to that the warlords and the Taliban and you will have trouble in the vacuum that will develop as the Western community withdraws support from Afghan media," Mujeeb said.

■ ■ ■

Afghan media won't be able to turn to their impoverished government for help. "The government's attitude toward media has been mixed and inconsistent," said human rights activist Ahmad Nader Nadery, now at the Free and Fair Election Foundation of Afghanistan. "Its response seems to be driven more by individuals than by a broad or coherent policy. There has been no systematic attempt to restrict media, but individuals within the government working on their own group's political agendas have made attempts," he told CPJ in his office in central Kabul.

Several of those attempts came in 2012, when the government tried to revise the Mass Media Law. Journalists like Najafizada, Tolo's head of current affairs, worry that the proposed revisions would restrict the ability of media to debate or report on areas such as national security and religion; the rules are vague and the government could hand down punishment for any report or talk show it might not like, using national security as an excuse. Other media watchers wondered why the law needs revising at all when media has thus far thrived. "Why not leave well enough alone?" was an attitude I heard frequently in Kabul.

What has helped Afghan media stand up to pressure from all sides has been their professional identification and solidarity. "They have responded collectively—even while they remain competitors, they have stood firm together. But that unity needs to be strengthened as their revenue pool shrinks," said human rights activist Nadery. "The danger is that they will start fighting each other for the shrinking resources available to them."

The problem is not lost on the people heading Afghan media outlets. NAI's Mujeeb has put forward a practical plan to help independent media stay alive in the coming drawdown. First, start to rationalize the media landscape. Small operations should combine with others of a similar size to form larger, more viable organizations. After that, stabilize the labor pool: Several sources put forward a figure of about 700 journalists without jobs around mid-2012. Independent media owners believe these journalists form a talent pool ripe for recruiting by the new, well-funded foreign employers emerging as players in the media market. Managers said that lowering reporters' wages by half, from approximately $400 per month, to bring them in line with government workers' salaries, might keep more journalists employed. Reporters said they were not thrilled with the prospect.

In some ways, journalists' organizations have been the victims of the same largesse of the international aid community that established

so many of the news organizations they work for. As many as six organizations vie for aid to fund a nationwide professional journalist group.
With their eyes on the pool of funding rather than the well-being of
their profession, Afghan journalists have been unable to come together
to form a coherent national representation. But they do self-identify as
a professional group. At the local level, particularly in the larger cities,
reporters and field crews have been more successful at unifying themselves and taking group action to protest abuse, be it from the government, anti-government forces, international forces, or even their own
employers. And local groups demonstrate in support when colleagues
in other cities come under attack.

Journalists in Kandahar, where violence is highest, have proven
to be notably well organized. "We have been going through such an
ordeal," Taimoor Shah, the *New York Times* reporter in Kandahar, told
CPJ. "We have problems with government, NATO, and the Taliban.
Coverage for news outlets is tremendously limited due to the existing
dangerous situation. We cannot travel to the outskirts of town for news
coverage."

Shah added, "Everywhere journalists go they are facing big threats
of IEDs [improvised explosive devices], kidnapping, and personal
intimidations in their day-to-day lives."

In one bid for solidarity and continued independence, three news
organizations—the Killid Group, Pajhwok Afghan News, Saba TV
and Radio Nawa network, owned by the Saba Media Organization—
founded the Afghan Independent Media Consortium in March 2012.
At their opening news conference, the group said it was time for
Afghan media to take control of their own destiny, and not to allow the
public debate to be defined "by the insurgency on one side and the U.S./
NATO/Afghan government on the other side," all filtered through
the focus of the Western media. It's a valid and admirable goal, but the
nascent group will be hard pressed to prevail in the coming economic
downturn.

The future looks fraught for Afghan reporters and their traditional
news organizations, but there might be some cause for hope. Internet
penetration is very low: The International Telecommunications Union
put it at 5 percent as of 2011. But, rather than a threat to independent media, Mujeeb sees great potential in social media platforms.

Empowering citizen journalism and street journalism through social media—not only on enhanced 3-G platforms but also simple texting on basic cellphones—might be the route to keeping independent media alive. There are some 15 million Afghans with mobile phones and 85 percent of them live within range of a cellphone tower. Just as cellphone technology leapfrogged traditional telephone landlines in many developing countries, smartphone distribution could bypass traditional media, even those reliant on Internet cabling, to ensure a free flow of information. Though the future may not bode well for the mainstream press, emerging technologies may be able to ensure that independently supplied news reaches a wide segment of Afghans, as it has been doing for more than 10 years.

Bob Dietz, coordinator of CPJ's Asia program, has reported across the continent for news outlets such as CNN and Asiaweek. He has led numerous CPJ missions, including ones to Afghanistan, Pakistan, the Philippines, and Sri Lanka.

Oil, Money, and Secrecy In East Africa

By Tom Rhodes

O fficials in East Africa are gushing with anticipation over potential oil revenue: A new production agreement has been reached in South Sudan; fresh discoveries have been made and drilling deals signed in Kenya and Uganda. But if the potential for economic growth is great, so is the capacity for corruption and environmental degradation if journalists are not allowed to report on contract details and resource allocation. And each of the East African nations has notable blemishes on its press freedom record, including government-sponsored violence in Kenya and Uganda, and suppression of in-depth reporting in South Sudan.

Oil accounts for almost all of South Sudan's government income, and although the country has wrangled with Sudan over who owns the oil and how much each side should pay to transport it, Africa's newest country has a wealth of untapped reserves, the World Bank says. In Uganda, estimated reserves of 3.5 billion barrels have the potential to double the country's economy, and in Kenya new reserves have been discovered in the northern county of Turkana and near the Ethiopian border.

Whether all this oil will benefit the average citizen depends largely on whether extraction deals are handled in an open, transparent manner. A comparison between Brazil and Nigeria is instructive. The South American country provides detailed monthly updates on oil production on a state website. Brazil became the seventh-largest economy in the world with the help of oil output, with 2011 per capita income of $12,594, according to World Bank statistics. In Nigeria, five decades of oil output have been mired in secrecy and conflict. Although the country's oil exports are comparable to those of Brazil, its per capita income is just $1,452.

■ ■ ■

So far, the authorities in Kenya, Uganda, and South Sudan have released occasional press releases and basic information on government websites about drilling locations and production expectations. But there are few specifics on how much private companies and governments are investing in the oil projects, how revenues will be shared, and what tax rates are applied. "Detailed information about contracts and compensation is not readily available to journalists. It takes a lot of effort to obtain such information," said Ugandan journalist Joe Nam, who reports on oil drilling and contributes to the daily New Vision. "In most cases it is not available at all unless it is leaked by a source in confidence."

Journalists in Uganda and South Sudan have some legal recourse to obtain information on oil production, but the authorities in both countries often skirt access-to-information rules. While Uganda's 2005 Access to Information Act theoretically covers documents between the government and private companies, oil contracts typically have special provisions whereby both parties must consent before information is given to a third party, according to Gilbert Sendugwa, coordinator of the Africa Freedom of Information Centre in Uganda. The secrecy clauses prevent even parliament from getting key information, according to Dickens Kamugisha, chief executive of the Africa Institute for Energy Governance, a Kampala-based think tank that advocates for transparent energy policies.

The Information Act did not help reporters Angelo Izama and Charles Mwanguhya, of Uganda's leading independent Daily Monitor, who sued for access to oil contracts on the grounds of public interest in February 2010. Chief Magistrate Deo Ssejjemba ruled that the petitioners had not proved the public benefit of disclosing the information, according to the journalists and news reports. Two other access-to-information cases filed by journalists and civil society organizations have been pending before the High Court of Uganda for four years, Kamugisha said.

Since few Ugandan authorities comply with requests under the access law, few journalists bother to use it. Sendugwa noted that all government ministers are required to report how they implement the information act. "We decided to test the law and sent an information request to parliament in November 2010 asking for the ministers' reports on their implementation of the Access to Information Act," he said. "To this date, none have complied."

Similarly, the Ugandan lands ministry is required by the Land Acquisitions Act to establish a policy for compensating those affected by oil development, but this has never been done, according to Kamugisha. "As a result, the citizens must continue to rely on the discretionary powers of government to determine compensation," he said. Uganda's 2012 Oil and Gas Revenue Management Policy contains a small section on transparency, saying that "all parties involved in the management of oil and gas revenues shall observe the highest standards of transparency," but it does not specify how this should be undertaken. Journalists place little faith in three petroleum bills proposed in parliament in 2012. None of the three bills—the Petroleum Resource Bill, Value Addition Bill, and Revenue Management Bill—contained clauses specifying access to oil contracts, according to reporter Edward Ssekika of the *Observer* newspaper. The anti-corruption research organization Global Witness also analyzed the bills and concluded that all three lack guarantees on contract and financial transparency.

In South Sudan, Minister of Petroleum and Mining Stephen Dhieu Dau says the nation's Petroleum Act ensures that members of the public "are able to know where our resources come from, how they are handled, and where the revenues go." Though the act offers broad assurances that oil information is public, a provision allows the ministry to determine whether or not a particular oil contract is published, said Dana Wilkins, a campaigner for Global Witness. No contract had been made public as of late 2012.

South Sudan gained independence from Sudan in July 2011, acquiring two-thirds of the former Sudan's oil, but Khartoum retained the processing and export facilities. Drilling in South Sudan came to a standstill in January 2012 after a dispute over how much South Sudan should pay Sudan in transit fees. The two countries reached agreement in September 2012 to end the gridlock on production and transportation, but the pact falls short of providing public access to financial data, according to Global Witness. "Sudan and South Sudan's citizens are the ultimate owners of their countries' natural resources," Wilkins said in a statement. "Yet they have been totally cut out of this new oil deal, with no way to verify the amount of oil and money that will be transferred between their governments." South Sudanese journalist Richard Ruati said he is not surprised by the lack of transparency in the latest agreement, since the press has been kept in the dark all along. "So far, no proper press conference has been organized to brief both the national and international media on regards to oil deals or contracts," he said. "But it seems there are already oil companies in the oil fields drilling clandestinely." South Sudan does not have a freedom of information law.

In Kenya, where oil exploration is at an earlier stage, there is also no freedom of information law, but journalists hope the country's robust new constitution, adopted in August 2010, will ensure that yet-to-be-signed oil contracts will be open to the public. "It's too early to tell yet, but luckily the new constitution does not allow executives much room to do secret contracts," said Charles Onyango-Obbo, an executive editor at the Kenyan Nation Media Group. The constitution says that transactions involving the grants of rights or concessions for exploitation of any natural resource must be subject to parliamentary ratification, according to business journalist Cathy Mputhia. The document also states that agreements related to natural resources must be published by 2015.

Prospective oil contracts were presented in parliament in June 2012, and the government plans to put information on oil deals on an online open data platform. "We are seeking to get the data," said the Kenyan Information Ministry's permanent secretary, Bitange Ndemo. "Most departments have not quite understood the new constitutional dispensation but we are determined to get the information and upload it." So far, journalists have had incident-free access to report on communities near oil drilling sites in Turkana, northern Kenya, according to William Oloo Janak, chairman of the Kenya Correspondents Association. "But when oil production starts, that's when potential problems for journalists and Kenyans at large may begin in terms of secrecy and possible environmental concerns," Janak said. In the past, journalists have been harassed or arrested for reporting on opposition to major development projects, most recently when freelance photographer Abdalla Bargash had his notes and memory card confiscated in March 2012 as he tried to cover local community members on Lamu Island opposed to a port project that includes an oil pipeline.

■ ■ ■

Ugandan and Southern Sudanese journalists say that attempts to interview residents near oil drilling sites in those countries are often blocked by local officials. The *Observer*'s Ssekika, who lives near one of the sites in Buliisa, western Uganda, said he has not attempted to interview locals about oil drilling since December 2011, when he was told he needed clearance from the district internal security officer, who in turn said the journalist would be allowed to work only with a police escort. After Ssekika declined an escort, the security officer told him he needed clearance from the mining ministry in Kampala to conduct interviews with local residents. "Personally, I have worked with journalists who I guide to the oil region, but they get arrested and deported from the oil districts to Kampala," said Kamugisha of the Africa Institute for Energy Governance. "The crime they commit is trying to ask the local people their challenges."

Obtaining information from local officials and residents of oil-producing regions of South Sudan is equally challenging. "I have tried asking officials in Unity state about the required funds for compensating locals, but none give me clear information," said freelance journalist Bonifacio Taban Kuich, who is based in the oil-rich state bordering Sudan. "Most people here, especially those in areas of oil production, do not have the slightest clue about oil income in South Sudan."

Officials and oil companies in Uganda try to control the message by providing organized tours of oil drilling facilities. The Ministry of Energy and Mineral Development's 2011 communication strategy paper recommends two media tours of the Albertine Graben oil-drilling area each year. "Sure, it's easy to go to oil areas for oil company-organized events," Ssekika said. "You can talk to district officials, etc. But when you go alone with your own view, that's a different story."

Oil companies, which benefit from minimizing costs and expediting production, may see few benefits to transparency. Taimour Lay, a journalist who covers oil production, said companies have pushed East African authorities to sign agreements without public debate, claiming they need quick approval to drill or they will work elsewhere in the oil-rich region. "When China National Offshore Oil Corporation [CNOOC] struck a deal with Tullow Oil to develop Uganda's fields, it warned [President Yoweri] Museveni that there wasn't time to wait for parliamentary debates over the issue—pausing now could mean Uganda losing its winning lottery ticket to Kenya," Lay wrote on the *African Arguments* news website. Tullow's communications manager in Kampala, Cathy Adengo, disputed that depiction. "Tullow did not push the Ugandan authorities into doing anything, considering we had a two-year wait to ratify the deal with CNOOC," Adengo said.

While offering general endorsements of transparency, oil companies typically defer actual requests for contract and other information to governments. "I have tried to communicate with them but they instead refer me to local government officials," said Kuich, the South Sudanese freelance journalist. Levi Obonyo, chairman of Kenya's independent Media Council, says bluntly that oil companies hide behind governments to avoid public scrutiny. "Unfortunately, with regard to oil companies, the demand for accessing information has been directed at the government and public sector rather than the private sector," Obonyo said. "Too often we tend to treat the private enterprise as an untouchable."

Adengo of Tullow Oil told CPJ that it is up to the Ugandan government to determine whether a contract should be published, although the company "would welcome publication of all our contracts with all governments." The French oil giant Total, which bought one-third interest in Tullow's Uganda oil exploration sites in February 2012, supports transparency in oil revenues, but the decision ultimately lies with the government, said Ahlem Friga-Noy, manager of public affairs and external communication. "Publishing the oil contract is a decision which pertains to the government and not to the company," she said. "Total is ready to publish the contract if the Ugandan authorities decide to do so."

Oil companies have sometimes paid a price for being opaque and running roughshod over local communities. In 2009, the Dutch oil giant Shell reached a $15.5 million settlement in a lawsuit filed in the United States over human rights violations in the Niger Delta. The company was accused of financing militias that used deadly force against local residents protesting Shell's presence. The company has faced further lawsuits over pollution in the Delta and alleged ties to the Nigerian military, according to Reuters. "Imagine, it took a court case launched in America before activities of oil companies were discovered," said Omoyele Sowore, publisher of the anti-corruption website *Sahara Reporters* and a former Niger Delta resident. The legal disputes resulted in an estimated loss of one million barrels of oil a day for the Nigerian government and private companies, according to Nigerian writer Orikinla Osinachi.

Secrecy and corruption have marked more than 50 years of oil production in Nigeria, obscuring and likely limiting the financial gains to citizens and leading to significant environmental degradation. Oil revenues count for 80 percent of the national budget, yet the government is unable to determine the amount of oil extracted from its territory, according to Alex Awiti, an ecologist at Aga Khan University in Nairobi. A 2011 study by the U.N. Environment Programme found widespread hydrocarbon pollution in soil, air, and water of the Delta, and said local drinking water is contaminated with 900 times the World Health Organization guideline for benzene, a carcinogen. Yet Nigeria still uses state security as a pretext to keep information on oil deals secret, Sowore said.

Nigeria's situation is not unique. Although Angola is the second-largest oil producer in Africa with an annual GDP of $101 billion and per capita income of nearly $9,000, more than two-thirds of its 8 million people live under the $2-a-day poverty line, according to the World Bank and news reports. These statistics, said Awiti, are rooted in the lack of transparency in Angola's oil production—leading to corruption, millions of dollars being stashed abroad, and revenue sequestered in a secret "parallel budget." In 2012, the International Monetary Fund attributed a \$32 billion gap in Angola's state funds from 2007 to 2010 to "quasi-fiscal operations by the state-owned oil company."

■ ■ ■

Already, allegations of corruption in oil dealings have arisen in Kenya, Uganda, and South Sudan. In October 2011, Ugandan Member of Parliament Gerald Karuhanga accused three officials—Prime Minister Amama Mbabazi, former Foreign Affairs Minister Sam Kutesa, and former Energy Minister Hilary Onek—of receiving billions of shillings in bribes from Tullow Oil Uganda. All three individuals and Tullow Oil deny wrongdoing. A commission of inquiry was set up to investigate the allegations but had not reached any conclusions by late 2012, according to local reports.

In Kenya, two MPs in Turkana County want an inquiry into allegations that a small firm owned by a cabinet minister made a fortune trading in oil prospecting licenses. They told parliament that shady deals might have fleeced the country and Turkana County of more than 3 billion shillings (about US\$35 million), according to news reports. "We demand to know all the companies involved, how much money the government made, and how land and rights were mortgaged," Turkana MP Josephat Nanok was quoted as saying in local media.

Lack of transparency in oil deals means that even allegations of graft can be frustratingly obscure. South Sudanese President Salva Kiir Mayardit accused government officials in June of stealing \$4 billion from government coffers, but he did not name any individuals or provide details. If true, the stolen funds would equate to more than 30 percent of oil revenue received by the government since 2005, particularly egregious given that oil accounts for nearly all national income. Also in South Sudan, the authorities are legally bound to ensure that a percentage of oil profits are used to develop communities in the drilling areas but, as freelancer Kuich said, "I have yet to see development within the communities in the oil areas even though it belongs to them."

Local communities in Upper Nile, Warrap, and Unity states in South Sudan have not benefited from the oil wealth in their backyards because the authorities have kept them in the dark concerning output, says Jok Madut Jok, executive director of the Sudd Institute, a policy research center. "The communities do not have an idea about the scale of production, the price of the barrel, the national net proceeds, and how they are distributed, and therefore are unable to hold the government to its responsibilities to use some of that money for the benefit of communities directly affected by oil production," Jok said. Instead, he said, many have suffered. "For example, the fencing-off of the territories previously used for grazing, future investment in farming over this land, pollution of their drinking water sources, and the displacement of people are all things that happen without any consultation with these communities," he said.

With oil output still in early stages in East Africa, the region has time to learn from other oil-producing countries. Chad has drilled oil since 2003, with the contracts kept secret. "The fact is Chadians do not know how many barrels are actually produced and where the money goes," said former *N'Djaména Hebdo* journalist Augustin Zusanne, who now works for the United Nations. Without such information, residents can hardly press for more development. "Even the oil-producing region, Doba, does not benefit from oil revenues. The population of this area lives in poverty," said Eric Topona, a journalist with the state broadcaster. However, things might improve, as Chad is now a candidate for membership in the Extractive Industries Transparency Initiative (EITI), an international forum that seeks openness by ensuring that oil payments are published annually. Government officials, oil companies, and civil society organizations oversee the process.

Kiir announced in December 2011 that South Sudan would join the initiative; a proposed Petroleum Revenue Management Bill would also require the finance ministry to report oil revenues on a quarterly basis and have independent audits of production costs and revenue expenditures. In its 2008 Oil and Gas Policy, Uganda said it would apply for membership in the EITI, but it did not say when and nothing has been implemented, according to news reports. "The way the EITI section is drafted clearly shows a government that is not sincere or ready to implement—it's so vague," Kamugisha of the Africa Institute for Energy Governance said in describing the Ugandan policy. Kenya has made no commitment to join the Initiative. Eddie Rich, deputy head of the EITI secretariat, confirmed that South Sudan and Uganda have made public commitments to implement the initiative and said "international partners are working with those governments to progress toward official applications." None of the African countries working with EITI are disclosing information on compensation to local people affected by oil production, Rich said.

There are a few other reasons to hope governments will become less secretive. Yusuf Bukenya-Matovu, communications director for Uganda's Energy Ministry, said his department is "working very closely with the Ministry of Water and Environment and the Uganda Wildlife Authority to ensure environmental protection while oil and gas extraction activities are going on." An environmental impact assessment of the oil-rich Albertine Graben region was also expected to be made public soon, although local journalists said they were skeptical this would happen on schedule.

Global Witness's Wilkins says these measures are still a long way from matching transparency models such as Brazil's, where monthly oil production statistics are published on a state website and transparency is considered by many to be stronger than in the United States. But East Africa does not have to look overseas for mentors: Ghana, Liberia, and even the Democratic Republic of Congo publish oil contracts. "It took years, but contracts are now in the public domain," said Ghanaian development economist Charles Abugre, who vigorously campaigned for publication. Now Abugre and other individuals from Ghana are meeting with civil society leaders in Turkana to help them contend with the new oil discoveries in their remote region of Kenya. "In Turkana, they do not really understand contracts or the transparency obligations so they don't know how far to push," he told CPJ.

Coming late to the discovery of oil reserves may provide East Africa with the advantage of hindsight. "There must be a reason why God made us wait to discover oil," said Ndemo, the Kenyan Information Ministry official. "Perhaps he wanted us to learn from other parts of the world while at the same time working on an appropriate legal and institutional framework."

Tom Rhodes is CPJ's East Africa consultant, based in Nairobi. Rhodes was a founder of the Juba Post, *southern Sudan's first independent newspaper. He was the author of the 2012 CPJ report "Murder in Remote Kenya Reverberates Across Nation, World."*

In Government-Media Fight, Argentine Journalism Suffers

By Sara Rafsky

Guillermo Moreno, Argentina's secretary of domestic commerce and one of the government's most colorful figures, has been spotted with a range of striking accessories. In Congress, he was seen handing out traditional Argentine mini-cakes. In a picture taken on a government airplane, a balloon floats above his head. And during his state trip to Angola in May 2012, an aide was photographed distributing socks to poor children. All of this paraphernalia bears the same white background emblazoned with the simple words "Clarín Lies."

Grupo Clarín, which owns the country's most widely read daily newspaper, *Clarín*, as well as radio stations, broadcast and cable television outlets, and an Internet service provider, is Argentina's principal media conglomerate and one of Latin America's largest. It is also the principal adversary of President Cristina Fernández de Kirchner in a battle pitting her and media outlets aligned with her government against those opposed to it. The government's primary weapon is financial: It props up, through advertising, outlets with favorable editorial lines, while withholding that support from others, like *Clarín*. Critical media, in turn, relentlessly hurl reproach at the administration.

The consequence of this bitter fight is an intensely polarized press. On one side, Kirchner's critics accuse her of stifling press freedom by rewarding allied media and punishing—with regulation as well as advertising manipulation—unsympathetic outlets. On the other side, many believe that Clarín has too much power and leverages its huge media holdings to further its private business interests. Horacio Verbitsky, a renowned Argentine journalist and former CPJ International Press Freedom Awardee who has been closely aligned with the Kirchner administration, told CPJ that Clarín and another major media owner, La Nación, "started this fight, and they did it in defense of their own political-economic interests."

"Are we not going to investigate corruption?" countered a visibly angry Martin Etchevers, spokesman for Grupo Clarín. "Are we not going to say that the inflation numbers the government publishes are false? That's not polarization or political opposition," he told CPJ, slamming his hand on the table. "That's journalism." Actually, the credibility of journalism is at stake as outlets on either side devote increasing coverage to discrediting each other. Argentina's citizens are unable to trust publications and broadcasters for objective information on vital issues, such as corruption, inflation, crime, the safety of infrastructure, sputtering economic growth, and whether Kirchner will seek a third term in office. Since Argentina has no federal right-to-information laws, the lack of sources for objective news is especially damaging to the public. Mónica Baumgratz, a coordinator for the local press group Foro de Periodismo Argentino (FOPEA), told CPJ the situation is troubling. When all news gathering has been discredited, even the truth becomes suspect, she said.

It wasn't always this way. During the presidency of Kirchner's late husband, Néstor, who governed from 2003 to 2007, and early in Cristina Kirchner's first term, Clarín enjoyed a privileged relationship with the executive branch. Graciela Mochkofsky writes in her book, *Original Sin: Clarín, the Kirchners, and the Fight for Power*, that Nestor Kirchner was "genuinely fascinated" with Héctor Magnetto, the powerful longtime chief executive and president of Clarín, a liking that was reflected in regular, shared lunches and in the scoops Clarín was granted on government decisions. And it was Néstor Kirchner who approved the 2007 merger that gave Clarín control of one of the biggest cable companies in Latin America. The relationship changed in 2008, when the government increased farming export taxes and Clarín's coverage sided with the farmers striking in protest. The government accused the group of being biased because of its own economic interests in the agricultural sector. Clarín and La Nación, which owns several print and digital publications as well as its flagship newspaper, are the principal organizers of Expoagro, the country's largest annual agricultural fair.

Before their falling-out, Clarín received substantial advertising from the federal government, according to "Quid Pro Quo: Official Advertising in Argentina and its Multiple Facets," a report published by the nonprofit Poder Ciudadano in December 2011. But the author, Martin Becerra, an Argentine researcher and professor of communications at the universities of Quilmes and Buenos Aires, found virtually no federal government advertising on Clarín-owned channels between May and October 2011.

Government advertising—or "official publicity," as it is called in Spanish—is common in Latin America; its intended function is to keep citizens informed of public services and policies. Under Article 13 of the Inter-American Commission on Human Rights' Declaration of Principles on Freedom of Expression, discriminatory placement is prohibited, meaning it is not supposed to be used as reward or punishment for coverage of the government. A 2008 report by the Open Society Institute, however, found that the practice is widely unregulated and abused in the region, to the point of being a form of "soft censorship." In June 2012, President Rafael Correa of Ecuador said he would suspend all government advertising in Ecuadoran private media outlets with which he has been engaged in his own fierce conflict.

■ ■ ■

In Argentina, the distribution of and criteria for official advertising are unregulated and opaque at the federal, state, and local levels and across party lines. (The exception is the province of Tierra del Fuego, which adopted regulations in 2008.) Only two of 23 provinces fully answered information requests from Poder Ciudadano for reports on official publicity spending, Becerra told CPJ.

According to Andrés D'Alessandro, executive director of FOPEA, the use of government advertising has been a systemic problem for Argentine journalism throughout the country's history. Media outlets have long been susceptible to retaliation for critical reporting in the form of fluctuating official advertising, regardless of political affiliation. It has come into sharp focus recently, he said, because state spending on advertising under Cristina and Néstor Kirchner dramatically increased.

Becerra found that in 2010, the federal government became the country's principal advertiser, surpassing the corporations Unilever and Procter & Gamble to account for 9 percent of the total advertising market. That year, the national government spent roughly $278.6 million, compared with $10.5 million in 2003. The 2010 numbers rose sharply from the previous year due partly to the number of ads shown during the "Soccer for Everyone" program, which in August 2009 wrested away from Clarín the rights to broadcast top-tier soccer matches in Argentina. Clarín had shown the games on its cable sports channel for nearly two decades, and held the rights through 2014. The decision to make the matches available on public television was extremely popular, but critics said the move was intended to hurt Clarín while providing the government with primetime advertising opportunities in the year preceding the 2011 election. The matches are still flooded with government advertising that lauds the Kirchners and attacks the opposition.

Discrimination in ad placement has affected other media companies. Editorial Perfil, the country's largest magazine publisher, sued the government over its advertising policies and in March 2011, the Supreme Court of Justice ruled in Perfil's favor, saying the government must apply reasonable balance in its distribution of advertising. But seven months later, Perfil alleged, the government had placed only eight advertisements in its weekly publication—including one that stated: "The publisher of this newspaper has honored businesses that are being investigated . . . for human trafficking and slave labor." In March 2012, the Justice Department fined the executive branch for noncompliance, and on August 14 a federal appeals court upheld the decision and imposed a fine of $215 a day on the government.

Local governments have also engaged in ad discrimination. According to Becerra's report, the city of Buenos Aires—led by Mayor Mauricio Macri, a Kirchner foe—favors media groups like Clarín and La Nación at the expense of public media and pro-Kirchner outlets. Macri's government, however, represents only 1 percent of the advertising market in Argentina. According to FOPEA, the situation is worse for smaller, provincial media outlets, many of which are almost completely dependent on official advertising and therefore vulnerable to government pressure over their coverage. Marisa Rauta, director of the daily *Diario de Madryn*, told CPJ that when the provincial government of Chubut pulled all of its advertising in December 2010 after critical reporting by the daily, she had to cut the news staff in half and eliminate several sections. In March 2011, a local court ruled that the government had to reinstate advertising, but Rauta said the newspaper is still operating at reduced capacity.

The flip side of official advertising is that being friendly to the government pays. According to a study cited in several publications, the four newspapers belonging to Grupo Uno, a former foe-turned-ally of Kirchner, received $8.2 million in federal advertising in 2011, up from about $830,000 in 2010. The consultant separately found that the pro-Kirchner media group Veintitrés received $6 million—the most of any group—in the first four months of 2012. In comparison, Clarín received $109,000, down 61 percent from the same period in 2011. Clarín spokesman Etchevers has called the amount of resources given to these and other groups a "colonization of the media space," and an attempt to use public resources to build up a vast network of outlets which, depending on their level of commitment, are "para-official," "co-opted," or "pro-government" and depend entirely on official advertising to survive. (None of the articles named the private consultant who carried out the study. Some media analysts alleged the consultant was hired by Clarín, a claim the group denies.)

Roberto Caballero, director of *Tiempo Argentino*, a pro-Kirchner daily owned by Veintitrés, said that while he is troubled by official advertising's potential to "create zombie journalists" without editorial independence, he doesn't see a problem with the government giving his newspaper advertising at the expense of groups like Clarín and La Nación. "I think official advertising distribution should be regulated and egalitarian, but always in such a way that it benefits small media outlets" that receive less private advertising, he told CPJ. He noted that Clarín didn't object to the way advertising was distributed during earlier administrations, when it benefited and other newspapers suffered. "They are the ones who gorged gluttonously on the advertising pie for 40 years and now they want us to share the bit we have?" he asked. Grupo Uno did not respond to phone or email requests for comment.

A broad spectrum of journalists, academics, and civil society members interviewed by CPJ mostly said that censorship is not a concern in Argentina. But in a survey of 1,000 Argentine journalists conducted in 2011 by FOPEA, dependence on government advertising was ranked the third-most serious challenge facing journalism after low salaries and lack of professionalism. Fifty-eight percent of the subjects said they thought journalism in the country was "conditioned" and 72 percent said they thought the business departments at their outlets had influence in the newsroom.

The Secretary of Public Communication, which is responsible for the government's media policies, directs state media, and acts as the president's spokesperson, did not reply to repeated requests by phone or email seeking an interview. Publicly, the Kirchner government has dismissed concerns by stating that, at 9 percent, federal advertising is an inconsequential part of the overall advertising market.

■ ■ ■

In any case, the government has other tools at its disposal. In addition to handing out props that paint Clarín a liar, Kirchner's administration has accused the group of being a monopoly and even of committing crimes against humanity during the country's brutal military dictatorship of 1976 to 1983. Both Clarín and La Nación have been criticized for being silent about the crimes of the dictatorship, and many Argentines believe that alignment with the junta allowed them to build undue influence.

The Kirchners—widely credited with continuing the process initiated by President Raúl Alfonsín to bring some leaders of that dark era to justice—have accused Clarín and La Nación's ownership of colluding with the dictatorship to force the sale of Papel Prensa, the country's only newsprint manufacturer, from its original proprietor (whose family was later arrested and tortured by the junta). The newspaper groups have denied the charges; Clarín told CPJ in an emailed statement that the case was a "bastardization of the cause of human rights." An investigation by a federal court is ongoing. Clarín's owner was also accused of illegally adopting the children of people killed by the regime; those charges were disproved by DNA tests.

"The Argentine press never made a mea culpa for its journalistic coverage during the dictatorship. Clarín and La Nación, to varying degrees, never did either," D'Alessandro told CPJ. "So they have this open wound for [their detractors] to keep hitting and criticizing them and linking everything they do in the present with their role in the dictatorship." Clarín, in its statement to CPJ, said, "Within the context of that period, *Clarín* did have spaces for questioning [the junta] that were not exactly common in the press at the time," citing denouncements of persecution in the cultural sector and coverage of visiting delegates from the Inter-American Commission on Human Rights. La Nación did not respond to requests for comment.

In December 2011, Hebe de Bonafini, head of the legendary Argentine human rights group Madres de Plaza de Mayo—who has been criticized in some circles for being too closely aligned with the Kirchner governments—enacted a public trial against Clarín in Buenos Aires's main plaza for its alleged complicity with the junta. Public shaming of anyone associated with Clarín particularly incenses Miguel Wiñazki, *Clarín*'s editor-in-chief. "The business side of the company can defend themselves," Wiñazki told CPJ. "But the smearing of individual journalists is discrediting the entire field."

Much of that criticism has played out on publicly funded media. The most prominent forum for attacks is the television show "6,7,8," where hosts and their guests delight in insulting high-profile journalists such as Joaquín Morales Solá—a columnist at *La Nación* who spent over a decade at *Clarín*—who was targeted with sardonic medleys insinuating unseemly actions during the dictatorship and featuring superimposed pictures of his head on the body of a gorilla. Jorge Lanata, one of Argentina's most critical journalists, is another frequent target. When Lanata declared on his then-cable television show that the world was "laughing" at Argentina because of its government, "6,7,8" leapt to Kirchner's defense, running a montage of favorable international headlines.

Critics complain that this highly politicized content is broadcast with taxpayer dollars on a public station. D'Alessandro noted that lack of regulations for public media is a long-standing problem in Argentina. Verbitsky told CPJ: "It should behave neutrally and pluralistically, which it does not. If it was the only source of information, the situation would be intolerable." However, Verbitsky added, one must take into the account the vast media landscape in the hands of Clarín.

Kirchner has not been afraid to join the fray. She and her camp have classified opposing journalists and media executives as "Nazis" and "mafiosos." But many Argentines say that the critical media are also guilty of excessive, even absurd, rhetoric. Lanata has accused "6,7,8" of being "pure Goebbels" and the government of "being bothered by freedom" for saying they would go after him for smoking, illegally, on his network television show. Even Caballero, the director of the pro-Kirchner *Tiempo Argentino*, protested that he was "constantly being attacked in *Clarín* and *La Nación*."

Laura Zommer, a journalist with *La Nación*, said the climate is so charged that journalists are censoring themselves out of fear of how their reporting will be interpreted. When "everyone is classified as a friend or enemy, many prefer to stay quiet," she told CPJ. FOPEA agreed that this atmosphere is detrimental to the exercise of journalism. "You lose your sources, [the government] doesn't invite you to cover public events, they don't answer your questions at press conferences, and they launch smear campaigns against you," D'Alessandro said. Prominent reporters have complained about the scarcity of presidential press conferences (five in Kirchner's tenure as of late 2012) and allege that officials purposely deceive them. Kirchner told the Casa Rosada (Pink House, as the executive mansion is called) press corps in an informal chat that "for official information, there are my speeches. I'm not going to speak against myself," according to news reports. At the provincial and local level, CPJ research shows, journalists have also been at risk of physical violence for criticizing local governments.

■ ■ ■

A couple of government moves have brought the battle into the legislative and judicial arena. In December 2011, new legislation established newsprint as a commodity of public interest regulated by the government, and set productivity requirements for Papel Prensa, of which Clarín and La Nación are majority owners (the state is a third partner). The two media groups denounced the measure as another attack on the government's principal critics. Many analysts, however, described the move as necessary to counteract the companies' monopoly control over the newsprint market.

Similarly, a broadcast law passed in 2009 to replace a law dating back to the dictatorship era, is aimed at curbing monopolies and democratizing ownership and access to radio and television outlets, the government said. Opposition politicians said it was a means for the government to exert greater control over news content and force Clarín to give up some holdings. Under parts of the law, the company could lose a significant chunk of its assets, which include at least six dailies, eight magazines, four network television channels, six cable channels, five radio stations, a cable company, and an Internet service provider, as well as other businesses. As of December 2012, the divestment provision was held up in court as Clarín challenged its constitutionality. Clarín also claimed the government was not enforcing the provision among media groups with sympathetic editorial lines. "They are not looking to create new voices, they are looking to silence voices," Etchevers said. Kirchner has said the government will not make any groups divest until the legal fight with Clarín, which stands to lose the most, is resolved.

The pace of implementation has frustrated media analysts, including those who argued that breaking up Clarín was essential to make room for new media voices. Becerra, author of the study on government advertising and a staunch advocate for the legislation, told CPJ that all parties have played a part in the delay. "It's the government's responsibility for being so obsessed with the fight with Clarín that it is distracting them from implementing the law. They are only focusing on the aspects that go against Clarín," he said. At the same time, Clarín, who he said is "used to the government legislating in their favor," has impeded progress with its "army of lawyers." And the political opposition, which is aligned with Clarín, refused until 2012 to join the new media regulatory body created by the law.

Claudio Schifer, a director of the regulatory body, told CPJ that while "it takes some time to construct a new house," the government was advancing with its goal of opening up access to media outlets, citing the creation of university television stations and 14 radio stations run by indigenous communities. Journalists and analysts from across the political spectrum have praised programming on new state television stations devoted to education and culture.

To be sure, the Kirchners have made at least one big move for press freedom; even the most staunchly anti-Kirchner journalists praise the decriminalization of libel in cases of public interest in 2009. "Personally, I was probably more persecuted under Menem," said *Clarín* Editor-in-Chief Wiñazki, referring to former Argentine President Carlos Saúl Menem, who in the 1990s launched a series of criminal defamation complaints against critical journalists.

And an important factor in the outlook for Argentine journalists—one that sets the country apart from some other Latin American nations where the press is besieged by thin-skinned governments—is its independent judiciary. As shown by the Perfil decision, judges are not afraid to rule against Casa Rosada. Still, the government has shown no intent to comply with that decision and, other than fines, there are no apparent repercussions for noncompliance, media analysts said.

For many journalists, the most serious consequence of the dispute is not the blaring of headlines or the ownership of assets, but the long-term standing of the profession itself. In July 2012, after the critic Lanata and the pro-government journalist Víctor Hugo Morales—two of the most prominent figures in the Argentine press—traded a series of nasty allegations about each other on the airwaves, one journalist titled his piece about the episode, "Journalism loses."

Sara Rafsky is research associate in CPJ's Americas program. A freelance journalist in South America and Southeast Asia, she was awarded a 2008 Fulbright Grant to research photojournalism and the Colombian armed conflict.

Why Transparency Is Good for Business

By Matthew Winkler

T he notion that business is best where there is a free press probably provokes the same jaded response that Jake Barnes gave
a wistful Lady Brett Ashley in *The Sun Also Rises*: "Yes. Isn't it
pretty to think so?"

For all of the skeptics who say business has no need, much less a
desire, for a free press in the globalized economy of the 21st century,
there is evidence from China to Europe and North America to India
showing the opposite: Multinational companies are most successful
when they are grounded in countries where democracy and capital-
ism are dependent on a vigorous press. Any glance at the 50 largest
companies as measured by market capitalization shows the majority of
them originate where reporting is timely, rigorous, and deep. That's
because successful companies—and, in turn, robust markets and national
economies—rely on the confidence of shareholders and creditors.
These investors can't prosper without a diet of reporting that is accurate
enough to be actionable.

Investors must also feel assured that all buyers and sellers are on the same information diet; if data have been prematurely leaked to selective players, the investor in the dark has a higher chance of finding himself on the losing end of a trade. Potential investors in China have been wary of just that. Though that nation, the world's second-largest economy, was spared the reckless speculation related to the opaque and toxic debt that infected North America and Europe during the first decade of the new century, China's stock market still suffers from the perception that insider trading is rampant. The Shanghai Composite Index declined about 38 percent from November 2009 to November 2012—a disappointment attributed in part to premature disclosure of government data that benefits a handful of short-term traders at the expense of long-term investors.

Bloomberg reporters following markets in Beijing, Shanghai, Frankfurt, and New York revealed a pattern of insider trading on many of the key China National Bureau of Statistics data, including quarterly figures on gross domestic product, monthly industrial production, and the monthly producer price index. Too many government offices became accustomed to seeing the statistics before they were made public, He Keng, a former deputy head of the bureau, told Bloomberg. With no historical precedent for punishing insider trading on the government's economic indicators, the integrity of the markets became easily compromised.

News reports of such behavior have prompted an encouraging response. The National Bureau of Statistics now says it will punish anyone who engages in unauthorized release of data, which it says violates the Statistics Law. Those breaking the law are subject to warnings, demotions, or dismissals, the bureau says. The head of the department, Ma Jiantang, told Reuters in March 2011 that it would also reduce the number of people with access to the data before publication and narrow the window between their calculation and release. In 2012, there were no reported anecdotes of insider trading on government data such as the consumer price index.

In Europe, where financial and commodities markets are most active, the historic indifference to insider trading on national economic statistics is diminishing. The German government recently acknowledged that it deploys fewer people to compile monthly unemployment figures as a way to limit leaks, Bloomberg reported. Britain similarly changed procedures so that its Office for National Statistics now shares data among government officials 24 hours before publication instead of more than

40 hours in advance, as it did in 2008. Enforcement of insider trading laws, including the prohibitions on deliberate unauthorized disclosure, is a strong deterrent to abuses. John Youngdahl, the now-deceased Goldman Sachs senior economist, was sentenced to 33 months in prison in 2004 for sharing government securities data before official release.

If U.S. Federal Reserve Chairman Ben S. Bernanke established anything during the global financial crisis, it is the concept that transparency increases accountability, which is essential for business to be successful. The Fed initially resisted disclosing information about its unprecedented loans to domestic and foreign banks, before complying with court orders affirming the public's right to know the recipients of taxpayer dollars deployed in the rescue. When the Fed belatedly complied with Freedom of Information Act requests by Bloomberg News, the revelations contributed to a robust understanding of the flow of money around the world, helping to pave the way for a recovery of the U.S. financial system. The Standard & Poor's 500 Index appreciated 86 percent from the first week of March 2009—which can be considered the market's bottom in the aftermath of Lehman Brothers' September 2008 bankruptcy—to the first week of November 2012.

■ ■ ■

Increased transparency has given the markets a boost in India. Duvvuri Subbarao, governor of the Reserve Bank of India, or RBI, is presiding over the biggest communications overhaul in the central bank's history. The RBI had long struggled to keep up with India's surging economy, with central bankers preferring to issue lengthy—and ambiguous— policy documents. Today, the RBI is more transparent in communicating decisions about interest rates, reducing the opportunity for insiders to trade on advance word of monetary policy. It had good reason to undertake the changes: The RBI has to be concerned about its standing in the government bond market, where foreign purchases have increased sixfold since Subbarao became governor in September 2008. At the same time, press reports showed that the central bank had been remote to most Indian citizens.

Now the RBI holds eight scheduled monetary policy meetings each year, or double the number from a few years ago. An increasingly vigorous financial press prompted the RBI in February 2011 to release the minutes of the 12-person technical advisory committee on monetary policy, which includes seven outside advisers, the governor, and deputy governor, Bloomberg reported. The records showed that the governor occasionally vetoes his external counsel, as he did on January 24, 2012, when he left borrowing costs unchanged for a second month after most outside advisers predicted a rate reduction. The RBI still has communication lapses, giving contradictory signals in January 2012 on the requirements it would place on lenders' cash-reserve ratios.

Still, "there is more clarity in the language of the policy statements and forward guidance on policy actions," N. S. Kannan, chief financial officer and executive director of ICICI Bank Ltd., India's second-largest lender, told Bloomberg. Subbarao "has made the RBI more transparent through an effective communication policy."

More information for global investors has led to more investment in India, accelerating economic growth and helping lift millions of people out of poverty. The drive to make the debt market more accessible and with fewer obstacles to overseas investment is paying off. Foreign purchases of government and corporate bonds increased to a record $31.5 billion in February 2012, from $5.1 billion in September 2008, the month Subbarao became RBI governor, according to data compiled by Bloomberg. "The changes are part of the opening up of India's economy and markets to the world—a necessary process if India is to meet its aspirations of becoming a global power," Bimal Jalan, who led the RBI for almost six years, until September 2003, told Bloomberg.

India's gross domestic product is now 10th in the world, up from 15th in 1993, according to International Monetary Fund data. "Earlier the RBI was quite secretive; even the language was very unclear and guarded," Tushar Pradhan, who manages about $1 billion as chief investment officer at HSBC Asset Management (India), said in an interview with Bloomberg. "The RBI has found that more information helps."

Matthew Winkler is editor-in-chief of Bloomberg News and a member of CPJ's board of directors.

9

THE INTERCONNECTED WORLD

How the Americas Failed Press Freedom

By Carlos Lauría

E cuadoran President Rafael Correa descended on the 42nd
general assembly of the Organization of American States in
Cochabamba, Bolivia, with a show of force and a determination to shatter precedent. Arriving with a delegation of several dozen
Ecuadoran officials, Correa was the only head of state besides the host,
Bolivian President Evo Morales, to attend the OAS assembly, traditionally a gathering of foreign ministers. But merely breaking protocol was
not his goal.

Shouldering aside what was supposed to be the assembly's main
agenda item, food security, Correa blasted the human rights arm
of the OAS and urged the organization's 34 member states to enact
drastic changes. "Neocolonialism is over," he declared in a confron-
tational, hour-long speech that cast the Inter-American Commission
on Human Rights (IACHR) and its special rapporteur on freedom of
expression as foreign policy tools of the United States that trample on
the sovereign decisions of member states.

That Correa and an allied OAS bloc would make such a case was not surprising. The Ecuadoran president has been at odds with the commission ever since it denounced his use of criminal libel laws to retaliate against critics in the press. But Correa accomplished far more. He and his allies won preliminary decisions that could gut the system that protects human rights and press freedom. And he did it with the tacit support of regional heavyweights such as Brazil.

"It is extremely grave that a group of countries with serious human rights and institutional problems are seeking to dismantle the Inter-American system," said Santiago Cantón, who served as the human rights commission's executive secretary until leaving office shortly after the June 2012 Cochabamba assembly. "Countries that should be leading the defense of the system—Brazil, Argentina, Colombia, and Peru—unfortunately are not doing so for various reasons," said Cantón, who now directs the Robert F. Kennedy Center for Justice and Human Rights.

In sum, the Ecuador-led bloc won initial approval for a series of changes that would prevent the rapporteur's office from publishing in-depth reports on freedom of expression, bar it from seeking independent financial support, and place it under greater control from member states. The changes are part of a broader overhaul of the IACHR's mandate that will come before the General Assembly for debate in 2013. As now outlined, the overhaul would limit the commission's ability to issue recommendations, known as precautionary measures, that call on member states to take immediate, corrective action in cases of grave human rights abuses.

Although in theory the plans could be derailed, many analysts believe some dismantling of the human rights system is inevitable. "The commission's autonomy suffered a big blow," said Peruvian journalist Ricardo Uceda, executive director of the regional press group Instituto Prensa y Sociedad, or IPYS. Under the plans, he said, the very governments being monitored for potential human rights violations would be allowed to set the terms of the monitoring. "From now on," Uceda said, "governments will be able to grab scissors and make custom-tailored suits."

■ ■ ■

Throughout its long history, the OAS human rights system has served as the last line of defense for citizens facing abusive treatment throughout the hemisphere. It has intervened directly in cases of imminent danger—ordering governments to provide security for threatened journalists, for instance—and issued in-depth reports that shine a light on systemic human rights abuses. Widely seen as an international model, the commission and its rapporteur have upheld such fundamental democratic principles as due process, separation of powers, and freedom of expression.

Yet the human rights system did not simply fall victim to an aggressive onslaught by regional leaders who oppose its core mission. It was also left undefended by other regional leaders who had individual grievances with commission decisions and who appeared dissatisfied with the commission's recently expanding portfolio.

The charge to weaken the system was led by Ecuador and the bloc known as the Bolivarian Alliance for the Americas or ALBA, which also includes Venezuela, Bolivia, Nicaragua, Cuba, Dominica, Antigua and Barbuda, and Saint Vincent and the Grenadines. At the Cochabamba meeting, the ALBA members threatened to pull out of the human rights body if it was not restructured to their liking (and, in fact, Venezuela announced its withdrawal from the American Convention on Human Rights in September 2012). Several ALBA countries have poor press freedom records. Correa's government, for example, has enacted a series of laws to restrict free expression, smeared critics as liars, and filed criminal cases against detractors. Many of his actions mirror ones taken by the Venezuelan government of Hugo Chávez. Cuba has among the harshest anti-press laws in the world, while the Bolivian and Nicaraguan governments have fashioned policies adversarial to journalists.

The sort of proposals promoted by Ecuador and the ALBA bloc would normally have been examined by the IACHR itself, which would then make its own decision whether to adopt them. The process is designed to insulate the IACHR from political pressures brought by member states that, invariably, come under criticism from the commission from time to time.

But in Cochabamba, ALBA took advantage of member states' weakening support for the human rights system, persuading the

General Assembly to allow its proposal to move forward outside the usual review process. Instead of having the IACHR make its own determination, the OAS Permanent Council, made up of ambassadors from member states, has been charged with drafting a statutory overhaul that will encompass the ALBA recommendations. The full General Assembly is scheduled to take action on the overhaul in March 2013.

ALBA also exploited the OAS practice of deciding issues by consensus, rather than by roll-call voting. Only Costa Rica, the United States, and Canada went on the record in Cochabamba defending the human rights system and urging that the ALBA proposals go through the normal review process. Other nations were effectively silent—and their silence amounted to support for the Ecuador-led plan.

Most notable in its failure to defend the system was Brazil—whose leaders were still angered by a 2011 IACHR ruling that called on President Dilma Rousseff's government to suspend construction of the Belo Monte dam in northern Brazil. Scheduled for completion in 2015, the $17 billion hydroelectric project had been a source of controversy since indigenous communities and environmental activists argued that it could flood an estimated 195 square miles of Amazonian rain forest and displace thousands of people. Officials disputed the contention and countered that the dam would provide electricity for 23 million homes.

In its decision, the IACHR found the Brazilian government had not properly consulted with indigenous groups and recommended it take steps to protect local tribes and make environmental and social impact statements available in local languages. An angry Rousseff, who had overseen the project as energy minister before becoming president, suspended Brazil's annual contribution to the OAS in 2011 and withdrew the country's OAS ambassador. (Brazil also ignored the IACHR's recommendations, although a domestic federal court halted dam construction in August 2012 on similar grounds that indigenous groups had not been properly consulted.)

"Brazil overreacted and has since launched a systematic attack against the commission," said José Miguel Vivanco, director of Human Rights Watch's Americas division. "It is disappointing that a country that aims to take over global responsibilities, including on human rights issues, continues to boycott the commission after it requested information on the impact of the dam on indigenous populations."

Brazil has tried to draw a distinction, saying that while it supports the human rights system, the commission has overreached. Brazil's OAS mission did not respond to CPJ's request for comment, but in an op-ed published in the Argentine daily *Página 12*, Rousseff adviser Guilherme de Aguiar Patriota argued that it is not the commission's job to interfere in the construction of a dam. He appeared to challenge the integrity of the commission's precautionary measures, saying the recommendations should be "substantiated" and based on "objective" criteria.

In the past decade, the IACHR has chosen to expand its portfolio, adopting a more ambitious agenda that includes labor, indigenous, and gay rights issues of exclusion and inequality, and deteriorating institutional practices among democratic states. "This new agenda has created tensions with governments as economic development programs clash with human rights issues, for example in the case of Brazil," said Roberto Saba, dean of the law school at Palermo University in Buenos Aires, Argentina.

Argentine officials, while saying they support the system, have hinted at such tensions. Federico Villegas Beltrán, human rights director at the Ministry of Foreign Affairs, said the system is in crisis because communications between the states and the commission have failed. "There is also a lack of reflection within the system that has affected the IACHR. The commission has to adapt itself to the new political reality," said Villegas, alluding to the growing influence of nations unreceptive to the OAS' human rights mission. He said Argentina would "avoid anything that debilitates the system," and defend the commission's autonomy and independence.

Still, Argentina's passivity in response to the ALBA offensive was significant. "Argentina has been the commission's strongest supporter since the restoration of democracy in 1983," said former IACHR executive secretary Cantón. "Now, after 30 years, it has changed its position. It is a step in the wrong direction." Peruvian press leader Uceda was dismayed as well. He said that while Argentina used politically correct rhetoric, its inaction allowed the restrictive ALBA proposal to advance.

Without the support of Brazil and Argentina, the system's staunchest defenders were the United States and Canada. They are also perhaps its most ineffective. Neither country has ratified the American Convention on Human Rights, reflecting their beliefs in the pre-eminence of their own legal systems. That position has left them incapable of parrying nations such as Ecuador, which also invokes sovereignty in making its case to rein in the regional human rights system.

The IACHR may act in contentious cases against all OAS members, including Canada and the United States; in fact, it has issued critical reports on U.S. immigration policies, executions, and Guantánamo Bay detentions. But Canada and the United States are outside the reach of the OAS judicial arm, the Inter-American Court of Human Rights. The distinction is not merely bureaucratic. The court is the primary means of enforcing IACHR recommendations when member states are reluctant to follow through on their own.

■ ■ ■

OAS Secretary General José Miguel Insulza, a Chilean, said publicly that he would oppose efforts to weaken the human rights system, but his actions in Cochabamba were not consistent with those statements. In response to the ALBA offensive, Insulza proposed an overhaul of the statute that governs the IACHR's actions. His proposal broadly outlined changes that would allow governments to set the terms of IACHR monitoring, impose delays in the publication of IACHR findings, and restrict the IACHR's power to issue precautionary measures.

Although the details were to be hashed out at the Permanent Council, the contours of the discussion had been set in Cochabamba. Cantón, the IACHR's former chief, is highly critical of Insulza's role. "He has been the main critic of the commission and the driving force behind the calls for change," Cantón said. Efforts by Insulza to limit the commission, Cantón said, are worse than the offensive by ALBA given the secretary general's position and his stated respect for human rights.

Insulza's broad proposal, if adopted in detail, would debilitate the human rights system, said Vivanco of Human Rights Watch. "Both the commission and its rapporteur on freedom of expression will become irrelevant," he said. "A vital layer of human rights protections for citizens throughout the region will be stripped if this happens, and people will be vulnerable to violations." The proposal would also set a precedent, representing as it does the first changes in IACHR's mandate not to be adopted by the commission on its own. "This decision would break the rule of the commission's autonomy by giving states, some of them declared enemies of the IACHR, the possibility of introducing changes," said Vivanco. "It legitimatizes the weakening of the system."

Insulza did not respond to CPJ's written request for comment. In Cochabamba, Insulza said, "The OAS and its member states need an autonomous and strong commission and an autonomous and strong court of human rights. But these bodies also need to take into consideration, in the course of their work, the points of view of the democratic governments of the hemisphere." He said he hoped the "assembly will adopt, with the necessary prudence" the recommendations set in motion by ALBA.

Nations such as Mexico, Panama, Chile, and Uruguay could play an important role in softening final details of the overhaul when the OAS assembly convenes in 2013, some analysts said. Those four nations, which have expressed general support for the commission's autonomy, could join with the IACHR's strongest supporters to turn the consensus against the most repressive bloc. "It is important to work at the national level to oppose those countries with an agenda aimed at debilitating the system," said Argentina's Saba.

The IACHR, created in 1959 and composed of seven independent members elected by the OAS General Assembly, played a key role in documenting, and reporting abuses committed by dictatorial regimes in the 1970s and 1980s. As democracy took hold in the region, the system began to address the legacy of the dictatorships and their impact on democratic institutions. The commission was instrumental, for example, in documenting and condemning the systematic disappearances and torture that occurred under Peru's Alberto Fujimori in the 1990s.

The special rapporteur on freedom of expression, created in 1997, has emphasized the need to end impunity in crimes against the press, denounced government censorship, campaigned against criminal defamation laws, and promoted access to information. Thanks to its efforts, laws criminalizing *desacato*, or disrespect, have been repealed in Paraguay, Costa Rica, Peru, Chile, Honduras, Panama, Nicaragua, Uruguay, and Bolivia. Mexico has decriminalized defamation laws at the federal level, while Argentina eliminated libel and slander on matters of public interest. Through the 2000s, the office highlighted indirect censorship brought about by inequitable distribution of government advertising and radio and television licenses.

"In a period where freedom of expression is at stake in the Americas, the weakening of the rapporteur will have extremely negative consequences for free expression," said Cantón, who was the IACHR's first rapporteur. The rapporteur has also had a significant impact on the lives of individual journalists. When Colombian journalist Claudia Julieta Duque discovered in 2009 that she was being followed and her communications intercepted by the national intelligence service, for example, the IACHR intervened and called on the state to guarantee her personal safety.

The nine-year legal battle of Mauricio Herrera Ulloa, a reporter with the Costa Rica–based daily *La Nación*, also serves as an example. Herrera was convicted of criminal defamation charges in 1999 after his articles in *La Nación* cited European press reports of alleged corruption by former Costa Rican diplomat Félix Przedborski. A local court ordered Herrera to pay Przedborski a fine equivalent to 120 days of wages and put the journalist's name on an official list of convicted criminals. After the Costa Rican Supreme Court rejected *La Nación's* appeal in January 2001, the newspaper and the journalist filed a petition with the IACHR. In effect, they said, Costa Rica was making it a crime to question the conduct of a public official.

In 2003, the IACHR submitted the case to the Inter-American Court and asked it to dismiss the verdict against Herrera. A year later, in a landmark decision, the court found that Costa Rica had violated Herrera's right to freedom of expression under the American Convention. The court ordered Costa Rica to dismiss Herrera's conviction and pay the reporter US$30,000 in damages and legal fees.

"If it weren't for the court's decision, I would have been neutralized in my work as a journalist, stigmatized, and would have abandoned the profession," said Herrera, who today is the director of the weekly magazine *Semanario Universidad*. Herrera said the court's decision gave *La Nación* and the entire Costa Rican press corps the confidence to do in-depth reporting on matters of public interest. In fact, *La Nación* went on to conduct investigations that led to the prosecution of three former presidents on political corruption charges.

The case shows why individual leaders of member states would have a powerful incentive to undermine an independent human rights monitor. But it also underlines the far greater value in protecting the rights of all citizens. "The ruling was not only important for me personally and for the Costa Rican press," said Herrera, "it was essential for the public and ultimately for the democratic system."

Carlos Lauría is senior coordinator for CPJ's Americas program. He has led CPJ missions to Ecuador, Venezuela, Argentina, Brazil, and Bolivia.

Repressive Hosts Tarnish The Olympic Image

By Kristin Jones and Nina Ognianova

S ochi, a Russian resort city that sidles up to the Black Sea, is preparing to give the world an eyeful in the Winter Olympics of 2014. Figure skating fans are already speculating on Kim Yu-na's chances for another gold. Lindsey Vonn has tested the ski terrain, and Russians are pinning hopes on their hockey team's chances in the new Bolshoy Ice Dome. But all that is yet to come. In 2012, the dominant image from Russia for many global audiences was a glass cage confining members of the feminist punk rock band Pussy Riot, on trial for "hooliganism" in connection with their protest against President Vladimir Putin. Three band members were convicted, and two were sent in October to remote prison camps.

These competing images present a challenge not only for the organizers of Russia's first Olympics in the post-Soviet era, but also for the International Olympic Committee, or IOC. In Beijing, the IOC found itself in the crosshairs for a summer Olympic Games whose gleaming success was set on a stage of tired repression. The contrast renewed debate over the role of human rights and the free exchange of information in granting and organizing a prestigious international event like the Olympics: Does the IOC have an obligation to hold host governments to account for repression, censorship, and human rights abuses? Can host-city obligations to allow news media the freedom to report on the Games be met in an environment in which journalists' physical safety is threatened or dissent is silenced?

In Russia, a crackdown on free expression and a strong anti-foreign climate threaten another collision with the Olympic goals of peace and mutual respect, and the guarantees of media freedom to report on the Games. And the debate is not limited to Sochi. Among the three finalists to host the 2020 Summer Olympics is Istanbul, where a government anti-terrorism campaign has lately landed dozens of journalists in jail and put serious constraints on the free flow of information. The IOC will have an opportunity when it chooses the 2020 host, and again when it negotiates its contract with the organizers, to take a stronger stance on these issues.

■ ■ ■

The Olympic Charter, a foundational document at the heart of the Games, sets out goals much broader than simply holding sports competitions. The charter espouses "social responsibility and respect for universal fundamental principles." The Olympic goal, as the charter puts it, "is to place sport at the service of the harmonious development of humankind, with a view to promoting a peaceful society concerned with the preservation of human dignity." It says any person or organization belonging to the Olympic movement—including national Olympic committees and host-city organizing committees—"is bound by the provisions of the Olympic Charter and shall abide by the decisions of the IOC."

Among the principles enshrined in the Olympic Charter is media freedom. "The IOC takes all necessary steps in order to ensure the fullest coverage by the different media and the widest possible audience in the world for the Olympic Games," Rule 48 of the charter decrees. "All decisions concerning the coverage of the Olympic Games by the media rest within the competence of the IOC."

Olympic officials say they take these objectives seriously. "The International Olympic Committee strongly believes that the Olympic

Games are, above all, a force for good, which can have a positive impact on the social development of a country," IOC spokesman Mark Adams told CPJ. However, being a force for good "does not mean the Olympic Games are a panacea for all ills and can solve all of the world's problems," Adams said, reaffirming statements made by IOC president Jacques Rogge in Beijing that the IOC is not a political body.

When it comes to media freedom, the IOC has, at least publicly, limited its involvement to those journalists specifically accredited to report on the Games. "The media were able to report freely from Beijing during the Games," Adams said. And few would argue that China starved them of the most striking competitive moments, such as Usain Bolt's world-record 100-meter sprint. But this approach under-estimates the extent to which journalists—foreign or domestic, accred-ited or not—share an ecosystem. "It's not possible just to guarantee the right to report on sporting events" and not other news, said Minky Worden, director of global initiatives at Human Rights Watch. "That's not even a wall that can be enforced."

The thousands of journalists who traveled to Beijing for the sole purpose of covering the Olympic Games felt the immediate effect of censorship. They arrived to find that they couldn't retrieve some news, information, or opinions, including from some international outlets, because certain websites were blocked—as they are for everyone in China. "It was an unprofessional working environment," Worden said, "and the IOC was responsible for that."

More crucially, between July 2001, when the IOC granted Beijing host city status, and August 2008, when the Games started, China jailed dozens of domestic journalists, fired or demoted progressive editors, and suppressed critical coverage. CPJ met twice with IOC officials to relay concerns about censorship and the treatment of journalists, but they made clear to CPJ that this was not their problem. "It is not within our mandate to act as an agent for concerned groups," Olympic Games Executive Director Gilbert Felli told CPJ in Lausanne in 2006.

Just before the Games, mainland journalists received a 21-point set of do-not-report instructions, including a specific edict not to report on food safety issues, Hong Kong's *South China Morning Post* said at the time. This was deadly timing. In September, after the Games were over, Chinese media broke the news that infant formula and other dairy products sold across the country were contaminated with melamine, an industrial chemical. Six infants died, and more than 50,000 infants and young children were hospitalized, the World Health Organization said later. A functioning local press could have prevented the tragedy; the first complaints had come as early as June.

In the run-up to the Games, the government also promised to give international correspondents greater latitude. On paper, the authorities relaxed travel restrictions in January 2007; foreign journalists were told they no longer needed advance permission from provincial authorities to conduct every interview, and that they were free to visit "places open to foreigners designated by the Chinese government." Nonetheless, international reporters continued to be harassed and occasionally detained, and they were blocked from reporting fully on protests, ethnic riots, and arrests in western China and Tibet.

And after the Games, local authorities returned to their more repressive ways, said Melinda Liu, who was president of the Foreign Correspondents Club of China from 2005 to 2008. "Access became more unpredictable, and foreign correspondents increasingly found themselves turned away, detained, harassed, and relieved of documents or reporting paraphernalia," Liu said. "In the months and years after the Games, the pendulum swung back toward greater restriction of media access."

■ ■ ■

The conditions for Russia's press are in many ways different from the Chinese media environment. Rather than running up against official censorship or jail, Russian journalists have historically been more likely to face threats, attacks, and even murder for reporting on corruption or human rights abuses. Russia ranks ninth-worst worldwide on CPJ's Impunity Index, which spotlights countries where journalists are murdered regularly and killers go free. The apparent lack of will to prosecute attacks on journalists hints at a link between political power and criminality, and the climate of fear results in diminished investigative reporting.

The Games will be held at a time of narrowing freedom for domestic journalists and official suspicion of international actors. President Putin's third term in office kicked off in 2012 with the passage of restrictive laws as well as harassment and prosecution of dissenters, including the jailing of Pussy Riot. In July, Putin signed a new criminal defamation law—reversing a 2011 measure that had decriminalized the offense—and set a maximum fine of $150,000, a prohibitive amount for news outlets not affiliated with the state. The same month saw passage of a new Internet law allowing the authorities to block websites that meet vaguely defined criteria, such as "making war propaganda" and "inciting inter-ethnic hatred." The blacklist of websites will be in the hands of a government agency, and the new law gave rise to many questions about its technical and legal implementation. A third newly signed law requires nongovernmental organizations that receive funds from overseas to register as "foreign agents."

Also in 2012, Russia expelled international organizations, such as the United States Agency for International Development and UNICEF, the United Nations children's agency. In November, Putin signed legislation that broadened the definition of high treason and gave the authorities wide-ranging rights to criminally prosecute individuals who consult with foreigners. The law—which was introduced by the Federal Security Service, successor to the Soviet-era KGB—could spell trouble for local journalists who work for international media outlets.

As in China, Russian authorities have a tendency to squeeze the press in the name of national security. In Beijing, the Olympics empowered security agencies to act with fresh zeal against protesters and critical domestic journalists. "You could very easily see a similar thing happening in Russia," said Worden of Human Rights Watch.

Holding the Olympic Games does require intensive security efforts to protect the athletes and the thousands of other visitors. But in Russia, legitimate efforts to augment security have too often bled into attempts to suppress nonviolent critical voices. This is particularly true in the North Caucasus—a group of Russian republics near Sochi. The volatile region, where Russia has long fought a separatist movement, is plagued by violence committed both by armed guerrillas and Kremlin-supported local authorities. Fearing a popular uprising like the ones that toppled governments in Ukraine and Georgia and, most recently, in the Arab world, security forces have worked hard to shape public opinion. In recent months, Russian authorities have "inundated the Internet space with so-called news sources that portray the North

Caucasus as a chaotic, lawless region" where violence is endemic, said Nadira Isayeva, former editor of the embattled Makhachkala-based newspaper *Chernovik* and a recipient of CPJ's International Press Freedom Award.

"Against this backdrop, any forceful actions by federal forces in the Caucasus can be justified easily as necessary to preserve calm in a dangerous, violent region," Isayeva said. At the same time, "the process of isolating and eliminating independent journalists and media outlets in the North Caucasus has been completed already," Isayeva said. A series of unsolved journalist murders has eviscerated the nonstate media, leaving no independent watchdog to monitor government or guerrilla action in the area. In at least two of the murders, suspicions have fallen on the administration of Chechnya, CPJ research shows.

In Sochi, Human Rights Watch has noted several abuses specifically related to the large-scale Olympic preparation, including forced evictions and demolitions, exploitation of workers employed to construct venues, and arrests of villagers who have protested the building of a massive power plant. Journalists and activists who have drawn attention to these issues have come under attack, the organization has reported.

Publicly, the IOC is sanguine about Sochi organizers' ability to grant complete media freedom in this context. "Sochi pledges, in its bid book, excellent working conditions for the media at the Games," Adams told CPJ. "It also promises the media an open dialogue with the Organizing Committee, so that their needs are met, in their words, 'openly, honestly, and promptly.'"

These promises may not inspire universal confidence, given recent history in Beijing. But, Worden said, there are important ways in which international Olympic organizers have shifted their stance since 2008. Human Rights Watch believes that its persistent, long-term engagement with the IOC and with key national Olympic committees and corporate sponsors has produced results. With an eye toward near-term impact in Sochi and long-term reform, Human Rights Watch participated in the 2009 Olympic Congress in Copenhagen, the first time a human rights group had done so, according to Worden. The organization also submitted a formal proposal for a standing IOC committee on human rights that would set and apply human rights benchmarks for potential Olympic hosts.

It took two years, but in September 2011, partially responding to the Human Rights Watch proposal, the IOC issued a set of commitments, including that "the IOC will intervene … in the event of serious abuses, such as: mistreatment of people displaced due to Olympic venue construction; abuse of migrant workers at Olympic venue construction sites; child labor; improper restrictions on the media's freedom to cover the Games, including cultural aspects." Another commitment says that the IOC "will establish a system for correctly identifying and dealing with 'legitimate complaints' from official sources."

The IOC "has tons of power," Worden said. But it has to be persuaded to use it.

Both "governments and the IOC are most responsive when their image risks being tarnished," she said. "This is why the role of the media is so crucial—it helps amplify the 'name and shame' strategy."

■ ■ ■

Organizing the Olympics carries significant benefits for the host, such as attracting economic revenue and boosting a country's global standing. In return, the IOC adopts a formal role in providing standards and making assessments. In this context, it already demands strict compliance to a host of requirements—many of them commercial, such as rules on branding, corporate contracts, and hotel and transportation prices.

The IOC's main mechanism for holding host cities to its very specific requirements comes in the form of a legally binding contract. In the case of the 2012 Games in London, this contract—made public through a Freedom of Information Act fight in the U.K.—consisted of a 47-page document stipulating London's broad responsibilities, along with lengthy technical manuals describing specific obligations in detail. The IOC has the right to exact financial penalties, in the form of withholding revenue, if the city or the national Olympic committee fails to comply.

The technical manuals are adjusted every few years for different cities and situations. A public version of the technical manual for written and photographic press—written in 2001 and amended in 2005—is 187 pages long. It includes detailed demands related to media accommodation, specifying, for instance, that 24-hour food catering services should provide at least one hot dish at all times. It requires that media transport be provided free and that Wi-Fi be available in all Olympic media locations. It gives the IOC ultimate authority on media accreditation, and contains specific language on local press access.

Some technical manuals contain specific dated milestones to be met. They also nod toward broader social goals with assurances like this one: "As a responsible organization, the IOC wants to ensure that host cities and residents are left with the best possible legacy in terms of venues, infrastructure, environment, expertise, and experience."

Through the host contract, the IOC already intervenes—broadly and in detail, with implied and explicit judgments, and with legal authority. The question is not whether it intervenes in media access and protection, but how. Hot meals are nice. But complete freedom to report—on the Games or on anything else of importance—hangs more crucially on whether the country's journalists are jailed for their work, whether the Internet is free, and whether independent media are allowed to survive.

Istanbul is one of three candidate cities for hosting the Summer Games in 2020, along with Tokyo and Madrid; the IOC will announce the winner in September 2013. When it is assessing the ability of the potential hosts to guarantee the media's freedom to cover the Games, the IOC would be making an incomplete evaluation if it didn't consider the broader media context. Over the past three years, Turkey has used vaguely worded penal code and anti-terror statutes to imprison dozens of journalists in retaliation for their work. With at least 49 in prison as of December 1, 2012, Turkey is the world's leading jailer of journalists, surpassing Iran and China. Many of the jailed have spent months, even years, in detention without a court verdict, kept in limbo by a judicial system in urgent need of fundamental reform.

At the same time, Prime Minister Recep Tayyip Erdoğan has adopted a hostile attitude toward critical media, publicly chastising individual journalists and media outlets; instructing media owners to discipline critical reporters and commentators; suing columnists for defamation; and discouraging press coverage of the longstanding conflict between the Turkish military and the outlawed Kurdistan Workers

Party. Aslı Aydıntaşbaş, a columnist with the Turkish daily *Milliyet*, told CPJ that Turkey has not yet had a debate about the Olympics in relation to freedom of expression. "While I think it is important to link Turkey's press freedom record to its overseas outreach and reception, such a link has not yet been made."

The IOC will have the chance to ask its bidders hard questions. How can Istanbul guarantee complete media freedom to cover the Games when its recent history suggests authorities' discomfort with a free press? Does it plan to extend this freedom to all domestic media, including long-persecuted Kurdish journalists? What steps will organizers take to ensure that Olympic-accredited journalists will be working in an environment in which information is unconstrained? And how do officials plan to handle the security measures that the Games may require without cracking down bluntly on civil society and the exchange of ideas?

Aydıntaşbaş said she and her colleagues would "welcome any outside intervention to remind Turkish leaders that their stifling of free speech and redesigning of the media is costing Turkey a lot. It is reducing the quality of our democracy and taking away from the 'prestige' they are keen on building."

■ ■ ■

The IOC's hesitance to promote human rights is partly in deference to the vast diversity of cultures represented in the Games, said Bruce Kidd, a professor of kinesiology and physical education at the University of Toronto who has written extensively about the Olympics. The IOC "has intervened selectively. It's been slow, reluctant to push the fullest envelope of human rights," Kidd said. "That's largely because its overarching goal is to bring the world together for peaceful intercultural exchange. And if you create too high a bar, you can't get the whole world."

Kidd was an Olympic athlete himself. He competed as a distance runner in the 1964 Games in Tokyo, and has remained active in the Olympic movement. He's an honorary member of the Canadian Olympic Committee and was involved in preparing the bid for the Winter Olympics in Vancouver in 2010. Still, he believes that human rights and athletes' rights to expression and full participation took a beating in Beijing, while Olympic officials came out looking complicit. "As somebody who has identified with the Olympic movement, I was embarrassed," Kidd said.

Despite its professed policy of nonintervention, Kidd notes, the IOC historically has intervened when pushed—sometimes to great effect. He notes that an international campaign against apartheid forced the IOC to act—hesitantly at first, and then more forcefully—by expelling the National Olympic Committee of South Africa and preventing Olympic members from segregating sports by race, even on their own soil.

More recently, the IOC has publicly pushed its participating members to field female athletes and credited itself when each national team did so in London 2012. But its stance was the result of a hard-won fight waged first from the outside. A feminist organization called Atlanta Plus had few allies when it launched in the mid-1990s—when 35 national Olympic teams included no women.

Taking a more muscular, consistent stance on basic rights of expression would bolster the IOC's position, not erode it, Kidd said. More than a century after the start of the modern Olympic Games, he argues, the goal of bringing the world into the same tent has been met. More than 200 countries now participate in the Olympics, and the entire world has signaled support for the U.N. Declaration of Human Rights.

"Now that everybody's there, let's gradually raise the bar," Kidd said. "One way to do this is to ensure the freest and fairest exchange of information."

Kristin Jones, a New York-based reporter, was lead author of the 2007 CPJ special report "Falling Short: As the 2008 Olympics Approach, China Falters on Press Freedom." Nina Ognianova, CPJ's Europe and Central Asia program coordinator, was the lead author of the 2012 CPJ special report "Turkey's Press Freedom Crisis: The Dark Days of Jailing Journalists and Criminalizing Dissent." Ognianova reported from Moscow for three months in 2012.

Beyond Article 19,
A Global Press
Freedom Charter

By Joel Simon

The right to seek and receive news and express opinions is enshrined in international law, regional human rights agreements, and national constitutions the world over. The right has never been fully respected in practice, of course, and journalists have long faced imprisonment, violent attacks, and even murder in reprisal for their work.

But today, even as technology fuels a global communications revolution, a range of governments are challenging the very concept of press freedom, arguing that it is not a universal right at all but must be adapted to national circumstances. China, which has increased domestic censorship and surveillance, is leading the charge internationally. Freedom of expression groups need to raise the stakes with governments that are increasingly asserting that speech should be curtailed to accommodate culture, heritage, and threats to national security.

Consider Turkey, which CPJ has determined to be the world's leading jailer of journalists, with 49 imprisoned in direct reprisal for their work as of December 2012. The government of Prime Minister Recep Tayyip Erdoğan says it is not cracking down on free expression. Rather, it claims to be responding to a significant threat to national security.

In a country with a history of coups and insurgencies sometimes backed by elements in the media, the government's claims cannot be dismissed out of hand. But an October 2012, a CPJ special report found that most of the detained journalists were being prosecuted under vague laws that equate covering terrorism with aiding terrorism. The evidence in many cases consists of journalism itself: published stories, phone calls to sources, and discussions with colleagues.

Nedim Şener, a leading investigative journalist, faces up 20 years in prison on charges that his critical reporting somehow furthered an anti-government plot. Şener, who already spent more than a year in jail awaiting trial, says the government is trying to persuade the public that "the normal rules of law do not apply."

Limits on critical expression in Turkey go well beyond alleged threats to national security. Reporting seen as insulting the Turkish people or influencing court proceedings is also outlawed. And if Erdoğan had his way, insults would be off-limits as well. The prime minister told CNN's Christiane Amanpour in a September 2012 interview that while he accepts criticism he will not tolerate insult, apparently reserving for himself the authority to distinguish between the two.

■ ■ ■

In Latin America, President Rafael Correa of Ecuador also reserves the right to personally determine the limits of acceptable criticism and claims that efforts by the human rights body of the Organization of American States to uphold international legal standards are a threat to his country's sovereignty. In one well-documented instance, Correa brought legal action against one of Ecuador's leading dailies, *El Universo*, that resulted in prison sentences for top editors and a fine of $40 million. After the verdict was upheld by the country's Supreme Court, Correa issued a pardon, vowing he would "forgive, but not forget."

The criminal conviction of the *El Universo* journalists—based solely on critical speech—was challenged by the OAS special rapporteur for freedom of expression as a violation of the American Convention on Human Rights. Correa not only lashed out at the special rapporteur and the Inter-American Commission of Human Rights (IACHR), but he also bridled at the very notion that Ecuador was bound by international legal standards.

Joining forces with a bloc of like-minded Latin American leaders, including Hugo Chávez of Venezuela and Daniel Ortega of Nicaragua, Correa won preliminary approval from OAS member states for an initiative that would greatly limit the authority and range of action of the IACHR and the special rapporteur. The rules will go into effect if approved by the General Assembly in 2013. Venezuela, meanwhile, has taken the unprecedented step of withdrawing from the American Convention on Human Rights, a largely symbolic but highly charged gesture.

"Chávez sees the American Convention on Human Rights as an obstacle for his vision of Venezuelan society," said Claudio Grossman, dean of the American University College of Law and a former president of the IACHR. Grossman acknowledged the significant threat posed by Correa, Chávez, and others to the regional human rights system that has safeguarded freedom of expression throughout the Americas, but concluded, "I don't believe they will carry the day."

Threats to the international legal system that protects freedom of expression are emerging from many quarters. Leaders in the Islamic world have long asserted the right to restrict expression that offends religious sensibilities and have advocated within the United Nations for various resolutions condemning defamation of religion—an effort that, if successful, could make blasphemy an international crime. The debate over the limits of free speech and religion reached the floor of the U.N. General Assembly in September 2012 in the aftermath of the provocative video "The Innocence of Muslims" that mocked the Prophet Muhammad.

Speaking at the United Nations, U.S. President Barack Obama argued that freedom of expression is not an American or Western value, but a universal ideal. Obama said that "at a time when anyone with a cellphone can spread offensive views around the world with the click of a button, the notion that we can control the flow of information is obsolete." Egyptian President Mohamed Morsi pushed back, arguing that it was unacceptable for U.S. freedom of expression standards to be imposed through the Internet on the entire world and asserting that Egypt had no obligation to tolerate speech that incites hatred, deepens ignorance, or disregards others. Morsi's position was endorsed by many other governments, particularly those from the Muslim world.

The Chinese also view the global nature of the Internet as a threat—although their focus is on national security and stability—and say the United Nations should intervene. The Chinese vision is that the Internet should operate a bit like a national highway system that is part of the global network but subject to the specific laws and mores of each country. They have used a variety of means to realize this vision inside their borders: filtering foreign content (including recent exposés from international media outlets on the personal wealth of Chinese leaders) while censoring, intimidating, and prosecuting domestic critics.

China's job would be much easier if there were a centralized system of Internet administration beholden to the interest not of individual users but of sovereign states, inverting the current paradigm. Beijing's proposal for a U.N.-administered Internet is supported by many other nations, including Iran, which is trying to use Chinese technology to produce what it calls a "halal" or authorized domestic Web free of subversive political speech and religious criticism.

China does not reject outright international standards of freedom of expression, says Sharon Hom, executive director of the advocacy group Human Rights in China. Instead, it asserts that such standards must be adapted to "national circumstances" and that in China's case, restrictions are justified because of national security concerns. In the international arena, China shrewdly exploits Western concerns about the threat posed by cyberattacks and cybercrime, while building support for a global system of Internet control in the developing world by casting the Web as an essential piece of global infrastructure dominated by "U.S. hegemonic interests."

Hom argues that if Western democracies fail to confront China, Beijing's ability to build a global coalition that supports—or at least tolerates—Internet control and monitoring will be immeasurably strengthened. Democracies "cannot allow themselves to be held hostage to their fears," she said. "You can't allow the debate over the Internet to be captured by statist rhetoric."

■ ■ ■

Article 19 of the Universal Declaration of Human Rights adopted in 1948 states simply that "Everyone has the right to freedom of opinion and expression; this right includes freedom to hold opinions without interference and to seek, receive, and impart information and ideas through any media and regardless of frontiers." The International Covenant on Civil and Political Rights, a multilateral treaty adopted by the U.N. General Assembly in 1966, broadly reaffirmed this language but also outlined permissible restrictions to protect the rights and reputations of others, national security, and public health, so long as such restrictions are codified in law.

"That little phrase, 'regardless of frontiers,' is extraordinary even in the world of human rights agreements," points out Timothy Garton Ash, a professor at Oxford University and an expert on modern European history who is writing a book on global free expression. "Most human rights agreements are obligations and demands put on states regarding the way they treat their own citizens."

The transnational nature of the right to freedom of expression is echoed in regional human rights treaties such as the American Convention on Human Rights, whose Article 13 contains an explicit prohibition on prior censorship within the Americas. Though the nature of permissible restrictions has been a source of discussion and debate, regional human rights bodies such as the European Court of Human Rights and the IACHR have a strong record on freedom of expression issues. But with the legal principles that undergird press freedom under attack from many governments around the world, the risk that basic standards could be rolled back is real and increasing.

The key challenge is that the Internet and other modern communication technologies have made real the once-abstract ideal expressed in Article 19: that the right to freedom of expression transcends borders.

"Freedom of expression was extended with the spread of democracy in the latter half of the 20th century," noted Ash, who helped establish the website Freespeechdebate.com, which hosts a global discussion on freedom of expression in the digital age. "Today we have an emerging superpower, China, which has a 19th-century norm regarding state power. For many countries this view is attractive. They are very interested in China's example. Post-colonial countries across the board are able to say, 'Yes, you do have to pay regard to our frontier.'"

The Internet disrupts in two ways. First, it makes it difficult to control ideas, information, and images entering a country from outside. Some of the material available to Internet users around the world—from pornography to anti-religious screeds to exposés on human rights violations and corruption—are shocking or even destabilizing in countries that have long controlled the flow of information. Second, technology makes it easier to share news and information domestically and for political movements to build communities of opposition. The Arab Spring is the most striking example, but the Internet has proven a disruptive political force in countries from Iran to Vietnam. Governments in many places are seeking to control the Internet itself while simultaneously cracking down on individual online dissenters, including journalists.

But a 2011 report from the U.N. special rapporteur for freedom of expression, Frank LaRue, determined that the specific language of Article 19 anticipated the development of new information technologies. Thus, the same principles of international law that have long applied to the traditional media also apply to all Internet users the world over.

And although international law permits certain restrictions on the basis of threats to national security, there is no legal basis for the broad and sweeping restrictions imposed by countries like Turkey in the name of fighting terrorism. In 1985, a group of legal scholars developed the Johannesburg Principles on national security and freedom of expression. They declare: "No restriction on freedom of expression or information on the ground of national security may be imposed unless the government can demonstrate that the restriction is prescribed by law and is necessary in a democratic society to protect a legitimate national security interest. The burden of demonstrating the validity of the restriction rests with the government."

International law also does not permit restrictions on the expression of ideas that offend or shock religious beliefs, although advocacy for "national, racial, or religious hatred that constitutes incitement to discrimination, hostility, or violence" can be banned. But efforts to define what constitutes hate speech in an international context have been challenging, and governments have abused the concept to justify restrictions on legitimate and lawful criticism. Many African governments, for example, have argued that unfettered "Western"-style press freedom accentuates ethnic divisions. In Rwanda, where the role of local radio stations in fueling the 1994 genocide has been well documented, critical journalists are regularly prosecuted under laws criminalizing "incitement to tribal hatred" and "divisionism" and jailed or forced into exile.

Morsi and other leaders in the Islamic world have essentially made the same argument—that the global nature of the Internet imposes Western standards of free expression on nations that don't want to see their deeply held religious beliefs mocked and denigrated. Morsi has a point, but the converse is also true: Restrictions on freedom of expression imposed in the name of religion in Egypt, Pakistan, or Iran represent a form of global censorship that deprive the world of relevant and timely information that would otherwise be available online to international decision makers and global citizens.

The basic consensus supporting freedom of expression in international law is strong enough to push back firmly against autocratic leaders who seek legal and political cover for their restrictive policies. Simply put, there is no basis in international law for distinguishing between criticism and insult as Turkey's Erdoğan suggests; no basis for restricting speech that "deepens ignorance" or "disregards others" as Morsi proposes to do; and no basis for the broad restrictions on Internet content that China seeks. The criminal defamation lawsuits that Ecuador's Correa has used to bludgeon his media critics violate basic principles enumerated in Inter-American law. Correa's petulant attacks on the IACHR for upholding these rights are unwarranted and dangerous.

■ ■ ■

International law and jurisprudence are critical to the realization of the ideals expressed in Article 19, but so is political action. Defenders of freedom of expression must unite behind a clear, concise, and accessible statement of what the exercise of those ideals means in practice. What is needed is a global freedom of expression charter.

Precisely what should be included in a charter needs to be determined by civil society groups in consultation with legal experts. Certainly, government perspectives on issues like national security should be considered, and to the extent possible dialogue between national freedom of expression organizations and government officials needs to be encouraged. But there can be no compromise when it comes to the ideals enumerated in Article 19—ideals that unite people all over the world who are struggling to express themselves or access independent information.

Though there are various statements, principles, and declarations on freedom of expression and Internet freedom, many are technical, legal, regional, or narrow in scope. What is needed is a new document that does not merely restate principles that are long established in international law, but translates those principles into concrete and verifiable terms.

At a minimum a global freedom of expression charter should make clear that prior censorship, government control over the Internet, criminal defamation statutes, criminal blasphemy laws, and libel suits brought by high officials are incompatible with Article 19 guarantees. Threats or violent acts carried out by governments to curb the expression of criticism or ideas are always unacceptable and must be condemned. In fact, governments have an obligation to investigate crimes against freedom of expression, including attacks on journalists.

The charter should be formally endorsed by the global freedom of expression community, and individual governments should be pressured to declare their public commitment to its principles. Some leaders will readily embrace it; others can be compelled to do so; and many others will resist. The idea is to eventually build broad enough support that governments refusing to endorse the charter will be perceived as outliers. Governments that commit to the principles, meanwhile, should also agree to undergo a periodic independent assessment to evaluate compliance.

The growing attacks from intolerant leaders on the universality of the ideals enumerated in Article 19 of the Universal Declaration threaten not only critical journalists but also people everywhere who are using new technologies to express their ideas and stay informed. A consensus forged by civil society and converted into clear, attainable, and verifiable standards will not only support the work of the media but also help people everywhere realize the full potential of the information revolution.

Joel Simon is executive director of the Committee to Protect Journalists. He led two CPJ missions to Turkey in 2012.

10

TRENDS AND DATA

CPJ Risk List: Where Press Freedom Suffered

By Karen Phillips

E cuadoran law forbids the presidential family to benefit from state contracts. But after Christian Zurita and Juan Carlos Calderón's book, *Big Brother*, revealed that President Rafael Correa's brother had obtained $600 million in government contracts, they were the ones in trouble with the law. Zurita and Calderón were found guilty of defaming the president and ordered to pay $1 million in damages apiece. Correa later pardoned the two, having accomplished his goal of intimidating the nation's press corps. "It was clear that no small or medium-sized media outlet was going to take on major critical reporting against the government," Zurita told CPJ.

Correa's use of defamation lawsuits to silence dissent is one of several repressive government tactics that propelled Ecuador onto the CPJ Risk List, which identifies the 10 countries worldwide where press freedom suffered the most in 2012. CPJ, which is publishing its Risk List for the first time, also identified Syria and Somalia, which are racked by conflict, along with Iran, Vietnam, and Ethiopia, nations that are ruled with an authoritarian grip. But half of the nations on the

Risk List—Brazil, Turkey, Pakistan, and Russia, along with Ecuador—practice some form of democracy and exert significant influence on a regional or international stage.

In determining the list, CPJ staff examined six press freedom indicators: fatalities, imprisonments, restrictive legislation, state censorship, impunity in anti-press attacks, and journalists driven into exile. Countries named to the Risk List are not necessarily the world's worst places for journalists; such a list would include nations like North Korea and Eritrea, where free expression has long been suffocated. Instead, the Risk List identifies the 10 places where CPJ documented the most significant downward trends during 2012. Those trends included:

- High murder rates and entrenched impunity in Pakistan, Somalia, and Brazil.
- The use of restrictive laws to silence dissent in Ecuador, Turkey, and Russia.
- The imprisonment of large numbers of journalists, typically on anti-state charges, to thwart critical reporting in Ethiopia, Turkey, Vietnam, Iran, and Syria.
- An exceedingly high fatality rate in Syria, where journalists faced multiple risks from all sides in the conflict.

Threats to press freedom were not confined within the borders of these nations. Four Risk List countries sought to undermine international or regional press freedom initiatives during the year. Russia pushed for centralized control of the Internet ahead of the World Conference on International Telecommunications. Ecuador led an effort, supported by Brazil, to weaken the ability of the Inter-American Commission on Human Rights to intervene in cases of systemic or grave press freedom abuses. Brazil and Pakistan were among a handful of countries that tried to derail a U.N. plan to improve journalist security and combat impunity worldwide.

Setbacks in Brazil are particularly alarming given its status as a regional leader and home to a diverse array of news media. But a spike in journalist murders, a failure to address impunity, and a pattern of judicial censorship have put Brazil's press freedom at risk, CPJ found. Turkey, too, has projected an image as a regional model for freedom and democracy. But although Prime Minister Recep Tayyip

Erdoğan has expressed a commitment to press freedom, his administration has wielded an anti-terror law as a club to jail and intimidate journalists.

Less surprising, but no less worrisome are setbacks in Vietnam, Ethiopia, and Iran. Though Ethiopia and Vietnam have been applauded for economic strides, both countries have lagged in terms of openness and freedom of the press. Conditions worsened in 2012, as Ethiopian and Vietnamese authorities ramped up efforts to stifle dissent by imprisoning journalists on anti-state charges. Iran, ignoring international criticism of its press record, has intensified an assault on critical voices that began after the disputed 2009 presidential election.

In Syria and Somalia, where journalists faced risks from multiple sides, the death tolls have mounted. Crossfire was the leading cause of death for journalists in Syria, although at least three journalists were assassinated, CPJ research shows. Both rebels and forces loyal to President Bashar al-Assad have been implicated in acts of violence against the press. All 12 journalists killed in Somalia in 2012, the country's bloodiest year for the press, were targeted in direct reprisal for their reporting. Both insurgents and government officials were suspected of involvement. In both countries, the ranks of young journalists, many with little training and experience, have been particularly hard hit.

Here, in alphabetical order, are capsule reports on the 10 nations named to the CPJ Risk List:

Brazil

Four journalists were murdered in direct relation to their work in 2012, exceeding the three murders recorded in the previous year and making the country the world's fourth deadliest for the press during the time period, CPJ research shows. Six out of seven journalists killed in the past two years had reported on official corruption or crime and all but one worked in provincial areas. Brazil's judicial system failed to keep pace.

"The lack of serious investigations in these crimes has given aggressors the notion that they won't be identified and punished," said

Mauri König, a veteran investigative reporter who CPJ honored in 2012 with an International Press Freedom Award. Brazil ranked 11th on CPJ's 2012 Impunity Index, which calculates unsolved journalist murders as a percentage of each country's population.

Judicial censorship remains a problem in Brazil, where businessmen, politicians, and public officials have filed hundreds of lawsuits claiming that critical journalists have offended their honor or invaded their privacy, CPJ research shows. Plaintiffs typically seek court orders to bar journalists from publishing anything further about them and to have existing online material taken down. In the first six months of 2012, Google said, Brazilian courts and other authorities sent the company 191 orders to remove material.

"Such lawsuits undermine Brazilian democracy and its press, and create a climate of legal uncertainty which, to some extent, is reflected in the quality of coverage of issues of public interest," König told CPJ.

Brazil also failed to support press freedom on the global stage. In March, objections raised by Brazil and a handful of other nations nearly thwarted a U.N. plan to improve journalist security and combat impunity worldwide. Three months later, Brazil supported an Ecuador-led offensive to weaken the Inter-American Commission on Human Rights and its special rapporteur on freedom of expression.

Ecuador

Newly enacted legislation bars the news media from promoting political candidates "directly or indirectly" in the 90 days before an election. The law, backed by the Correa administration, also prohibits news media from publishing or transmitting any type of information, photos, or opinions about an election in the 48 hours leading up to the vote. The move was widely seen as benefiting Correa in his 2013 bid for re-election.

The president has made a practice of demonizing the press, routinely calling journalists "liars" if they don't parrot his government's views. "The administration has adopted a policy of generating polarization between the media and the government," Zurita said. Facing legal harassment, three journalists fled into exile in 2012, marking Ecuador's first appearance on CPJ's annual exile report, which tracks journalists forced to flee their countries. (Two of these journalists were later able to return.) In September, threats forced journalist Janet Hinostroza to take a leave of absence from her show on the private network Teleamazonas, where she had been investigating allegations of banking improprieties involving a presidential relative.

Though the administration maintained one of the most extensive state media operations in the hemisphere, government regulators closed at least 11 private broadcasters during the year. Although officials cited regulatory violations, most of the stations had been critical of the government.

Ethiopia

Ethiopian authorities wielded a sweeping anti-terror law to silence critics. In late year, six journalists languished in prison, making Ethiopia the second-worst jailer of journalists in the region, behind only neighboring Eritrea. Most detainees were jailed under the anti-terrorism law, which criminalizes coverage of opposition and separatist groups, CPJ found. "We only have a handful of independent newspapers and no private broadcast media—and the anti-terrorism law is killing those few that exist," said an Ethiopian journalist who spoke on condition of anonymity for fear of reprisal.

Four journalists fled Ethiopia in the face of possible imprisonment, CPJ's 2012 exile report found. At least 49 Ethiopian journalists have been forced into exile since 2007, the third-highest total worldwide. CPJ research indicates that journalists in exile face major obstacles to their health and safety, and only 17 percent are able to remain in their profession.

The suppression of news was reflected by the information vacuum surrounding the lengthy illness that preceded the August death of longtime Prime Minister Meles Zenawi. The government, which insisted Meles was fine until his death, shut the one domestic newspaper that tried to examine his weeks-long absence from public view. Journalists said they are not optimistic that conditions will improve under the new leader, Hailemariam Desalegn. The government "wouldn't want to allow any threat to the new leadership," the journalist said. "The media is one of the biggest threats they would want to avoid."

Iran

The authorities maintained a stranglehold on the press, imprisoning 45 reporters and editors as of December 1, 2012—the second-highest total in the world—while censoring online media and forcing journalists into exile. Imprisoned journalists are subjected to horrific conditions that include extended periods of solitary confinement, deprivation of medical care, and torture. In November, imprisoned blogger Sattar Beheshti died in state custody shortly after he complained of severe mistreatment.

At least four journalists fled the country, according to CPJ's 2012 exile report, joining at least 64 colleagues already in exile. Only Somalia has sent more journalists into exile since 2007. In addition to facing financial and legal worries, most exiled Iranian journalists live in fear of retaliation from their government, according to CPJ interviews. Several living in Turkey and Iraq have reported being followed or harassed by Iranian security agents.

Iran ranked fourth in the world for government censorship of the media, according to a CPJ analysis released in May. The mass imprisonment of journalists is just one of several tactics used by Iranian authorities to stifle dissent. Iran's Internet censorship apparatus is adept at blocking millions of websites, thwarting anti-censorship programs, and intimidating reporters via social networks. The government also jams satellite signals, including those of the BBC Persian-language service.

Pakistan

With seven journalists killed in 2012, Pakistan was the world's third-deadliest place to report the news, CPJ found. Five victims were killed in targeted attacks and four worked in restive Baluchistan, where journalists are increasingly caught between separatist factions and Pakistani military forces. "Government is doing nothing. They just condemn and beyond that there is no concrete action," said Umar Cheema, a reporter for Pakistan's English-language daily *The News*. Cheema, who was abducted and assaulted himself in 2010, also faulted media companies for not doing enough to protect their reporters.

With 19 unsolved journalist murders in the past decade, the country is ranked 10th on CPJ's Impunity Index, which highlights countries where journalists are murdered regularly and the killers go free. The combination of violence and impunity drove six Pakistani journalists into exile, twice the number that fled the previous year, according to CPJ's 2012 report on exiled journalists.

In March, Pakistan was among a handful of nations that tried to derail a U.N. plan to combat impunity worldwide. Although the plan moved forward, the country's continued opposition could weaken its effect.

Russia

A press freedom climate that had improved modestly under Dmitry Medvedev deteriorated within weeks of Vladimir Putin's return to the presidency in May 2012. Putin signed a series of restrictive bills aimed at stifling dissent and curbing the work of civil society. The legislation included harsh restrictions on nongovernmental organizations, and strict limitations on public assembly. Two measures directly affect the press: the criminalization of defamation (which had just been decriminalized under Medvedev), and a restrictive statute governing online content.

The new defamation law sets a maximum fine of 5 million rubles (US$150,000), an exponential jump from the 3,000-ruble fine that had been on the books previously. The fine is prohibitive for many independent and pro-opposition media in Russia, and the statute makes all media vulnerable to politically motivated prosecution. The Internet measure allows the authorities to block sites deemed to have "unlawful content." The law's vague definitions of unlawful content include "making war propaganda" and "inciting inter-ethnic hatred."

Journalists worry that the law will be used to silence critical views on the Internet, which has recently emerged as a home for independent news.

"As they say in Russia, the authorities are tightening the screws," said Nadezhda Prusenkova, a spokeswoman for *Novaya Gazeta*, one of a handful of publications that investigates official corruption in Russia.

With 16 unsolved journalist murders in the past decade, Russia has the world's ninth-worst record for combating deadly anti-press crime, according to CPJ's Impunity Index. CPJ documented one work-related murder in 2012, along with numerous assaults, threats, and cases of intimidation. Kazbek Gekkiyev, a news anchor for state-owned VGTRK, was shot and killed in the North Caucasus city of Nalchik in December.

Somalia

In a country with a long record of deadly violence, fatalities hit a new high in 2012 when 12 journalists were killed in direct relation to their work, CPJ research shows. A particularly bloody string of assaults in Mogadishu left four journalists dead in a 24-hour period in September. Although crossfire deaths have been common in the past in the conflict-ridden country, all of the journalists killed in 2012 were victims of targeted attacks.

"Everyone is armed, so there is a constant threat," said Abdulaziz Billow, Mogadishu-based correspondent for Iran's Press TV. In such a climate, he said, reporting is limited. "If you investigate a person, the next day you can expect to get a bullet in the head."

There is little to deter would-be assassins in Somalia, second-worst in the world in combating journalist murders, according to CPJ's Impunity Index. Not a single journalist murder has been successfully prosecuted since 1992, according to CPJ research. "People who kill journalists continue to walk freely in town the next day," Billow said. "Without functioning government institutions, the killers of journalists are not prosecuted."

Unchecked violence drove at least seven Somali journalists into exile, more than any other nation in the world, according to CPJ's

2012 exile report. At least 78 journalists have fled Somalia since 2007, devastating the country's press corps.

Syria

As it spiraled into civil war, Syria became the world's deadliest place for journalists. At least 28 journalists were killed and two others went missing between January 1 and December 10, 2012, CPJ research shows. Local reporters and citizen journalists made up the vast majority of those killed, although at least four international correspondents also died on assignment. Photographers and videographers faced particularly high risk.

"When you try to take photos of violence, at any moment you could be killed either in shelling or crossfire," said Sami al-Rifaie, 23, a citizen journalist who works outside the city of Homs. "On the other side, you have the government that is trying to find you, capture you, and punish you to make an example out of you for other activists." Though CPJ research shows that government forces loyal to President Bashar al-Assad are behind many of the fatalities in Syria, some recent attacks against journalists and news outlets seen as pro-government have been attributed to rebel forces.

Syria ranked third on CPJ's list of most-censored countries this year as the Assad government sought to suppress independent coverage of the uprising. In addition to disabling phone networks, electricity, and the Internet, the authorities have been implicated in malware attacks against reporters and have used torture to extract the online passwords of journalists. At least 15 journalists were imprisoned when CPJ conducted its worldwide census on December 1.

Turkey

With 49 journalists imprisoned for their work as of December 1, 2012, Turkey emerged as the world's leading jailer of journalists, CPJ research shows. An October 2012 CPJ special report found highly repressive laws, particularly in the penal code and anti-terror law; a criminal procedure code that greatly favors the state; and a harsh anti-press tone set at the highest levels of government.

Kurdish journalists, charged with supporting terrorism by covering the views and activities of the banned Kurdistan Workers Party, made up the majority of the imprisoned journalists. They are charged under a broadly worded anti-terror law that allows the authorities to conflate reporting activities with engaging in a terrorist enterprise. More than three-quarters of the imprisoned journalists had not been convicted of a crime but were being held as they awaited resolution of their cases.

Erdoğan has made a habit of filing defamation lawsuits and lashing out publicly at critics in the press and calling on media owners and editors to rein them in. "We are at the mercy of the government," said one journalist, who spoke on condition of anonymity. "If I write something that [Erdoğan] gets mad about, he can get me fired the day after." In this context, self-censorship is the key to remaining employed and out of jail.

Vietnam

With at least 14 journalists behind bars, Vietnam is Asia's second-worst jailer of the press, according to CPJ's annual worldwide census. Many of those detained have been charged or convicted of anti-state crimes related to their blog posts on politically sensitive topics. A 2012 CPJ special report found that Prime Minister Nguyen Tan Dung's administration has targeted online journalism by imprisoning bloggers and enacting restrictive legislation.

The Communist Party–dominated government controls all traditional news outlets in Vietnam; the authorities meet weekly with top newspaper editors to prescribe the news agenda and identify banned topics. "In Vietnam, there are a lot of issues that are not right—corruption, social issues, political problems—that journalists are not allowed to write about," said Huynh Ngoc Chenh, a retired senior editor at *Thanh Nien* newspaper and a blogger.

Blogs and other online news outlets, once a relatively vibrant place for critical viewpoints, are the new targets of government censorship. Recent measures aimed at stifling online press freedom have included heightened surveillance of blogs, laws barring the posting of information viewed as a threat to national security or unity, and the deployment of security officials who pose online as ordinary Internet users and harshly criticize and harass bloggers, CPJ research found. A draft executive decree, if passed, would force international technology companies to set up data centers and offices in Vietnam, which analysts say would erode the security of IP addresses and make critical writers even more vulnerable.

Detailed reports on these and dozens of other countries are available at cpj.org/attacks.

Karen Phillips is a freelance writer working in New York. She previously served in CPJ's Journalist Assistance and Americas programs and is the author of the 2011 CPJ special report, "After the Black Spring, Cuba's New Repression."

CPJ Data

Where Journalists Are Killed

At least 66 journalists were killed in direct relation to their work from January 1, 2012, through December 10, 2012, according to CPJ research.

Location:
Syria: 28
Somalia: 12
Pakistan: 7
Brazil: 4
Thailand: 1
Iran: 1
Nigeria: 1
India: 1
Lebanon: 1
Ecuador: 1
Mexico: 1
Bangladesh: 1
Bahrain: 1
Tanzania: 1
Cambodia: 1

Philippines: 1
Indonesia: 1
Colombia: 1
Russia: 1

Type of Death
Murder: 32
Combat-related: 24
Dangerous Assignment: 9
Undetermined: 1

Type of Journalist
Local: 62
International: 4

CPJ investigates the death of every journalist to determine whether it is work-related. CPJ confirms cases as work-related only if it is reasonably certain that a journalist was murdered in direct reprisal for his or her work; was killed in crossfire during combat situations; or was killed while carrying out a dangerous assignment such as coverage of a street protest. Our data do not include journalists killed in accidents such as car or plane crashes. When the motive in a fatality is unclear, but it is possible that a journalist was killed because of his or her work, CPJ classifies the case as "unconfirmed" and continues to investigate. CPJ's killed database is available at cpj.org/killed.

CPJ Impunity Index

The CPJ Impunity Index calculates the number of unsolved journalist murders as a percentage of each country's population. Here are the 12 countries with the worst records of combating deadly anti-press crimes over the past decade.

1. **Iraq**: 93 unsolved journalist murders
   Rating: 2.906 unsolved cases per million inhabitants
2. **Somalia**: 11 unsolved journalist murders
   Rating: 1.183 unsolved cases per million inhabitants
3. **Philippines**: 55 unsolved journalist murders
   Rating: 0.589 unsolved cases per million inhabitants

4. **Sri Lanka**: 9 unsolved journalist murders
   Rating: 0.431 unsolved cases per million inhabitants
5. **Colombia**: 8 unsolved journalist murders
   Rating: 0.173 unsolved cases per million inhabitants
6. **Nepal**: 5 unsolved journalist murders
   Rating: 0.167 unsolved cases per million inhabitants
7. **Afghanistan**: 5 unsolved journalist murders
   Rating: 0.145 unsolved cases per million inhabitants
8. **Mexico:** 15 unsolved journalist murders
   Rating: 0.132 unsolved cases per million inhabitants
9. **Russia**: 16 unsolved journalist murders
   Rating: 0.113 unsolved cases per million inhabitants
10. **Pakistan**: 19 unsolved journalist murders
    Rating: 0.109 unsolved cases per million inhabitants
11. **Brazil**: 5 unsolved journalist murders
    Rating: 0.026 unsolved cases per million inhabitants
12. **India**: 6 unsolved journalist murders
    Rating: 0.005 unsolved cases per million inhabitants

For the 2012 index, CPJ examined journalist murders that occurred between January 1, 2002, and December 31, 2011. Only those nations with five or more unsolved cases are included on this index. Cases are considered unsolved when no convictions have been obtained. CPJ defines murder as a deliberate attack against a specific journalist in relation to the victim's work. This index does not include cases of journalists killed in combat or while carrying out dangerous assignments such as coverage of street protests. Population data from the World Bank's *2010 World Development Indicators* were used in calculating each country's rating. More data are available cpj.org/campaigns/impunity.

Where Journalists Are Imprisoned

At least 232 journalists were imprisoned worldwide when CPJ conducted its annual worldwide census on December 1, 2012. The tally is the highest the organization has recorded since it began conducting worldwide surveys in 1990.

Location
Turkey: 49
Iran: 45
China: 32
Eritrea: 28
Syria: 15
Vietnam: 14
Azerbaijan: 9
Ethiopia: 6
Saudi Arabia: 4
Uzbekistan: 4
Democratic Republic of Congo: 3
India: 3
Israel and the Occupied Palestinian Territories: 3
Rwanda: 3
Morocco: 2
Bahrain: 1
Burkina Faso: 1
Burundi: 1
Cambodia: 1
Cuba: 1
Gambia: 1
Italy: 1
Iraq: 1
Kyrgyzstan: 1
Somalia: 1
Thailand: 1
Yemen: 1

By Charge
Terrorism, subversion, or other anti-state charge: 132
No publicly disclosed charge: 63
Retaliatory charge: 19
Religious or ethnic insult: 7
Defamation: 6
Censorship violations: 3
False news: 2

CPJ's survey is a snapshot of those incarcerated at midnight on December 1, 2012. It does not include the many journalists imprisoned and released throughout the year. More data are available at cpj.org/imprisoned.

Journalists in Exile

Here are the countries from which journalists most often fled in fear of attack or imprisonment in the years 2007 to 2012, along with the nations where they most often resettled.

Top Countries From Which They Fled

1. Somalia: 78
2. Iran: 68
3. Ethiopia: 49
4. Iraq: 40
5. Eritrea: 27
6. Sri Lanka: 23
7. Cuba: 19
8. Pakistan: 15
9. Chad: 14
9. Rwanda: 14

Top Resettlement Countries

1. U.S.: 128
2. Kenya: 52
3. Sweden: 26
4. Uganda: 24
5. Turkey: 22
6. Djibouti: 17
6. France: 17
8. U.K.: 13
9. Canada: 11
10. India: 9
10. Germany: 9

Prospects in Exile
17 percent: Able to work as a journalist in exile
8 percent: Able to return home

Each year, CPJ compiles an assessment of exiled journalists to mark World Refugee Day, June 20. CPJ's 2012 survey examined the period June 1, 2007, through May 31, 2012. CPJ's survey counts only those journalists who fled due to work-related persecution, who remained in exile for at least three months, and whose current whereabouts and activities are known. It does not include the many journalists and media workers who left their countries for professional or financial opportunities, those who left due to general violence, or those who were targeted for activities other than journalism, such as political activism. More data are available at cpj.org/exile.

Most Censored Countries

Here are the world's 10 most censored countries as determined by CPJ staff. All nations were judged on 15 criteria that assess citizens' access to information and journalists' ability to move and report freely.

1. Eritrea
Only state news media are allowed to operate in Eritrea, and they do so under the absolute control of the Information Ministry.

2. North Korea
Virtually all print and broadcast content comes from the official Korean Central News Agency and focuses on the political leadership's statements and activities.

3. Syria
The government has imposed a blackout on independent coverage of the civil war, attacking local journalists and barring most international reporters from entering the country.

4. Iran
Authorities imprison dozens of critical journalists at any given time, block millions of websites, engage in electronic surveillance, and jam satellite transmissions.

5. Equatorial Guinea

Rigid censorship rules enforce positive coverage of the nation's leadership. All domestic outlets are owned by the government or its proxies. Security agents harass international journalists.

6. Uzbekistan

No independent media outlets are based in Uzbekistan. Independent journalists who contribute to news organizations outside the country are subject to interrogation and prosecution.

7. Burma

Despite Burma's historic transition to a civilian government, authorities retained the censorship agency and conduct official post-publication review of all newspapers.

8. Saudi Arabia

Authorities appoint senior editors in traditional media and approve editors for news websites. International journalists' movements and coverage are limited.

9. Cuba

All domestic news media are controlled by the Communist Party. The government subjects independent bloggers to detentions, beatings, surveillance, and smear campaigns.

10. Belarus

The government restricts the travel of critical reporters, raids newsrooms, and confiscates newspaper editions. Public access to the Internet requires government-issued identification.

CPJ compiled its 2012 Most Censored Countries list to mark World Press Freedom Day, May 3. To determine this list, CPJ staff judged all countries worldwide according to 15 benchmarks. Those benchmarks included blocking of websites; restrictions on electronic recording and dissemination; the absence of privately owned or independent media; restrictions on journalist movements; license requirements to conduct journalism; security service monitoring of journalists; jamming of foreign broadcasts; and blocking of foreign correspondents. All of the countries on the list met at least 10 benchmarks. More data are available at cpj.org, keywords "most censored."

Index